TANKS
ON THE
STREETS?

TANKS
ON THE
STREETS?

The Battle of George Square, Glasgow, 1919

Louise Heren

&

Gordon J. Barclay

PEN & SWORD
HISTORY

AN IMPRINT OF PEN & SWORD BOOKS LTD.
YORKSHIRE – PHILADELPHIA

First published in Great Britain in 2023 by
PEN AND SWORD HISTORY
An imprint of
Pen & Sword Books Ltd
Yorkshire – Philadelphia

ISBN 978 1 52678 265 6

Typeset in Times New Roman 11/13.5 by
SJmagic DESIGN SERVICES, India.
Printed and bound in the UK by CPI Group (UK) Ltd.

Pen & Sword Books Ltd includes the Imprints of Atlas, Archaeology, Aviation,
Discovery, Family History, Fiction, History, Maritime, Military, Military
Classics, Politics, Select, Airworld, Frontline Publishing, Leo Cooper, Remember
When, Seaforth Publishing, The Praetorian Press, Wharncliffe Local History,
Wharncliffe Transport, Wharncliffe True Crime and White Owl.

For a complete list of Pen & Sword titles please contact
PEN & SWORD BOOKS LTD
George House, Units 12 & 13, Beevor Street, Off Pontefract Road,
Barnsley, South Yorkshire, S71 1HN, England
E-mail: enquiries@pen-and-sword.co.uk
Website: www.pen-and-sword.co.uk

or

PEN AND SWORD BOOKS
1950 Lawrence Rd, Havertown, PA 19083, USA
E-mail: uspen-and-sword@casematepublishers.com
Website: www,penandswordbooks.com

Contents

Authors' Foreword

This is not just another book on Red Clydeside in the early twentieth century. There are many books on the subject on the shelves but this one is different from the others. We are writing about one of the most iconic events in the history of Red Clydeside – the 'Battle of George Square'. In late January 1919, the Forty-Hours Strike for a shorter working week culminated in a demonstration in George Square and the ensuing 'Battle' led many to believe the city was on the brink of revolution. Most books about the events in January 1919 have been at best superficial in their analysis or entirely misleading and, surprisingly, none have attempted to pull together all the available archival sources and to tell the story as it happened, as witnessed by those who participated in it.

Few subjects in modern Scottish history are as contested as the legend of Red Clydeside and particularly the Battle of George Square. There are many arguments: how Red were the strikers in 1919? Was there a possibility of revolution? Whose fault was the violence in the Square? In court, who lied under oath? Without a dispassionate forensic analysis of all the records, how are we to know? Throughout our research, we have discovered sometimes significant errors perpetuated from secondary source to secondary source as well as fantastical statements that simply have no grounding in historical truth. Many accounts of the events of Bloody Friday recycle half-truths told in the memoirs of the strike leadership, possibly because the authors sympathize with their political perspective.

We do not claim that anyone could write a definitive account of events in the last week of January or the subsequent trial in April 1919, but we believe this is the first time that all the sources discovered to date, all the voices, have been considered in detail and brought together to produce a coherent and readable narrative. However, it would be a difficult read if every time we needed to explain in detail how eyewitness accounts differed, we stopped the reader to point out the more egregious differences.

We met by chance in November 2018 in the cloakroom at the National Records of Scotland in Edinburgh. One of us was deep in thought taking a breather from research on sexual violence while the other was trying to negotiate the limited space to reach his locker. Pardons and apologies for being an obstacle led to a brief conversation. He had been photographing the trial transcript of Bloody Friday, which would inform two articles he was writing and she remarked she had been trying for some years to promote a television documentary on the topic. 'You're not publishing, are you?' she asked. 'Yes', he replied. Within five minutes we had agreed in principle to collaborate on this project and within nine months we had a commission to publish. Then began the 'getting to know you' phase of research.

Gordon is a Lowland Scot from Aberdeen, to whom Glasgow at times seems more foreign than Newcastle. He is the son of a policeman and has spent most of his professional life as a civil service archaeologist in the lower reaches of 'the establishment', spending much of the last five years of his career drafting speeches, policy documents and answers to parliamentary questions for Scottish National Party and Labour Party culture ministers in the Scottish Parliament. His experience is that public servants in general try to do their best, often in difficult circumstances. He finds objectionable the trivialization of the sometimes-extreme violence against the police so common in accounts of the Battle. He is a member of the successor party (Liberal) to which many of the 'establishment' protagonists in this story belonged. He believes strongly in the rigorous testing of hypotheses, and consequently that anyone writing about the past should actively seek out evidence that undermines their favourite theories.

Louise is the daughter of a marine fitter and granddaughter of a ship's boilermaker, both of whom worked in the Port of London from 1920 until 1970, and who experienced long periods of unemployment at the hands of the shipyard 'Management'. These were formative years that she believes led to her lifelong passion to understand history 'from the bottom up'. Thirty years in documentary television production have taught her that so-called 'facts' are easy to manipulate if the delivery is sufficiently compelling – which is why the myths of the Battle of Bloody Friday need to be debunked a century on. Louise's many years researching Scottish social history have resulted in her always arguing politics from the small 's' socialist perspective.

Together we adhere to Evans' test of good history: 'Evidence running counter to the argument cannot be omitted or distorted, but must be explained, even at the cost of amending the argument or abandoning it altogether'.[1] Thus, if we have displayed any biases in the researching and writing of this book, we hope we have ironed each other's out in the process.

Writing the mythology of Bloody Friday started at approximately 1.00 pm on Friday 31 January 1919. Since then, contemporary strikers' newspapers and the memoirs written by the strike leaders between 1935 and the 1980s have formed a largely unchallenged catechism: an unprovoked, or even pre-planned brutal and indiscriminate attack on a peaceful crowd, with the Government sending English troops to crush the strike, or even quash a rebellion. Some historical commentators have used the available evidence to support lines of argument they personally adhere to; others have selected their sources to achieve the same. Often, authors have not checked whether the version they have inherited from another writer is supported by the evidence.

From the beginning 'Bloody Friday' has been an emblem fuelling narratives of Capital versus Labour, grievance and victimhood and, more recently, Westminster or England oppressing the Scots. There appears to have been deliberate historical amnesia to use the history of Red Clydeside, and Bloody Friday in particular, to bolster the cause of Scottish independence.[2] These mythologies, we are told, are the reality – it is their 'meaning' that is important – and we are foolish to attempt to present an evidence-based account of events in 1919. As Evans has it: 'politically committed history only damages itself if it distorts, manipulates or obscures historical fact in the interests of the cause it claims to represent'.[3]

It is often claimed that Glasgow marked the first time a state used the new and frightening military invention – the tank – to overawe its population, but that assertion relies on a belief that there were tanks in George Square (there weren't), or that they were driven around the streets (they weren't). They were deployed to meet a worst-case situation that did not happen and thus the tanks remained under cover and unused against Glaswegians, or any other Britons. Indeed, Liverpool has a better claim, as tanks were visibly parked in the city centre there during opportunistic looting and rioting which occurred during the police strike of August 1919.

The Battle of George Square was not Glasgow's 'Tiananmen Square', nor Hungary's Rising in 1956, nor a Scottish 'Prague Spring' despite claims made on social media. The mythology becomes ever more pervasive as distance in time from 1919 grows and therefore we both believe the events immediately before, during and after 31 January 1919 deserve a dispassionate, critical dissection and robust testing of all the available evidence. After all, this approach is what the best histories are based on.

Over a hundred years have elapsed since the Red Clydesiders took to the streets in 1919. It's time to clean up the Clyde.

Acknowledgements

First, we must acknowledge our gratitude to Serendipity, without whose attentions our accidental meeting would not have occurred and neither would this book.

Our journey from research to publication would have been virtually impossible without access to archives and the assistance of the very willing archivists who give freely of their time to help with projects not their own. Our thanks go to Alison Lindsay, head of the Historical Search Room at the National Records of Scotland, Edinburgh and her friendly team. Alison responded promptly and fully to our Freedom of Information request for access to the High Court of Justiciary criminal papers relating to the Shinwell *et al* case and has advised on complementary sources throughout this project. We are also grateful for permission granted by the National Records of Scotland to reproduce extracts from the criminal case papers and trial transcript. Our thanks also to Dr Irene O'Brien at the Mitchell Library in Glasgow for providing access to Glasgow Trades' Council minute books and miscellaneous papers, and the Federation of Shipbuilders' minute books.

We are grateful for the help of staff at the National Archives at Kew and the Parliamentary Archives.

The Labour History Society kindly awarded us a grant, which has greatly assisted remote access to archives especially when they were closed to researchers during the pandemic.

Dr Robert Shiels' e-mails gently suggesting and attaching articles on the history of the procurator fiscal service and the trials of James Maxton and John Maclean have been very helpful and informative. His exactitude when reviewing the legal elements of our text has been warmly welcomed and his enthusiasm and encouragement for this project is much appreciated.

The late Councillor Malcolm Cunning of Glasgow City Council always had an interest in the mythologization of the 'Battle'. He and the then Deputy Lord Provost, Philip Braat, kindly facilitated and guided our visit to the City Chambers in 2019 where we saw places that played an important part in the events: the Lord Provost's office, the Library, various meeting rooms, the council chamber and the quadrangle, where Kirkwood and Gallacher, and later the army, were photographed.

Our thanks are also due to Dr Bill Knox for reading the first draft of this book. As a highly respected academic of Scottish history of the nineteenth and twentieth centuries, Dr Knox has himself written on this subject, and so we are grateful for his insightful and careful comments. His support, as ever, is generous and always welcomed.

Our research has been exhaustive, but not necessarily comprehensive as new sources continue to emerge. We very much welcome approaches from readers who have new material to add to this history. As ever, any errors are entirely our own.

Louise began research on 'Bloody Friday' in 2012 and it would not have come together in this form without Gordon's passion for unravelling popular historical myths and his forensic analysis of the facts as contained in the archives. Together, we have consulted several thousand pages of contemporary records and a secondary reading list which would fill the pages of an entirely separate book. However, our next collaboration is a forthcoming academic monograph on the same topic using the same sources which will analyze the events of January 1919 and will examine more extensively how, over the intervening one hundred years, historians have diverged from the facts as contained in the contemporary records.

And lastly, we would like to thank our families who have suffered us and our cast of characters for too long.

List of Illustrations

Unless otherwise stated, all photographs are out of copyright and are taken from newspapers and pamphlets which are the property of the authors.

1. Postcard showing George Square, looking from the south-east corner towards the Merchants' House. First decades of the twentieth century.
2. Postcard showing George Square, looking from the west side towards the City Chambers, showing the south-east corner (right). First decades of the twentieth century.
3. The procession from St Andrew's Halls to George Square, Monday 27 January 1919. (*Bulletin* 28 January 1919)
4. Crowds in George Square, Monday 27 January 1919. (*Bulletin* 28 January 1919)
5. Emanuel Shinwell and Harry Hopkins speaking to the crowd from the plinth of the City Chambers, Monday 27 January 1919. (*Bulletin* 28 January 1919)
6. The red flag flying from the corporation flag pole, George Square, Monday 27 January 1919. (*Bulletin* 28 January 1919)
7. The most frequently used image to represent the events of 31 January. In reality, the red flag in George Square five days earlier, on Monday 27 January 1919. (*Daily Record*)
8. A strikers' procession, Tuesday 28 January 1919. (*Bulletin*, 29 January 1919)
9. A placard in a procession on Tuesday 28 January 1919, showing a blackleg being hanged. (*Bulletin* 29 January 1919)
10. A strike picket at Weir's of Cathcart's works, Thursday 30 January 1919. (*Illustrated London News* 8 February 1919)
11. Kirkwood being brought round in the City Chambers quadrangle. (*Graphic* 8 February 1919)
12. Gallacher, bandaged, in the City Chambers quadrangle. Kirkwood, is just visible, still prone, at the bottom right. (*Illustrated London News* 8 February 1919)

13. A police casualty being put in an ambulance. (*Illustrated London News* 8 February 1919)
14. Kirkwood being batoned by Sergeant Steele between the door of the City Chambers and the Gladstone statue. Note that there is no crowd for Kirkwood to incite, as was claimed by Steele and others. The figure immediately to the right of Kirkwood is probably Neil Maclean MP. Reproduced by kind permission; Crown copyright. National Records of Scotland, AD15/19/11/7
15. Sheriff McKenzie (marked with a cross) shortly before reading the proclamation of the Riot Act. Assistant Chief Constable Mennie is on the right; Chief Constable Stevenson is third from right. Friday 31 January 1919. (*Bulletin* 1 February 1919)
16. The police withdraw after a baton charge in North Frederick Street. The barricade of boxes taken from George Binnie's lorry is visible. (*Illustrated London News* 8 February 1919)
17. George Square in the immediate aftermath of the riot. (*Graphic*, 8 February 1919)
18. The immediate aftermath of the Battle; the broken flagpole outside the City Chambers, and Gladstone's statue, from which the strike leaders addressed the crowd. (*Bulletin* 1 February 1919)
19. Soldiers guarding a railway bridge, 1 or 2 February 1919. (*Illustrated London News* 8 February 1919)
20. Mortars set up for the cameras in the quadrangle of the City Chambers, 1 or 2 February 1919. (*New York Times* 2 March 1919)
21. Soldiers guarding a railway bridge over the Clyde, 1 or 2 February 1919. (*Illustrated London News*, 8 February 1919)
22. Soldiers with fixed bayonets, some wearing steel helmets, escort a supplies cart, 1 or 2 February 1919. (*Illustrated London News*, 8 February 1919)
23. Troops marching in George Square 1 or 2 February 1919. Note the variety of headgear: flat forage caps; Tam o'Shanter bonnets; fore-and-aft caps; even a bush hat, such is the variety of units represented. (*Ilustrated London News* 8 February 1919)
24. A soldier sleeping in the City Chambers, 3 February 1919. (*Bulletin*, 4 February 1919)
25. A soldier inspects a damaged tram. (*Graphic*, 8 February 1919)
26. One of the smashed and looted windows of the Cable Shoe Shop, as joiners prepare to board it up, 31 January 1919. (*Graphic*, 8 February 1919)

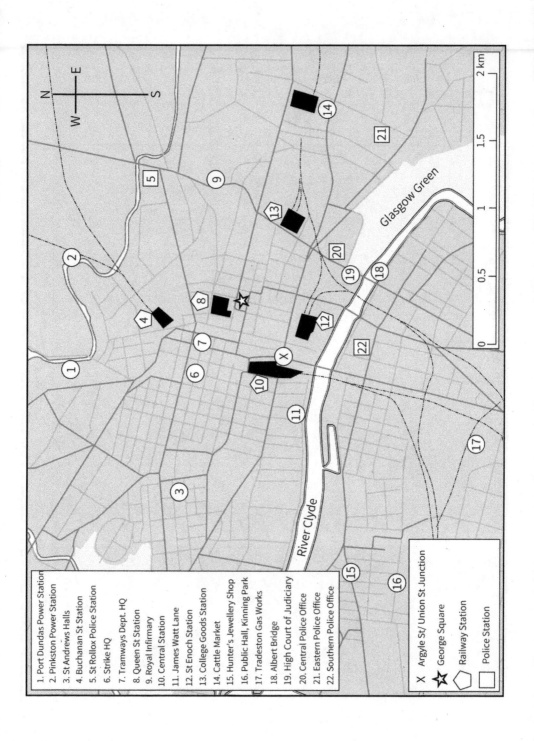

1. Port Dundas Power Station
2. Pinkston Power Station
3. St Andrews Halls
4. St Rollox Police Station
5. Buchanan St Station
6. Strike HQ
7. Tramways Dept. HQ
8. Queen St Station
9. Royal Infirmary
10. Central Station
11. James Watt Lane
12. St Enoch Station
13. College Goods Station
14. Cattle Market
15. Hunter's Jewellery Shop
16. Public Hall, Kinning Park
17. Tradeston Gas Works
18. Albert Bridge
19. High Court of Judiciary
20. Central Police Office
21. Eastern Police Office
22. Southern Police Office

X Argyle St / Union St Junction
☆ George Square
⬠ Railway Station
▢ Police Station

Glasgow Green

River Clyde

N
W E
S

0   0.5   1   1.5   2 km

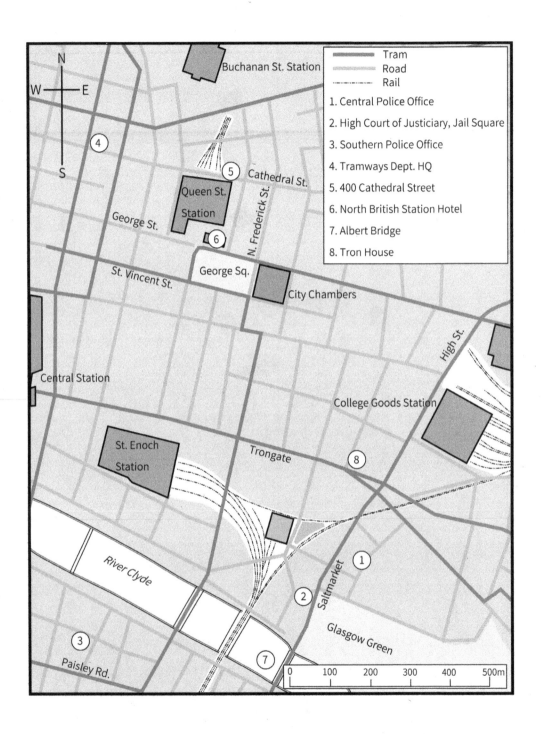

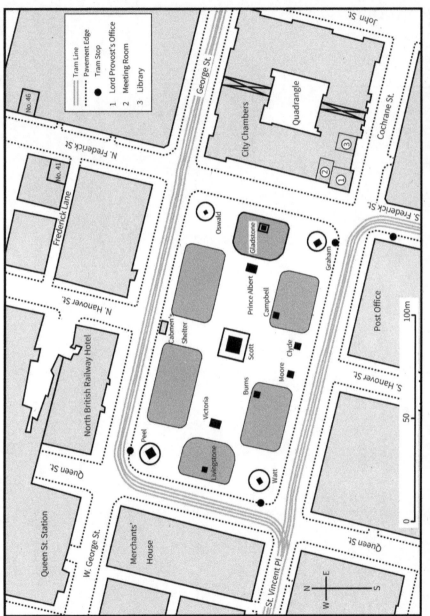

George Square, showing the location of the statues and the areas of grass and flowers. No.46 North Frederick Street is where the lorry-load of bottles was being delivered.

Introduction

> During the war, from press and platform, it was impressed
> upon the workers that if they only fought and worked, gave
> up their union rules, privileges, etc. and won the war, they
> would see the dawn of a new era. The experience gained in the
> trenches and workshops had wiped out all class distinctions,
> and the last had been seen of unemployment, long hours of
> toil, low wages, and all the misery result there from – so ran
> the fairy tale.[1]

Scotland the brave; Scotland the romantic land largely invented by
Sir Walter Scott; Scotland the tough and independent. Edinburgh the refined
capital; Glasgow the 'second city of empire', only forty miles distant but a
whole world away. Scotland has many facets: some imagined others real.
One of its most famous aspects is its heavy industries, most especially
Glasgow's shipbuilding yards, renowned for immense munitions output
during both world wars and its sacrifice of husbands, fathers, brothers and
sons. However, Glasgow is also infamous for its poverty, slum housing,
tough – sometimes toxic – masculinity and violence. That is where this
story is set: in the last week of January 1919 when wartime deprivations
and exhaustion, growing unemployment, homes unfit for heroes and
labour unrest collided in what some hoped – and others feared – would be
Britain's very own socialist, possibly Bolshevik, revolution. But it didn't
happen. George Square had been 'black with men' at midday on Friday
31 January 1919, but the strikers' anger cooled and by sunset they were
joined by opportunistic looters.[2]

In the Act of Union in 1707 Scotland retained its distinct legal, religious
and education systems. After the dynastic struggles and disruptions of the
Jacobite risings in 1715 and 1745, Scotland rebuilt itself and responded
glitteringly with the Scottish Enlightenment, forging a reputation for
philosophy, jurisprudence, medicine, science and a diaspora which took
the nation's thinking and its people to the far-flung corners of the globe.
Yet, from the late eighteenth century, as in much of Britain, rapid industrial

advances produced social problems. A rural population, often living in squalor, migrated to much worse urban degradation. Dislocation from the land for these new urban communities created deprivation, depravation and disease. By the late nineteenth century, Glasgow had become the centre for Scotland's rural dispossessed.

By the time of the 1921 census, of Scotland's almost five million inhabitants, nearly 60 per cent lived in towns with more than 5,000 residents, and of those nearly a million lived in Glasgow and the Clyde region.[3] Glasgow had been a magnet for Scots and Irish immigrants seeking work for over a century. A unique combination of wealth often built on slave industries, raw materials, maritime transport links and available workers coalesced so that by the end of the Great War, Clydeside was arguably the centre of Britain's global industrial empire. The belching heart of the shipbuilding industries, Clydeside accounted for 757,000 tons of new shipping in 1913 and over a million horse-power of marine engines – 49 per cent of the United Kingdom's total output.[4] When orders were buoyant, the yards were busy and the men's skills made the Clyde a by-word for quality and precision: 'Clyde-built' meant something around the world and to everyone who lived and worked on Clydeside too. Pride in the Clyde benefited everyone from wealthy shipyard owners to the poorest working-class families. But these heavy industries suffered cyclical depression and, arguably, if it had not been for the economic boom created during the Great War, Glasgow's reputation might have dwindled.

However, this economic success was accompanied by shame. Some of the skilled working class occupied better housing but, generally, Glasgow's tenements, the homes of its workforce, were so tightly packed that the officers of the *Royal Commission on the Housing of the Industrial Population of Scotland* reported in 1917 the need to light a match even in daylight to see their way to the front doors, with families of six or more living in a single-end, a one-roomed dwelling in a tenement block.[5] Conditions were cramped and lavatories were shared. Infant mortality in Glasgow was outstripped in the United Kingdom only by Dundee; working-class wards in Glasgow experienced infant deaths almost five times higher than middle-class districts such as Kelvinside.[6] An arduous working life, an inadequate diet with the risk of industrial injuries and disease, returning home in the evenings to an overcrowded single-end crawling with children resulted in nearly 50 per cent of men dying between their twenty-fifth and sixty-fifth birthdays before the Great War. Their wives fared slightly better. Life expectancy was fifty years for men and fifty-three for women.[7] Glasgow's working-class districts were described as 'earth's nearest suburb to hell'.[8]

The state of the nation's health exercised Westminster's politicians and Glasgow's City Council: what could be done to improve the workforce's housing and longevity? And would such improvements reduce crime and undermine the burgeoning growth of socialism? Both issues were bound up in notions of the respectable and the unrespectable poor. Drinking and other incontinent habits produced an underclass, a residuum beyond redemption who were believed to be responsible for their own situation, while the respectable poor appeared to be coping.[9] The city's medical officers made the correlation between ill-health and impoverished and insanitary living conditions, which the city's municipal leaders acknowledged, but what could they do?[10] For the working classes, respectable or otherwise, if welfare was not provided by the city authorities, then they would look elsewhere for assistance.

In 1888 Keir Hardie formed the Scottish Labour Party; by 1893 it had merged with the Independent Labour Party (ILP) and allied with the trade unions. The ILP's Scottish leaders were hardly Marxists; in fact Hardie was reported never to have read any of Marx's works, but their fervour for fairness and public ownership of the means of production made them socialists.[11] In the years before the Great War in Glasgow, campaigners and educators such as John Maclean and James Maxton, both of whom were ex-teachers, held evening classes and preached socialism from street corners to workers wishing to improve themselves. Combined with increasing trade union membership, this would start the cauldron of agitation bubbling on Clydeside. The most successful trade union in Britain was the Amalgamated Society of Engineers (ASE), which in Glasgow represented most of the skilled engineers in Clydeside's machine works. They formed a working-class aristocracy separate from their unskilled brothers, differentiated by apprenticeships and higher wages. By the last decade of the nineteenth century, Scottish engineers, miners and steelworkers comprised a third of the country's trade union members.[12] Unionization was a response to the vagaries of cyclical depression; by coming together members expected their representatives would negotiate on their behalf and there was also the limited hope of hardship relief from the union's welfare funds. It has been argued that the labour movement on Clydeside was both horizontal and vertical; horizontal, connecting working-class Glaswegians to short-lived widespread national discontent with workplace and domestic conditions, and vertical, creating a local movement with a century-long legacy.[13] At grassroots level, Glaswegians' socialist life began at Sunday afternoon classes progressing to night classes and workplace lectures; Tom Johnston's *Forward* newspaper kept the workers informed of socialist debates and working-class issues in their rare moments of leisure.

On Glasgow's City Council, Irish-born Catholic and socialist John Wheatley began the campaign in 1913 for improved housing with his pamphlet *Eight Pound Cottages for Glasgow Citizens*. But the city council shied away from razing Glasgow's slums, which largely belonged to wealthy landlords, and re-building with affordable housing. It was an intractable situation that coincided with Glasgow's working classes finding their voice and using agitation and industrial action to be heard. Their opinions were not necessarily consistent with a workplace hierarchy – engineers on top, the unskilled below – obstructing collective action, but Glasgow's reputation for 'municipal socialism' – public ownership of the means of power, transport and water supply – which had begun in the last century might gain a different momentum if life did not change soon.

Then war broke out.

Overnight, notions of regional and international working-class solidarity were largely replaced by widespread patriotism. However, left-wing politics and workers' organizations did not disappear. Many activists, such as James Maxton and John Maclean, opposed the war and the effort in Clydeside to supply it. As the importance of wartime shipbuilding and munitions manufacture became urgently apparent, Clydeside's industrial workers found a new voice which recognized their pivotal position in the war effort. They would not suffer the erosion of their craft working practices nor their prestige as skilled men by the dilution of their working practices by unskilled men and women in the shipyards and machine shops. Neither could their wives stump up hard-earned cash to pay for rising rents. The threat of strikes elicited visits from the likes of David Lloyd George and Winston Churchill, keen to cool tempers before anyone threw down their tools. An uneasy truce was agreed. In return for rent controls and post-war welfare and employment promises, Clydeside's workforce would continue to churn out the iron, steel, precision machines and tools and ships needed for the war.

And then Armistice was declared.

The population exhaled with relief, but two new questions were posed: if wartime manufacture had created full employment using women and the unskilled in semi-skilled occupations to fulfil government contracts, would these 'excess' workers be prepared to return to their previous lives? And if not, how could the country welcome home their military heroes if there were no jobs and the threat of a post-war slump? One solution which gained considerable traction among the skilled workforce was to reduce the number of hours worked while retaining their full pay to make space for demobilizing soldiers. Different parts of the country and different trade crafts pursued separate targets: in Belfast they wanted forty-four hours; some in Glasgow wanted thirty hours, but in the end the Clyde's workers opted for what became known as the Forty-Hours Week campaign. It caused conflict between the workers, the shipyard magnates and Glasgow's city councillors and senior police officers. It led to the event now recalled as 'Bloody Friday' – a cold damp last day of January that ended with insufficient blood to warrant its soubriquet and a high-profile trial, both of which have had an enduring impact on Glasgow's self-image.

Glaswegians can be surprised at how few Scots – and English – have heard about Bloody Friday; knowledge has only in recent years been extended by social media. Today, it is generally known as 'The Battle of George Square'. The cast of characters comprises workers and strikers, former soldiers, councillors, police officers and constables, tram workers, but most importantly the members of the Clyde Workers' Committee (CWC), other shop stewards and factory leaders. One side becomes the founding fathers of Red Clydeside, the other side disappears quietly.

The intervening years have had a remarkable impact on the re-telling of Bloody Friday and the 'legend' of Red Clydeside. Those charged with incitement to riot re-cast themselves as heroes and have been accepted as such at their own evaluation: the victims of a conspiracy by the 'establishment'. However, history is never so clear-cut. It is messy and nuanced, open to interpretation and sometimes bias. One thing that remains constant though is the archives.

In writing this book, we have returned to look in great detail at the contemporary sources: newspapers, images, film, oral history and most importantly the archival material. We recognize that the 'voices' contained in the archives are invariably mitigated across time by many actors: those who give evidence; those who decide in the moment which papers are kept; those in their future who select which records are preserved. The process of compiling archives is not without pitfalls. Therefore, it is the job of historians to listen to all the available 'voices' and never to judge the past by the values of our present.

The main archival source is the High Court of Justiciary (HCJ) papers held at the National Records of Scotland. In the weeks immediately succeeding the Battle, precognition statements – Scots Law's form of pre-trial witness deposition – were taken from several hundred witnesses. In Scots Law, no one can be prosecuted on the testimony of a single witness and therefore over a hundred of the precognitions do little more than corroborate others.

These papers are supported by extensive legal correspondence, reports and lists prepared for the trial and the trial transcript which runs to over a thousand pages. Under the guidance contained in the *Book of Regulations*, Scottish procurators fiscal – public prosecutors – must collect evidence as soon as possible after a crime is reported to them. They precognosce as many witnesses as they can discover, whose testimonies form the basis for any prosecution. It has been argued that a trial under Scots Law is more inquisitorial than adversarial, testing the evidence rather than counsels' debating abilities.[14] The minute books and other papers of the Joint and Executive Committees of the Engineers' and Shipbuilders' Associations, and the meeting books and papers of the Glasgow Trades' Council, held at Glasgow City Archives, complement the HCJ criminal case papers.

Another source on which previous writers have perhaps placed too much reliance are the published memoirs of the strike leaders; none of the 'other side' published. These fifteen or so memoirs (see chapter 10) provide a series of narratives that promote personal recollections and which adhere, often erratically, to the story told by the contemporary sources. After all, these memoirs were not intended to be history, but served to tell the authors' stories as they wished, perhaps ensuring their place *in history,* while occasionally casting aspersions on their colleagues. An extensive secondary literature, mainly written after 1980, has informed historical analysis.

Sadly, there are two important sources missing. First, to our knowledge, the defence precognition statements have not survived; instead, these witnesses' words are heard through the stilted structure of the trial transcript and, as with the prosecution, there would have been precognitions for many more witnesses than were called to give evidence. Second, the descriptions of events and opinions of the great mass of participants in George Square on 31 January 1919 survive in fragmentary oral history, rarely recorded and sometimes recounted to children and grandchildren, reducing in accuracy with each repetition. We continue to seek their written accounts of this event.

To narrate the events of the last week in January and its culmination in the Battle and subsequent trial, we have employed the archive in the following manner: chapters 1 to 6 rely mostly on precognition statements and newspaper reportage from the mainstream press and the strikers' publications, thus telling the story using the most in-the-moment and recent after-the-event material. Thereafter chapter 7 uses a range of precognitions, newspaper and other reportage, before chapter 8 recounts the trial using mostly the trial transcript and newspaper reports which offer both prosecution and defence voices. Chapter 9 is constructed from newspapers, memoirs and secondary literature. For anyone wishing to consult the criminal case papers, for the precognition statements original page numbers top and centre have been given in the endnotes as well as the witness's name. However, page numbering in the National Records of Scotland copy of the trial transcript is inconsistent, often offering several pencil and ink variations and, therefore, the witness's name only is given. The names of key figures are frequently spelled erroneously, often with variants on the same page: Maclean/McLean/MacLean; Gallacher/Gallagher. We have silently corrected the spelling to the versions apparently preferred by the men themselves and their families. Complete and lengthy direct quotes from the archival sources are sparingly used; however key words and phrases in the contemporary records are incorporated to convey the authenticity of the words spoken and reported by the main protagonists.

For 100 years the events we describe have been mythologized, in part deliberately, to create a useable history of an iconic event. We have been told that the mythology is now the reality and it is the event's meaning which matters more. We disagree. Many historians are perennially disappointed that they are never present when 'it' happens. Therefore, we must rely on the veracity of participants and eyewitnesses, on the integrity of the individuals recording the event and those preserving the archives, while always being aware of the agenda that each witness – labour leader, striker, passer-by, journalist, policeman and politician – may have had when describing events, near the time or subsequently. If we are accused of having an agenda, it is that we believe in evidence-based history.

Writing his account of Clydeside politics in 1936, William Gallacher claimed that a leader in the *Glasgow Herald* for 8 February 1919 had revealed the city and national authorities' fears: they anticipated a 'Spartacus Coup' as had just occurred in Germany and were 'prepared to suppress it at all costs'. He also claimed in his books and interviews that the workers had been prepared for a rising, but it had failed because 'the leadership had never thought of it'.[15] The 'leader' he quoted from does not exist and the possibility of a revolution is unevidenced, yet Gallacher's memoir continues to be quoted as if it were a reliable source.

In the intervening years, memories have emerged of tanks crawling through George Square to disperse or even crush the protestors, of howitzers on the City Chambers' roof and English soldiers patrolling Glasgow's streets as the sun set on the city's vandalized, looted and smashed centre. Yet, if the city's authorities had anticipated a socialist uprising, why was Westminster not more agitated? Were Clydeside's workers sufficiently 'red' to rise? As for tanks and troops, the archives tell us exactly how many tanks and how many troops were deployed to Glasgow and, more importantly, those records also contain the detail of when both men and materiel arrived and where they came from.

As we trawled the evidence, inevitably we began to judge the reliability of some witnesses. On both sides, some individuals slanted their evidence (the Lord Provost and Isaac Sim) or lied under oath (Sergeant Steele and Neil Maclean MP). In what follows, the words 'he claims' and 'he will later claim' highlight places where there are doubts, or where someone describes events that no one else in the vicinity saw.

It is 6.00 am on a dreich Friday morning in Glasgow, the last day of January 1919. Much of the region has been on strike since earlier in the week and yet, even if not at work today, the city is waking. Word went out yesterday for the workers to gather in George Square by midday today to hear what their leaders have to say about the Forty-Hour week. It's the last chance for both sides to prevent disastrous unemployment and as one man – the Scottish Secretary – would put it, a 'Bolshevist rising'.[16]

This is what happens next.

Chapter 1

Friday, 31 January 1919

Morning

The last day of January 1919 is no morning to rise early if you are not going to work and, this morning, much of Glasgow will not be arriving at the factory and shipyard gates at 6.00 am, but still they are rising. On Monday a general strike was called by the strike committee of the Clyde Workers Committee (CWC) and according to the newspapers the electricians came out immediately as well as the flour-mill workers, but not the municipal employees, which has become a bone of contention between the strike leadership and the city authorities during this tumultuous week.[1] An estimated total of 40,000 workers were out on that first day, but the strike has been patchy across the city's industries all week and on Wednesday the strike leaders paid a visit to the Lord Provost, Glasgow City Council's leader. They wanted to know what he planned to do about their demand for a forty-hour week and, more importantly, what Westminster might have to say. The question was, and the answer everyone awaits is: will the Government intervene? Today, many Glaswegians expect Westminster's response to be conveyed to them by their leaders from their usual gathering place in George Square. This is the place to be to hear the Government's response.

It is a dark and dreich morning, with a light north-easterly wind blowing. It is barely two degrees Celsius outside and little more indoors; no one wants to throw back the covers and poke the first toe out into the chilly air.[2] In single-ends and slightly roomier apartments around Glasgow's working-class districts, mothers and daughters are the first to brave it. As they vacate family beds, the men can stretch out for the remaining few minutes while the women bustle about. Gas stoves are lit, meagre curtains pulled back and once the men and boys have emerged, the daily grind begins of folding up bedding, up-ending beds and stacking them against the walls and dragging out the wooden dining table and arranging some chairs to sit down for breakfast.[3]

South of the River Clyde in Govan, Archibald Wallace's home is no different. This neighbourhood nestled on the south bank of the River

Clyde is densely populated and poor, where the number of people seeking shelter far exceeds the capacity of the exhausted tenement blocks. The area is threaded with small industries belching smoke and effluent and docks clanging and ringing throughout every day; even on a bright winter's day like this, Govan exudes dejection.

Archibald's family is already awake and busy. He is a sheet metalworker and has been out on strike all week with strike pay because his union sanctioned the stoppage. Archibald is a member of the Joint General Strike Committee involved in union business for the past twelve years. He had a late night attending a committee meeting to plan today's workers' processions through the city. This morning he will not be joining the other strikers from his street to march into the city centre; instead, he intends to lead the eastern section of his union to Cochrane Street reaching George Square in time for midday. The plan is that those coming from Govan will meet at the south of George Square while those arriving from Partick will take the west side and others from Dennistoun will congregate to the east. It has been planned that, once in George Square, each district will occupy a particular designated spot.[4] For Archibald, the march will be approximately three miles and should only take an hour, but first he must cross the river to reach his assigned union group; marshalling the expected crowds will also eat up time, so Archibald leaves early. As he walks across the Clyde, there is an opportunity for a breath of relatively fresh air.

Elsewhere around the city, families prepare for the day ahead. If not on strike, they may decide to join the marches and stand on the side-lines when they reach George Square. It is publicized to be quite an event. And, if intending to go to work, at least the trams are still running despite reported threats to cut the electricity and bring the city to a standstill.

To the east of the city Inspector Neil Gillies of the Eastern District police has been tasked with accompanying a procession heading to George Square from Whitevale Road in Dennistoun. The glass-fronted shops with apartments above hide the tenements clustered behind. Trams normally run along the centre of the shopping streets with their rails set into the cobbles, but the residents here cannot board a tram this morning because they are obstructed by the congregating marchers. Gillies has twenty-eight years' experience and knows a thing or two about estimating crowd sizes.[5] He reckons the march he joins is 700 strong. As they advance towards the Square they take a circuitous route, dropping south to Gallowgate, before heading west to the Trongate and on to Glassford Street. All the way the marchers hold up the traffic, many deliberately, meandering across the roads and they pay no attention to the police.[6] There is a holiday atmosphere, and everyone appears to be in good spirits. Gillies estimates it takes them an hour to reach Glassford Street just south of the Square.

To the west Constable Andrew Gallagher joins a procession at Charing Cross which he estimates at 8,000 or 9,000 strong arriving in formation and blocking the street, which he believes is deliberately done. They have come all the way from Partick and the constables accompanying them are unable to control the marchers.[7] Sergeant John Steele notices men repeatedly boarding passing trams and catching hold of the rope dangling at the back of the cars to pull the trolleys off their overhead wires. He has insufficient men to intervene. It is 11.30 am and together Steele and Gallagher join the procession, which is now singing loudly and, along with other constables walking along Sauchiehall Street to reach St Vincent Place to the west, head to the Square.[8] For Archibald Wallace, there has been a mix-up. He arrives south of the Square earlier than planned; his contingent of strikers is also unable to get beyond Glassford Street because so many protestors fill the surrounding streets. They wheel round and march up South Hanover Street to reach their allotted point: Cochrane Street. Archibald stands in the middle of an orderly but jostling crowd.[9]

It is now 12.00 noon and George Square throngs with thousands of strikers. The men have arrived from all over the city and its outskirts, seeking their designated spots in the Square. Sergeant Steele and his men join Inspector Gillies; they have been instructed in advance to join their forty or so colleagues already on duty in front of the Municipal Buildings. Stiffly upright inside their heavy uniforms, they are perhaps the only people able immediately to occupy their allotted location, because already some of the strikers are moving away from their designated sections and are heading towards the City Chambers. With the milling crowds shouting and singing, it is difficult for either Steele or Gillies to hear what is being said from the plinth of the Gladstone statue about eighty feet away from the front of the Buildings; Gillies feels the crowd's mood is now dangerous and menacing.[10] From his position at the entrance to the City Chambers, Chief Constable of the City of Glasgow Police James Verdier Stevenson has a wide view across the Square. As more processions arrive, he is satisfied his force, which will reach 140 policemen, are disposed where he anticipates they are most required.[11]

The Gladstone statue is cast in bronze cloaked with a long lawyer's gown atop a stone plinth, and clinging to the statue is William Gallacher wearing a dark coat and a workman's flat cap. He blends perfectly with the swirling crowds, his brown work boots level with their capped and bonneted heads. This ardent striker and leader of the CWC is speaking to the assembled crowd; he has a reputation for persuasion. Looking down, the paving stones appear wet and Gallacher will later mistakenly claim there has been overnight rain; the grass around the statue is muddy.[12] Hanging on to the Gladstone statue with him are fellow strike leaders David Kirkwood, Emanuel Shinwell and Harry Hopkins.[13] He shouts down to the crowd, but none of the policemen, who will later give evidence in court, hear what he says, except Lieutenant Lawrence Gray.[14] Gray will claim to hear Gallacher tell his companions to head into the City Chambers to listen to what the Lord Provost has to report. Before the delegation jumps down, Shinwell has one thing to ask the men below. He requests them to be on their best behaviour while the deputation interviews the Lord Provost.[15]

The Municipal Buildings, or City Chambers, occupy the entire east side of George Square and have loomed with late-Victorian grandeur over Glasgow's citizens for three decades, time for the white stone façade to turn a dirty shade of grey. The police manage to part the crowd and Lieutenant Gray watches as the deputation's leaders Shinwell and Kirkwood walk towards him.[16] Emanuel Shinwell is chairman of the Glasgow Trades and Labour Council and was instrumental in calling the strike on Monday. He is an experienced labour representative, committed to the men he leads, whether they are tailors, sailors or firemen, decisive and expedient. He is also chairman of the Joint Strike Committee which includes David Kirkwood now striding beside him. Kirkwood, or Davie to his workmates and later to his colleagues in the House of Commons, is certainly David to everyone around him today. Since the Great War started, Kirkwood has been Sir William Beardmore's intermediary smoothing relations between Parkhead Forge's workforce and Sir William, its owner. He is an engineer and union member and, on the whole, Glasgow's workforce trusts his judgement. History will deservedly treat him more favourably than the other strike leaders after today.

Shinwell and Kirkwood are joined by others from the previous deputation which visited the Lord Provost two days ago on Wednesday afternoon. Shouldering their way through the crowd, they walk up the Chambers' front steps and in through the towering doors. An unnamed woman who tried to accompany them on Wednesday is excluded again today. The clamour of the crowd now reaching 20,000 strong – some will later claim it has reached, improbably, over 70,000 people – fades slowly as the doors swing closed behind them.[17] Constable James Ritchie from Western District considers the crowd to be particularly dense in front of the Municipal Buildings, although there is no disorder. The Keeper of the Municipal Buildings shows them into his room before handing them to a council officer who escorts them to the first-floor library. This is where they met the Lord Provost two days ago and, despite giving him notice of their return today, he is not yet free to meet them.[18] All morning the usual business of the city council has continued uninterrupted; the Lord Provost is in a meeting and apparently cannot be disturbed. So, Shinwell and the delegation wait.

Since 11.00 am the Sheriff of Lanarkshire, Alastair MacKenzie, has been in consultation in the Lord Provost's room situated on the second floor of the Municipal Buildings. It has a view from one window over the Square and from another side window down onto the south-east corner where Cochrane Street meets South Frederick Street. He is joined by the Town Clerk, Sir John Lindsay, and Mr John Lamb, recently arrived from London. Lamb is Westminster's Scottish Office representative, despatched north yesterday to acquaint the Lord Provost and sheriff with the Government's policy towards today's demonstration and to communicate to London any developments in the situation.[19] The Lord Provost is currently with them. He is having a busy morning having already received a delegation from the Engineers' and Shipbuilders' Association. They have impressed upon him strongly their displeasure with the Corporation Electricity Department in cutting off the electricity supply without consultation.[20] Shortly, he will leave to attend a magistrates' meeting in the neighbouring room.[21] Occasionally, one of them rises from their discussion to observe the massing crowds outside, particularly groups gathering around South Frederick Street and the post office. With the Lord Provost, they received the Government's official response to the strikers' demands by telegram last night which the Government has also had published in this morning's newspapers. The Government has not informed James Stewart of their actions ahead of publication and what the men in the Lord Provost's room do not know is how many of the strikers and their supporters in the Square below have read the news already. It is likely most have, which is not helpful to the city's leaders. The Government refuses to intervene in the strike, which leaves the Lord Provost and his team fearful that the strike leaders will carry out their threat to use unconstitutional means to remove the trams from the streets today. What 'unconstitutional' actually means they are unsure, but as noon approaches the Lord Provost leaves a few minutes late for his scheduled meeting.[22] The town clerk and sheriff get up and move to the windows where they see a body of men gathered around the Gladstone statue and another congregating on both sides of the tram rails outside the post office. Sheriff MacKenzie observes that the pavement on either side of Cochrane Street where it becomes George Square and crosses with South Frederick Street is a most unusual location to congregate if expecting to listen to a

13

speech delivered nearer the statue. MacKenzie observes similar behaviour at the north-east corner and is worried. Where the men have gathered at the south-east and north-east corners are key routes for trams travelling east to west. He suspects they plan to stop the trams to fulfil their previous threat to bring the city to a standstill; to him their actions appear wilful and deliberate. Sir John agrees.[23]

Crossing the Square at this point is solicitor and city councillor Rosslyn Mitchell who will later act for some of the leaders in court. He is early for his 12.30 meeting with the General Finance Committee.[24] Rubbing shoulders with the crowd as he approaches the Municipal Buildings, he feels they are a good-natured crowd and has no difficulty getting through. Around him processions continue to arrive and, in particular, he notices the Maryhill Strike Committee's banner floating above the marchers' heads as they approach down North Hanover Street.[25] Also arriving from the same direction is the Springburn contingent headed by a brass band and a piper.[26] What they cannot see is what Archibald Wallace, who should have been with them, witnesses. Positioned beside a Royal Mail lorry which is reversing because the route through to Cochrane Street is blocked with people, Archibald cannot get any closer due to the lorry's difficulties; this delay prevents him becoming embroiled in what ensues.[27]

Detective Inspector Louis Noble stands near the Gladstone statue and, once the deputation leaves, he recognizes a fervent socialist, Andrew Smith, take over the proceedings. He hears Smith ask William Gallacher to address the strikers, who commences with a lecture on the 'Commercial Combines at Coat's Thread Combine' and how the workers have the right to combine and demand better conditions. It is a stentorian effort. He is just getting up steam when Smith's voice is heard above him. He calls out for the police to stop all the traffic immediately because a van passing in front of the Municipal Buildings appears to have injured two of the crowd, which is a detail Archibald Wallace does not witness because he is distracted by the post van still manoeuvring through the masses.[28]

Still on the Gladstone plinth, Gallacher will later claim to see the Square packed with strikers and gazing towards the post office at the south-east corner; he will recall a real scrum of people jammed together.[29] By now the police in front of the Municipal Buildings have formed what Gallacher later remembers as two rows facing out into the crowd.[30] Detective Inspector Noble feels the crowd swaying backwards and forwards around him as excitement begins to swell, but he does not remark on ranked rows of policemen or people pressed together.[31]

In the City Chambers' library, the delegation receives a message from the council officer that the Lord Provost will not be long. David Kirkwood can hear a great volume of shouting from outside but cannot see what is happening. Kirkwood is keen to find a window that will reveal what is going on and crosses the library to peer out on the mayhem below. The library's windows look on to Cochrane Street where he can see the south-east corner of the Square and a scrummage which has begun around a cluster of trams. While waiting for the Lord Provost to see them, evidently tempers outside have flared and police batons and strikers' heads are making contact; mud and debris flying. It's hard to tell what's happening let alone how it started.[32]

Stationed towards the south-east corner of George Square, Sergeant Norman McArthur of the Central District watches as a horse yoked to a lorry is held up on the west-going tram rails; he takes the horse by the halter and clears it from the road. Immediately afterwards, two tram cars heading east try to get through but the mob is now too dense or too obstinate to move and is covering the rails; for the moment they are at a standstill.[33] The first tram heading to Mount Florida is halted opposite the post office. Its driver, 30-year-old Margaret Buchanan, is running to timetable; by her calculation it is 12.08 pm. As she reaches the corner of the Square and Cochrane Street, several hundred protesters swarm onto the rails which prevents her from proceeding. Suddenly, a man in a grey suit emerges from the crowd, advances from the front to the rear of Margaret's tram where he tugs on the rope and pulls the trolley from the wire, and then calmly melts back into the sea of similarly monochrome protestors. Some men shout at her that they have gone out to France to fight and she is now preventing them from getting their jobs back. They use filthy and abusive language towards her and tram Inspector David Cree who rides with her. They are reported to yell 'Stop your *** cars. We are going to put you off the street'. Trying to steady his female driver, Cree advises caution to avoid any friction with the men.

Sergeant McArthur's superior officer, Inspector Sutherland, has been standing in front of the Municipal Buildings since 11.30 am and from what he has observed over the past half hour, he believes this crowd clustered in the south-east corner is intent on violence. If this group of men came with intent to start a riot, their wish may be about to be fulfilled. Sutherland steps forward and personally takes hold of some of the protestors who are now clinging on to Margaret's tram. Thick worsted coats have a long history of providing a policeman with a good purchase for collaring a resisting malcontent. Constable Samuel Ross is right beside him as a second tram car heading south for Mount Florida is forced to stop behind Margaret's tram. A passenger, elderly produce merchant James Cummings, cannot see why

15

the men are spilling onto the rails because, in his opinion, there is ample room for them on the south side of the Square. He interprets their actions as deliberate and cannot see how the lady tram driver has given them any provocation.[34]

Inside the stricken tram, it takes both Margaret and Cree to hold on to the power handles as some of the mob reach through the window and attempt to snatch them from her. Things are clearly getting out of hand and Inspector Sutherland advances with a dozen police. They do not yet need to draw their batons and manage to repel the crowd using just their hands and Margaret does not see them use any violence. Although no one lays hands on Margaret, some of the crowd attempt to pull Inspector Cree off the platform. At the rear of the tram, someone in the crowd shouts at the conductor, 26-year-old Frances Simeone. They order her to get off the tram or else they'll make short work of her. What that means she does not get the chance to discover because, thankfully, four soldiers, three of them Australians, dash forward to protect her, then they climb the tram stairs to replace the trolley on the wire. Safe for the moment but petrified, Frances walks through the tram to join Margaret and Cree on the front platform. Margaret has had her own struggles and has been rescued by a New Zealand Flying Corps officer and Private Cecil Naismith of the Royal Scots who remain on the platform beside her while she concentrates on getting the tram moving. Her tram escapes round the corner into South Frederick Street, but other trams remain held up. The whole experience takes just ten minutes and later there will be conflicting reports whether any windows on her tram were actually smashed despite descriptions of missiles flying through the air. Neither Margaret nor Frances witnesses the violence about to be unleashed.[35] But Inspector Cree does because he has jumped cars and now heads in the opposite direction on board a tram heading north up South Frederick Street into the Square. It is approximately 12.18 pm and he hears glass smashing and a heated shout go up from the surrounding mob: 'Go for the police'.[36] Still on Margaret's tram, Private Cecil Naismith also hears the crowd threaten the police in the same words. He alights at the Municipal Buildings and waits on the corner of George Square.[37]

Assistant Chief Constable Alexander Mennie watches as Margaret's tramcar trolley is pulled from the wire and then a second car's and a third. The crowd throws whatever they can lay hands on and the police are roughly handled. Still in charge, of his police contingent at least, Inspector Sutherland is now in the thick of it. He also hears members of the crowd baying to rush the police. His men tense, anticipating the onslaught. Sergeant MacKinnon ducks to avoid mud, bottles and nuts and bolts lobbed

16

at him and his colleagues. If those nuts and bolts get under the crowd's or the police's feet, George Square will become an ice rink. But it is too late for the police to react and, anyway, they are hugely outnumbered. Sutherland and his men are jammed against one of the tram cars, their backs protected but there is little they can do to defend themselves while their batons are undrawn. The mob nearest to them kick their shins. Even Sutherland's inspector's stripes do not save him, and he and his men are all generally abused. Sergeant David Murdoch is squashed against another tramcar with his men, and they, too, are kicked with workmen's hard-toed boots. He swears a window is smashed near him. Standing a little distance away, Sergeant McArthur hears the crash of glass as a window is broken. However, his greater fear is the surging and swaying crowd and a mob that is now thoroughly hostile to the police's presence.

Superintendent Matthew McCulloch of the Lanarkshire Constabulary stands outside 55 Cochrane Street and also claims to hear the words 'Go for them, into them, rush them, never mind their batons, get into them'. He looks up at the buildings and from the second floor he sees five men gesticulating from two separate windows. They are waving from inside the library and he interprets their gestures as hostile to the police. He recognizes one of the men as David Kirkwood whom he has met before at workers' meetings in Rutherglen. He is certain it is Kirkwood who has shouted the fateful words, because afterwards McCulloch considers the crowd becomes more violent and disorderly. And yet, the men standing with Kirkwood at the windows hear him respond to calls from below. They hear the crowd shout, 'For God's sake come down, they are batoning us'. Standing at the window beside Kirkwood, Neil Maclean thinks this is said by a woman with a child in her arms. Kirkwood cannot bear to watch anymore and goes to find the Lord Provost to get the violence stopped.[38]

Inspector Sutherland has not heard any of this exchange. He and his men are crushed against the trams with elements of the crowd continuing to encourage a rush at the police, stones and other missiles flying around their heads. Finally, and with some difficulty as they push their way through the mayhem, reinforcements arrive under the direction of Inspector Fraser. They are perhaps only ten or a dozen more men, but with little time to weigh up such a grave decision any longer, Sutherland orders his men to draw batons. Self-protection or to get the trams running again, at this stage it does not matter. His men have managed to release the first trams, but the situation is now dangerous. As the crowd surges back towards the trams in line with the police, they advance on the crowd with their batons raised.[39]

Still an innocent bystander, Archibald Wallace watches as the crowd around him runs down the adjoining streets; no one wants a police baton thwacked across their back, but he cannot see where the crowd can run. From his viewpoint, the crowd does not appear to be able to cross the street nor flee into the Square.[40] Yet, when the police advance on them, the crowd does manage to recoil towards the Square and the Municipal Buildings.[41] Watching from the upstairs window, Town Clerk Lindsay estimates 1,000 or 2,000 protestors attempt to run to the west and north of the Square to escape the police batons and, with his face pressed against the glass beside him, Sheriff MacKenzie can see trams now running round the corner below.[42] How they hear him above the shouting of the crowd and confusion is anyone's guess, but Inspector Sutherland orders his men to return their batons.

Forced back into the Square, the crowd scatters where it can. Many are pushed towards the Gladstone statue where Gallacher is speaking, others are funnelled towards the doors to the City Chambers where a line of police protects the entrance.[43] Everything is confused: is the mob attempting to storm the City Chambers as the police anticipate, or are these protestors those trying to get away from the police baton charge around the trams in the south-east corner? Standing in front of the Chambers, Sergeant Steele claims he hears the crowd shout, 'Rush the Buildings' which he believes will fulfil the threat made earlier in the week by the strike's leaders. It is a neat connection to make from a man whose evidence at court will later be viewed as unreliable. Steele is in the thick of the fighting as the police attempt to protect the buildings and themselves, pushing the crowd back the width of the street in front of them. So far, this is the second baton charge of the day. The crowd resents it violently and throws more stones and mud and kicks, but ultimately is pushed across the roadway away from the Buildings. In the space that has suddenly become clear, Steele sees a man exit the main entrance to the Municipal Buildings running down the front steps. He does not recognize him.[44]

Speaking from the Gladstone plinth, William Gallacher is unaware of the events in the south-east corner of the Square; all he can see is what he later claims looks like the police making a savage and unexpected assault on the rear of the crowd who have their backs turned to the Municipal Buildings while listening to him. He claims to see batons smashing right and left with brutal ferocity regardless of whether they make contact with men, women or children. As the crowd begins to move back towards the Chambers, Sutherland and his men drive the crowd back a considerable distance into the Square – this is their third baton charge – but from the statue, Sutherland's actions are interpreted by some as an unprovoked assault on the crowd from behind; this will become a pivotal claim for the defence at the trial.

Gallacher watches as men are laid low by the onslaught of the police and he claims to see a woman lying on her side with a muddy boot print on her face; no one else reports this. Standing at the base of the Gladstone plinth, Sergeant McClure remonstrates with Gallacher to get down, but Gallacher replies, 'I'm damned sure if I don't'. Beside him acting Detective Constable John Miller says he hears Gallacher shout in a wild and excited state for the crowd to rush the police. He helps McClure pull Gallacher from the plinth. Pulled off or jumped off as Gallacher will later claim, he is on the ground now with several of his comrades. While they tend to the unknown woman, Gallacher seeks out the chief constable. Lieutenant Gray, whose leadership of the second baton charge has placed him near the Gladstone statue, spots Gallacher rush at Chief Constable Stevenson. Gallacher remonstrates with Stevenson to stop the police but, with batons raised all around him as he claims, Gallacher is forced to duck and weave and then, getting close enough, inexplicably he throws a full powerful punch with his fist at Stevenson. Constable Melrose sees him do it. Constable Turner cannot be certain that a stick isn't used as well. Now batons rain down on Gallacher and when his efforts to resist arrest fail, he falls to the ground on his back. Struggling and losing strength as several policemen attempt to arrest him simultaneously, a nearby unknown striker throws himself across Gallacher and a blow that might have landed full force on his face instead knocks the man semi-conscious. Sergeant Murdoch of Central Division lays claim to the blow which removes Gallacher from the fight. Covered in blood and mud, Gallacher does not recognize his saviour as Neil Alexander, a boilermaker, reputedly a quiet fellow. Dazed but still squirming, Turner manages to keep hold of Gallacher with Constable Rennie's help and, unluckily, Constable Davidson is left to apprehend Alexander who flails around in a very infuriated state like a mad man.[45] Constable Gargan watches as Alexander decidedly resists arrest.[46]

Frustratingly, Lieutenant Gray cannot see what fells Gallacher and he also does not see Alexander's attempted rescue, but he does watch as the deputation leaves the Municipal Buildings with David Kirkwood at their front who dashes out waving his arms above his head. So does Sergeant Steele who claims to hear him shout 'Come on men, come on men, rally round men, rush the Buildings, rush them!' But Kirkwood's obvious intention is to appeal to the police and crowds for restraint. Steele will claim that he orders Kirkwood to leave and, when told 'to hell with you', will recount how he reaches for his baton and strikes Kirkwood on the back and shoulders. Kirkwood is 47-years-old, a robust man who has experienced long hours of physical labour since he began work aged twelve; he drops like a stone.[47] Following Kirkwood out of the Buildings, Neil Maclean witnesses what to him appears to be Steele's unprovoked assault on Kirkwood which is also captured by a newspaper photographer.[48] Constable Ritchie is right beside him as he crumples; he also claims to see and hear the exchange. Gallacher will later describe it as a vicious cowardly blow to Kirkwood's head, although in the moment the picture is taken, the policeman is shown striking Kirkwood's upper back. As Gallacher and Alexander are dragged into the Municipal Buildings' inner quadrangle, together Steele and Ritchie carry Kirkwood's limp body in the same direction.[49]

Having come by a circuitous route, stopping at workshops and yards to persuade men still working to join them, the Parkhead procession led by the Parkhead Forge workers' band arrives late. It is 12.30 pm according to Herbert Highton, one of the Parkhead strike leaders. His procession has been orderly all the way and actively avoided any friction with road traffic. But, as they are almost at the Square, they are diverted from South Frederick Street to South Hanover Street by Harry Hopkins, an engineer and union leader, who approaches with his hands up shouting excitedly. Herbert hears him say, 'For God's sake get them out of here'. It is also reported that Gallacher has been injured and arrested.[50]

No one knows what is happening in the courtyard inside the Buildings except the police gathered around Kirkwood's prostrate body and Gallacher with a bandage now wrapped around his head. It has stemmed the flow of blood, but not the haranguing he receives from his wife who has appeared in the quadrangle. The high imposing walls of the Municipal Buildings loom over them along with four policemen made taller by their high-domed helmets. The average height of a Glaswegian constable is five feet eleven inches, which is five inches taller than most Glaswegians, and so these four tower over Kirkwood and Gallacher.[51] There is another man in the quadrangle with them, an anonymous news photographer who has followed them in and who captures the moment. Three of the four policemen turn to look at him, their faces devoid of humour.[52] The stone walls insulate the quadrangle from the waves of growing clamour beyond.

Outside in the Square, news of Kirkwood's and Gallacher's arrest is broadcast by a tall man standing at the front of the Buildings. Private Naismith, who remains in the Square watching events, does not recognize him, but he hears him call the police 'blue-coated assassins'. It is a peculiar phrase for a working-class man to use against Glasgow's police;

more usually they are referred to as 'blue bottles' or 'blue locusts' by men expressing their hostility to their authority.[53]

Two floors above them inside the Municipal Buildings in the Lord Provost's office, Sheriff MacKenzie and Sir John Lindsay have also observed much of the violence so far.[54] MacKenzie has been sheriff of Inverness-shire, Renfrew and Bute over the years, and Sheriff of Lanarkshire since August 1917.[55] He has never encountered anything like this, but he knows an ugly and disorderly crowd when he sees one and decides they must be induced to depart. He wrestles with a decision which will be a pivotal moment in Glasgow's history. With only around 140 police on duty in the Square and tens of thousands of protestors, many of whom are angry, he decides on the ultimate sanction because he considers there are no other options available to him. Turning to Sir John, he declares rather formally, 'I am satisfied with what I have seen that mobbing and rioting is taking place and that the time has now arrived when I should act for the preservation of the public peace'. Sheriff MacKenzie determines to read the Riot Act.[56]

MacKenzie goes in search of the Lord Provost and finds him at the magistrates' meeting in the neighbouring room where he informs him of his decision and repeats his statement already made to Sir John. Their exchange is short and later Baillie Muir recalls a hammering at the door may have frightened the sheriff into making a decision that longer deliberation might have avoided.[57] However, they are in debate sufficiently long for someone in the room to suggest they use machine guns to clear the Square. Believing this is no occasion for the military to intervene, Baillie John Wheatley and his colleague Baillie John Stewart suggest they might be allowed first to speak to the crowd. The sheriff does not object and both baillies, the sheriff and Sir John prepare to go outside. The third baton charge – the second from the front of the City Chambers – has cleared space in front of the walls and the men are able to stand milling for a moment deciding how to proceed. It is sufficient time for Baillies Wheatley and Stewart to shout to the crowd that if they do not disperse the military will be called, but only a dozen or so of those closest to them can hear what they say. Not even Sir John standing with them hears their message to the crowd.[58]

Then Sheriff MacKenzie notices a lorry pull up in North Frederick Street. Some men and lads begin to unload boxes of bottles from it, but one man catches his attention as he bends down to take something from a crate on the ground. Surrounded by Chief Constable Stevenson, a guard of police and the Lord Provost, MacKenzie concludes an attack is imminent and resolves to read the Riot Act at the very corner where the attack may commence. Two bottles fly over MacKenzie's head and smash on the roadway behind him. He stops and gives the immediate crowd a warning that he intends to read the Riot Act. Instead of dispersing for fear of the severe consequences of being arrested after its reading, the crowd becomes louder and louder which the sheriff believes is done on purpose to drown out his voice. The group of gentlemen has been outside the Buildings for five, perhaps seven minutes by Sir John's estimation.

Unfolding the ominous sheet of paper on which the short 'Proclamation' of the Riot Act is printed, holding it up so that he can read it and the crowd can sense the imminent portentous ceremony, the Sheriff of Lanarkshire begins to read:

> Our Sovereign lord the King chargeth and commandeth all persons, being assembled, immediately to disperse themselves and peaceably to depart to their habitations ... .

It's pointless. No one can hear him and he does not manage to read beyond the word 'habitations', when a young man shouts, 'He's reading the Riot Act' and dashes forward, snatching the sheet from MacKenzie's hands before diving back into the crowd. He does not know the wording by heart, he has never had cause to learn it and so MacKenzie, his dignity bristling, skips a line and wraps up with a hasty 'under the pains of Law', respectfully adds 'God Save the King' and heads back to the Municipal Buildings.[59] The strikers stand and watch him depart, but Assistant Chief Constable Alexander Mennie is not so mesmerized by proceedings. He has not managed successfully to hold onto the man who interrupted the reading of the Riot Act, but his accomplice is now under arrest. No striker gets away with grabbing the assistant chief constable by the coat tails, holding him back from his duty, knocking off his hat and allowing him to be struck on the head. Mennie's head bleeds profusely and then someone stabs him on the inner side of his right knee.[60] While Mennie deals with his injuries, Chief Detective Inspector Andrew Keith catches hold of the man responsible, a slightly built man by the name of Loudon and assisted by Detective Sergeant Montgomerie, they take him into custody, depositing him in the quadrangle alongside Gallacher and Kirkwood.[61] It has all been so fast and confused, they are not sure they have the man who snatched the Riot Act from under the sheriff's nose or the man who hung onto Mennie's coat tails. They're also not sure it matters at this point.

With all the missiles already flying, the addition of a lorry-load of over a thousand bottles is cause for concern. Sir John sees the City Chambers' windows broken by a bottle lobbed from the crowd and heading back inside with him, Sheriff MacKenzie notices a young policeman's helmet knocked from his head by another bottle and then three more strike the wall near the entrance to the Buildings and shatter into small pieces. As they near the entrance, a group of police rush past them heading for North Frederick Street, their batons raised. Clearly reading the Riot Act has had no effect on the crowd's mood. Is there something different about this group of men chucking bottles on the north side of the Square? Are they opportunists, young apprentices and hooligans, or an influx of strikers driven here from deeper in the Square? It is hard to tell because everyone in the Square appears to be engaged in some form of tussle with those around them, even if their efforts are only to keep their footing and remain upright in the mayhem.

He has been hit on the stomach by a bottle, but Sheriff MacKenzie and Sir John reach safety on the steps of the Buildings and, leaving the tumult behind them, the two men proceed to the Lord Provost's room where Chief Constable Stevenson joins them. He has come from a quickly snatched conversation with Neil Maclean. The latter is a Member of Parliament who will later explain how he became involved in events throughout the week almost by accident; now he thinks the crowd might calm down and disperse if they could hear from Gallacher and Kirkwood. Could that be arranged? MacKenzie is the responsible official in charge now; he considers his options. It is a quick calculation because he is very much out of options. He needs to stop the mobbing without further trouble, risk or danger. So long as the two men make no attempt to deliver a rousing speech, he agrees. The message is conveyed to the police in the quadrangle and, shortly afterwards, Kirkwood and Gallacher appear in the Lord Provost's room. No one considers their injuries or that Kirkwood is recently recovered from being knocked unconscious. Constable Rennie offers Gallacher a glass of whisky which he refuses; he and Kirkwood have a duty to their city.[62] But Gallacher asks fellow striker John McBain who has come inside to enquire after them if he will try first. There is a shallow balcony on the second floor of the Buildings and someone opens the ceiling-height windows for them. Cold air and the commotion of the crowd rush in, and John McBain steps out. They interpret his words because there is no way they can hear him distinctly but, presumably in response to his orders, some of the crowd forms up into sections in readiness to depart. But these are their men and Gallacher and Kirkwood now step forward so they can be seen. Gallacher is accustomed to addressing a noisy crowd and usually his voice carries above the assembled heads, but not now. His head wrapped in bandages and blood on his collar, he asks the crowd to disperse, but they do not respond. Councillor Rosslyn Mitchell who arrived early for his meeting has been disturbed by the noise and is on an adjacent balcony. He witnesses Gallacher's attempts to disperse the crowd. He hears him call out: 'Now, men, clear away from here. Don't mind us, we are all right. Our only concern is for you, and we plead that you should form up in procession and go down to Glasgow Green'. They still do not respond. Gallacher appeals to them 'For God's sake to leave the Square and go to the Green'. The crowd appears to hesitate. They have kept their promise to the sheriff; neither strike leader says anything he could take exception to, but then Kirkwood becomes exasperated. They never meant for any of this to happen, did they? Surely this was not their plan?

A mass show of solidarity and the desire to hear the Government's response has turned into a riot. They have been assembled here since just before midday. Not one of them has seen or heard from their delegation since they disappeared inside. They may already have read the Government's response in this morning's press, but no one has addressed them here today to tell them what the plan is and that is precisely why they came. And now, even if anyone tries, they would not be heard. The sheriff, town clerk and chief constable stiffen as Kirkwood steps up beside Gallacher, a cap covering the bandages wrapped around his head – he does not want the crowd to use his injuries as an excuse for further violence.[63] He raises his arms to catch the crowd's attention. Perhaps they will hear him, listen to him, if he tries one last time? He leans as far forward as he dares. Spread out in front of him, the Square is black with men. They must leave George Square, this is not the opportunity they might think it is. He shouts out to them, 'Your time will come later on'.[64]

Just six words, the different interpretations of which will determine Kirkwood's fate and that of his strike colleagues in two months' time when they will defend their actions in court. It is one of several sentences spoken this week which the prosecution will use to attempt to prove that Kirkwood and the others incited a riot. It will become pivotal to understanding the legacy of today's events as the personal memories of those involved fade with time.

Within the hour, the sheriff will call for military aid. His decision will stamp an indelible mark on Glasgow's history.

Chapter 2

Monday, 27 January 1919

The Leaders

The promised strike has begun. On Friday the newspapers reported that a strike had been called for today in Glasgow despite efforts by the union national executives to avert a city-wide stoppage.[1] All weekend, the city has been tense, waiting to see what the impact will be. Last night, as he sat writing his column for this morning's press, the *Manchester Guardian's* journalist anticipated the nearest thing to a general strike ever to be seen on Clydeside, a region with a reputation for disturbance and aggression.[2] There are fears the electricity will be cut off, the trams cease to work and potentially the city may grind to a halt, held to ransom by the strikers. On Glasgow's dreich streets, idle men gather on corners, their workmen's bonnets damp, their woollen coats heavy with the atmosphere. Hard, nailed boots scuff against the kerb and young boys run messages between meeting halls. Over the weekend, meetings, debates and arguments have kept the men warm. But there can only be so much talk otherwise there is a risk of division and indecision taking hold. So, this morning, the strike is on.

So far, tens of thousands of men are confirmed to be out on strike, but the figures vary; some are out officially with their union's backing, some unofficially and some intimidated to join them. It is not a general strike yet, but the fear – hope among some – is it will become such. There are rumours the miners will come out, and some wild claims the police may join them. The strikers have the support of the Scottish Trades Union Congress and the Glasgow Trades Council, but not of the national Trades Union Congress, nor in every case their national representative unions, which makes this a peculiarly Scottish strike, for the moment. Without the national TUC's approval, Glasgow's strikers may not be able to negotiate with Government ministers. Negotiations in London between the TUC and Ministry of Labour make slow progress and will hardly calm the storm brewing on the Clyde. Some think it is Clydeside playing tough again, using their grip on the shipbuilding industry to negotiate with the Government, others interpret the strike as a battle with the unions' national executive and the employers.[3]

The strike is organized by the Clyde Workers' Committee (CWC) led by William Gallacher, Willie to his friends, and a stalwart of the Clyde's wartime struggles for pay and conditions, but he is viewed as ugly and violent in Westminster.[4] As president of the CWC, which evolved from the Withdrawal of Labour Committee in 1916, Gallacher could be viewed as a small-time agitator looking after his men's interests while the national union leaders play politics and prefer national bargaining to resolving local issues. For Gallacher, the unions have lost their allure; he is a socialist and a syndicalist spreading his doctrine workshop by workshop, man by man. It is a form of workers' organization begun during the war and which Government did not like then.[5] Then there is Emanuel Shinwell, an astute labour leader, president of the Glasgow Trades Council, city councillor and recently involved in a Clydeside sailors' dispute that had racist undertones. Sometimes, he pours oil on troubled labour disputes and at other times he lights fires and stands back to observe the resulting blaze. Unlike Gallacher, Shinwell does not wear his principles on his sleeve, if he possesses any.

The strikers' demands are for shorter hours for no reduction in pay, and Glasgow's shipbuilding and engineering workers are not the only workforce campaigning for improved post-war conditions. Despite the lack of national TUC support or approval, this is no local labour dispute. Pockets of unrest have flared around the country in the eleven weeks since the cessation of hostilities. Already the railwaymen have secured the Government's promise of an eight-hour day; the miners have a tradition of shorter working hours because of the conditions they labour in and are making claims for a six-hour day. Government is inundated with demands varying from forty to forty-seven hours with or without breaktimes included. The overarching message is that the nation's workforce needs a rest after four exhausting years of wartime working pace, or at least an easier time. They want to reap the rewards of the war even if they cannot benefit from the profits made by their employers.

Last week, the War Cabinet received a memorandum describing the countrywide situation. A 'National Agreement' for the engineering and shipbuilding trades, negotiated by the Amalgamated Society of Engineers and a federation of shipbuilding and engineering unions, has secured a promise of a forty-seven-hour working week which was meant to come into operation on 1 January 1919, but Glasgow's ASE and CWC leadership have other ideas. They remain undecided on their precise demands, while around the country many industries are making claims for reductions in their workers' hours, accompanied by calls for increased wages with paid annual leave, demands unknown before the war.[6]

On Clydeside, forty hours is insufficient for Gallacher. He has led the CWC throughout the war and his Marxist politics necessitate more for his men; his recommendation – to some it appears a revolutionary demand – is thirty hours. It would take someone with a more diplomatic approach and a longer view to persuade him otherwise, or a workers' vote, which Gallacher respects. At a meeting last week of 300 delegates representing the widespread interests of industrial Scotland and chaired by Shinwell, the issue of hours was put to the vote. The men responded in favour of thirty hours, but in order to appear more reasonable to the wavering minority, forty hours was agreed as the campaign goal.[7]

Unions and Government know that demobilizing soldiers will need jobs when they return home and it is anticipated there will not be as many as will be required. Only eleven weeks have elapsed since the Armistice was declared, and already the predicted post-war slump has hit Glasgow harder than most of Britain's industrial centres. For the past four years, Glasgow's citizens have enjoyed decent wages and full employment in wartime industries, but there is no longer as great a need for armaments and munitions or warships. Unemployment is rising and looks like doubling within the month, especially in engineering sectors.[8] A reduction to thirty hours might accommodate most of the returning men, but forty hours sounds more realistic.

Glasgow's working men have a reputation for hard work and hard drinking, and some for deep thinking. Numerous Glaswegians have spent the war attending John Maclean's Marxist night-school lectures, reading at home and brooding on what this new political model means to them in the shipyard, factory and society. However, no one knows how many men attended, how many have taken Maclean's teaching to heart, who is prepared to act and how many might happily maintain the *status quo*. But the Government does not care to countenance what might happen if the workforce falls idle after so much effort. Ministers are less concerned with domestic troubles with bored men recently returned from a brutal war cooped up in overcrowded homes alongside their wives and children feeling worthless and enervated. Men congregating on street corners and in public houses with potential political grievances are far more worrying. The Government has a correspondent in Glasgow right now – probably an over-excited member of Special Branch – reporting that the revolutionary movement appears to be gaining traction. He thinks John Maclean is mentally unstable, but Maclean's audiences are growing and this agent is convinced the 'Social Revolution' will happen this year. In London, the Minister for Labour, Sir Robert Horne, explains the Clyde's current irritation by the lack of beer and its poor quality.[9] Despite these worrying reports from their men on the ground, the Government appears relatively unconcerned.

A gentleman at his breakfast reading some of the more excitable morning papers would be forgiven for thinking Britain is on the verge of revolution, and a labourer picking up Friday's copy of *The Worker* will be looking forward to forcing his own conditions on the employers if sufficient of them join the campaign for the forty-hour week. William Gallacher's front page column is incendiary. He calls for solidarity because if the men agree to anything less than forty hours they will betray their own class and every man idle on the streets is a man desperate for work to support his family who potentially may take your job for less pay. He enjoins them to stand fast with the soldiers who have done the fighting and in return now expect their share of the nation's wealth. To sweep away the profits of power, to agitate, educate and organize is the only way, and for anyone who reads as far as the second page the connection to the Russian people is clear: workers of the world unite against the old order. Westminster is alive to these sentiments too, keeping a careful eye on the influence of recent events in Russia on home-grown extremists.[10]

It is desperate in Belfast, too, where the workers have organized themselves into 'soviets'. It is a new word and Westminster is anxious to understand what this really means: is it emulation of the recent Russian upheavals? Or simply an appropriated term keeping the Belfast strike topical? Its use seems unrelated to what is really happening here because Belfast's strikers endeavour to keep their protest non-political. Belfast has been on strike for a week already demanding a forty-four-hour working week and, crucially, with the municipal workers joining the strike, gas and electricity supplies have been interrupted. The authorities have managed to persuade the strikers to allow electricity to be generated for use in Belfast's hospitals, but the tram network has ceased operations.[11] Belfast is at a standstill and even if its citizens wished to go to work, there is no transport. Even the streetlights have been off since Saturday to conserve gas.[12] The sun sets in Belfast just before 5.00 pm at this time of year, plunging the city's residents into chilly, joyless darkness.

Over the weekend a representative from the Glasgow strike committee has been in Belfast, but so far the two cities have not joined forces, although cohesion across mainland Britain has gathered pace since Thursday last week. Despite the Minister of Labour's attempts to intercede, Sir Robert Horne failed to secure a wholesale promise of resumption of work for trades already threatening strike action. In Scotland that means the engineers employed at Mirrlees Watson's ironworks south of the Clyde have agreed to stick with the forty-seven hours negotiated by their union and not to strike unless there is a change of heart at executive level. Yet, their neighbours at shipbuilders Harland and Wolff are in favour of stopping work today; in fact, all departments at their Govan works are in favour of the stoppage.[13] The trades councils at Coatbridge and Airdrie have voted the same. The iron moulders and brass moulders are in sympathy and are out today. A hurried meeting in the Good Templars' Hall on Friday night failed to establish Glasgow Corporation's tram-workers' position. The workers present rejected the idea of coming out on a show of hands which their pro-strike officials wanted. There is to be a ballot and another meeting, but for the moment they are not keen to join the strike and their support for it remains in the balance.[14] The Corporation's traffic department alone employs 32,000, nearly half of whom are women.[15] Corporation engineering workers at Coplawhill's tram maintenance depot have demanded a forty-hour week for fifty-four hours' pay and they're striking today. At 6.00 am this morning, the Coplawhill works were open for any employees wishing to turn up for work. At present, it is unknown how many have. All the while, the employers have remained publicly silent, although the minutes from the meeting of the executive committee of the Engineers' and Shipbuilders' Associations last Monday reveal their nervousness about today's strike.[16]

Its imposing red sandstone tower looming over an anxious Friday night crowd, Shinwell declared at Greenock Town Hall two days ago to an estimated audience of 8,000 that today's strike would be the greatest ever to take place since the industrial world began.[17] It is quite a claim. Early counts suggest 40,000 men are idle in Glasgow's shipyards and engineering shops, about half the workforce called upon to strike. Similar smaller strikes occur in Edinburgh, on the east coast at Arbroath, Aberdeen and Dundee with some of Fife's miners also out.[18] But this morning, another Glasgow newspaper, *The Bulletin*, reports the stoppage is not on the scale expected, or promoted by Shinwell, although the situation remains critical.[19]

The weekend has been busy for anyone managing the city's meeting halls. There have been many gatherings and speeches as individual yards have held meetings and unions have summoned members to vote. Last night the Albert Hall in Bath Street, normally home to Glasgow's enthusiastic palais-goers, housed the Electrical Trade Union's members. Their officials called them out on strike for today. In response, the tramways' manager and his colleague the chief engineer in the city's electricity department confirmed that Glasgow's Corporation power stations would remain operational: trams, streetlights, hospitals and homes would continue to function.[20] As important as power to the city, the bakers have been exempted from the general appeal to strike, but they are in two minds. Their Scottish executive advised against it, but the bakers themselves desire better conditions, at least an agreement on a forty-hour week. In the city's bakeries, last night was a fog of flour and sweat in preparation for today's baking and what they have agreed is that they will not strike without giving notice to Glasgow's citizens. A lack of bread has been the catalyst for revolutions in the past. However, the big news is that the stoppage is unanimous at Beardmore's Parkhead and Dalmuir sites.[21]

Messrs Beardmore, iron forgers in Glasgow's East End, employs 20,000 men and women. It is a vast site that has produced naval guns before sending them down the water to Beardmore's shipbuilding site at Dalmuir. All of Clydeside has contributed to the war effort, but Beardmore is where David Kirkwood works, and he has been pivotal to the workers' movement on Clydeside, helping to gain his employer's factory its reputation across the country. Kirkwood is 47 years old and, since he was 20, he has been a member of the ASE. He is a skilled engineer respected for his diligence and good sense and known for saying exactly what he thinks. He called his first strike in 1895 at Beardmore's Parkhead Forge because two labourers were caught doing an engineer's job at labourers' wages. The encroachment on skilled workers' status not only undermines their position and wages, but eventually leads to the labourer being abused, as employers realize they can get engineers on labourer's rates.[22] It has been an issue throughout Kirkwood's working life in Glasgow's engineering shops and cropped up most recently during the war when dilution was mooted – another attempt to pay lower rates for skilled work. He will not have it. Despite his reputation for strikes, Kirkwood is not such a staunch socialist as his colleague Gallacher.[23] He enjoys a co-operative relationship with Beardmore's owner, Sir William Beardmore. Kirkwood is Sir William's interpreter; he listens to the management and conveys their messages to the workforce. He is the chairman of Beardmore's shop stewards where he also listens and tells Sir William what they want. He can be collaborative, but he is no company man. Popular among his engineering colleagues, he rose to prominence just before the war when he demanded that engineers' wages go up by two pence (2d) an hour. Even the ASE chairman refused to support him, and then the war began, and the issue died down until Christmas 1914. If the employers refuse to pay an extra 2d an hour to Scotsmen, why would they bring over a gang of engineers from the United States, agree to pay them the higher rate and give them a bonus to boot? That is what they did at Weir's of Cathcart, the Clyde's famous pump manufacturers. Pumps in

Persian pipelines, marine engineering consultants to the Clyde's shipyards, of course Weir's engineers came out on strike and so did the rest of the Clyde's engineers, as did the Americans, not wishing to upset their fellow men.[24] But timing and public opinion are everything. Kirkwood was leading a strike which the public viewed as undermining to the war effort; even their own union executive demanded a return to work. The compromise of 1d pay rise solved the issue. The men went back and seemingly there was no bad feeling. Kirkwood considered his friendship with Sir William was as harmonious as ever, but there would be more trouble with the unions in Beardmore's works.

This morning it appears all the engineers at Beardmore's at Parkhead are out, responding to the call to strike for a forty-hour week. Is this because they are all in agreement across all the trades employed at Beardmore's or is it because the electricians have come out and none of the machinery will now function?[25] Whatever, this is good news for Emanuel Shinwell as he prepares to take the stage at St Andrew's Hall. The venue is Glasgow's West End concert hall, more used to popular music performances than inflammatory speeches. The last time a rousing speech was heard before a capacity audience here was Christmas 1915, an auspicious day for Glasgow's working men and their leaders.

They had defied David Lloyd George, then minister of munitions, and established the Clyde as troublemakers. In these early months of the war, if the British Army stood any chance of survival, they needed more munitions at the front; productivity needed to increase and was only possible with a larger workforce. The Government had felt compelled to legislate in the form of the Munitions Act which had been introduced in March 1915. On the Clyde, the workers' response concentrated on two key elements of that Act: leaving certificates and dilution of the workforce. The Act's prohibition on striking did not seem to concern Clydeside's leaders at this stage. Clydesiders were among the world's most skilled workers, proud of their achievements and renown, who considered themselves free to sell their labour to the highest bidder, but the Act prohibited them from changing employers. Why should they be forced to remain with their employer when wages were going up and a skilled tradesman could negotiate? The fact that many skilled men, like Edgar Board, a fitter for thirty-nine years at Yarrow's in Scotstoun, had worked for one employer all their working lives and did not wish to swap one yard for another was beside the point; the principle of workers' freedom was at stake.[26] Added to that insult was dilution, the introduction of unskilled men and women into the workforce to increase production. That seemed a logical approach to increase the workforce, but the skilled men had feared the newcomers would replace them at lower rates. It was 1895 all over again. The CWC had wanted to retain control of dilution's implementation to protect their skilled workers' valued status and standard of living by maintaining wages.[27]

In early December 1915 Lloyd George had already spoken to employers in Manchester where he had defied the unions to interfere with plans to introduce unskilled workers into skilled roles. At another meeting later in the month in Newcastle, he met two of Glasgow's permanent trade union officials. They invited him to visit their city to speak to their men. He had agreed but refused to acknowledge or meet the CWC. Either he had not understood the allegiance of Glasgow's workforce to the CWC or he intended to be confrontational. And it was clear by agreeing to exclude the CWC the trade union officials were equally out of step with the men they represented; the men's loyalty to the CWC shop stewards threatened union influence and they did not wish to give the CWC a platform alongside Lloyd George. By the time he arrived in Glasgow on 22 December, Gallacher was adamant the Welsh Wizard's eloquence and charm would get nowhere, although, in Parkhead Forge, Kirkwood had been invited to meet Lloyd George. After all he was the reasonable face of Clyde labour in contrast to Gallacher. Kirkwood was also easier to locate.

Lloyd George's telegram, simply addressed to Kirkwood at 'Parkhead Forge, Glasgow', requested a meeting with Kirkwood and the shop stewards at Sir William's premises. That afternoon Lloyd George had kept Kirkwood and his men waiting for forty-five minutes without apology and when he entered Sir William's office Kirkwood let rip, as he later admitted disrespectfully. His men had been dressed in their work clothes while Lloyd George's team were clean and smart, but the two men shook hands and the meeting began.[28] Kirkwood supported dilution so long as the women were not paid the same as the men, and had arrived prepared to listen to the minister, but speechifying about their brothers in the trenches and his wish for their efforts to rain shells on the Germans was not what Kirkwood's men had come to hear. Kirkwood did not need reminding of the Clyde's contribution to the war. Instead, he had preferred to hear the minister's plans for compromise on the Munitions Act, but Lloyd George refused to move on the issue of Scotsmen 'enslaved' to their shipyard and workshop. All that could be agreed was a meeting for Christmas Day and some years later Kirkwood will recall that it would include the detested CWC; he had ensured that. Gallacher's version is that Lloyd George had moved on from Beardmore's to Weir's where the shop stewards had refused to meet him without CWC representation. Gallacher will also recall that the Christmas

Day meeting was devised while Lloyd George was still in Newcastle at the beginning of the month because, on Thursday 23 December, why else would Gallacher and his colleagues gather to distribute tickets for the event? Either way, it was another meeting where Lloyd George was strongly rebuffed. By the time Gallacher and the men left, little had been agreed except a promise of transport home had been extracted. As Gallacher emerged from the central hall before midnight, ranks of taxis with their lights glittering in the damp dark were lined up ready to take the delegates home, one cab for every man.

On Christmas Eve Gallacher and Kirkwood set forth their position on dilution: they were not against it; they understood why it was necessary, but who was going to control the process – the men or the employers? Lloyd George was clear, he only wanted to win the war, so Kirkwood answered for him: the men would control dilution. The meeting was considered over until Christmas morning, but not by Gallacher. Calling him back for one last assurance that all would go smoothly in the morning, Lloyd George draped his arm round Gallacher's shoulders and purred that it would be a shame if anything were to go wrong, but Gallacher was no mesmerized mouse. His response was clearly infuriating because the minister stormed out.[29]

And so, last time St Andrew's Hall had enjoyed so many men under its roof, it had been decked out in Union flags with young girls dressed in khaki and a choir singing patriotic songs. With uniformed police in the throng, the mood was set from the start. With 3,000 gathered on the floor, they had raised the roof with their rendition of the 'Red Flag' and became louder when Lloyd George uttered Keir Hardie's revered name in a misguided attempt to quieten them. Kirkwood had stepped forward to silence the hall so the minister could be heard, but, instead of addressing their concerns on dilution, Lloyd George had attempted to rouse their patriotism, which they did not consider to be lukewarm. According to Kirkwood, the meeting had been a fiasco and from Lloyd George's perspective his usual charm had failed. No journalists had been allowed to attend and so, on 27 December, the national press carried only a short official report, supplied to them prior to the meeting, to avoid discussion of the minister's lack of success.[30] Word had travelled as far as Paris where a brief French news article had exhorted Glasgow to pull out the stops, but, by noon on New Year's Day, the workers' own report on the meeting's outcome had been silenced, the offices of their newspaper *Forward* ransacked by the authorities, printing machines dismantled, and every copy of their version of the event confiscated. The unforeseen victory for the CWC, in light of the suppression of Glasgow's left-wing press, was the impetus to publish the first edition of their own paper *The Worker,* a hurriedly distributed newssheet which appeared by mid-January 1916 carrying the CWC's voice direct to the men's homes.[31]

Dilution had been approved on the men's terms, conditions which Kirkwood readily agreed to at Parkhead Forge and thereafter other shops followed suit. Their victory was the formation of a committee appointed by the workers and accepted by the employers to administer the detail of the Munitions Act as it affected Clydeside, none of which should have been a problem if relations between men and employees had been resolved before the war.[32] However, it had taken the conflict and the confidence of Clydesiders to resolve labour disputes to their benefit, this time, and they had proved their ability to negotiate rather than use belligerence to win.

The word went out two days ago on Saturday lunchtime about this morning's strike. The call to strike is hard to miss: it is published in the newspapers, the socialist press, discussed in the pubs and chalked on pavements in front of the workshop gates since Friday night. Now, in St Andrew's Hall, Shinwell steps forward. The venue is designed for performances so he should be heard above the clamour of the crowd's agitated voices. He spoke at length on Saturday evening at Greenock and today he continues at full oratorical strength in front of 3,000 men inside and a crowd claimed to be 27,000 strong in the streets outside. Shinwell is their leader, so he speaks first.[33] He is known for rousing speeches. He intends to drive the strike's chances of success on the first day with a blistering oration to those who can actually hear him, because the police scattered among the swaying crowd of dark-suited men outside cannot. From reports arriving from various yards and works, Shinwell understands the sectional nature of the strike so far. It is better than sporadic, but solidarity among the same trades is yet to materialize and, while some men are out in support of the forty-hour campaign, others have downed tools because of lost wages when the working-week was reduced from fifty-four to forty-seven hours. Now his task is to rally the men in front of him, to coalesce around the Forty-Hour campaign, to instil in them the resolve to come out, to remain out and to encourage them to help their working brothers to join them.

The platform party approaches the stage. The men gathered before them are emotional and someone starts to sing as the party slowly appears. Socialist agitator Harry McShane listens as the tune catches on and voices join in around the hall. This is not a revolutionary song, it is not even 'red', just a popular tune to which everyone seems to know the words. Its effect is terrific, pulling the men together in one voice, forging one mind.[34] As the party climbs the platform, the audience is with them whatever they have to say.

The rustling of wool coats, men coughing, boots shuffling, the hall is hardly quiet as Shinwell addresses them. Immediately someone proposes from the floor that they form a mass picket to bring out reluctant workers. As quickly as proposed, the motion is adopted, but Shinwell cautions the men to good behaviour, to conduct themselves in an orthodox and orderly manner, to maintain a legitimate fight in a clean fashion and to keep on the side of moral suasion if they form pickets. Only if the Joint Committee instructs otherwise can they employ other measures.[35] Gallacher chips in to say they might take their non-striking brothers by the hand and guide them away from the evil presence of their masters.[36] He raises a laugh. Everyone knows what he hints at, but Shinwell's injunction to maintain discipline keeps them sober.

Gallacher is talking about picketing and coercing non-strikers into joining them. The strike only began this morning and until they can understand how widespread the stoppage is there is no need to resort to such tactics. However, 'other methods' are already being employed. On Friday 24 January, at the North British Railway Company's Cowlairs Works, where iron turner George Lingard has worked for twenty-five years, a vote was taken about joining the strike. He was not present but heard that the men had decided almost unanimously to remain at work. Now this morning there is another vote, effectively to see if anyone has changed their mind. To Lingard, it seems they will keep voting until the ASE branch secretary gets the decision he wants. Lingard is at work this morning but he is fearful of what will happen if pickets come knocking at his door.[37]

Now in St Andrew's Hall Gallacher, who reporters describe as representing the unofficial movement, proposes a motion to withhold rent and income tax until the Forty-Hours movement succeeds. Another cheer before Harry Hopkins, Glasgow District Secretary of the ASE, re-emphasizes the mass meeting's key resolution: no resumption of work until the forty-hour week with no reduction of pay has been conceded. The police have not managed to elbow their way inside the hall, but later Constable Turner believes he heard Hopkins say they will use drastic measures to make the strike a success and Constable Andrew Gallagher hears him suggest the newly-formed police union will be out before the end of the week.[38] The crowd's confidence, enthusiasm and unanimity are palpable.[39] From this moment on, Shinwell's job is easy.

Before he resumes his speech, another man on the floor calls out, 'What about the reporters?' He wants to know which newspapers they represent. Are they trusted to report fairly on this morning's proceedings? Already there has been some intimation in the press that the strike is in the hands of political extremist Bolsheviks.[40] Shinwell explains clearly that the strike's Joint Committee has decided the press should be allowed to hear what they have to say but in no way is the strike leadership actually dealing with the press. He recounts how in the past week the press has misrepresented the strike, how the authorities have cavilled with them and their own executives in London have been fainthearted. If their union officials are afraid to lead, although he assures them he is all for constitutional action, but if that does not work, then more expeditious measures might be adopted.[41] This morning they are closer to unity than the trade unions have ever brought them; he informs them a telegram from Edinburgh brings news of the Forth supporting the Clyde. Lanarkshire's miners are out this morning. Where there has not been a positive response, then it is the task of those here today to see to it they join them. Keeping his voice measured and calm, Shinwell informs them this cannot be a long strike and the issue of strike pay cannot stand between them. To make this a success, they must adopt other measures.[42] As the crowd cheers at each staccato instruction to stand firm, Shinwell suggests they take a nice walk, somewhere spacious enough for them to congregate and listen to more rousing speeches before dusk.

Now the police might get a chance to hear what is happening. As the crowds outside take up processional formations, those inside pour out on to Kent Street. There are thousands of men milling about, all intent on heading in one direction: to George Square. Steering them through Glasgow's streets is impossible for the handful of police on duty. The crowd swarms through the city's broad thoroughfares, blocking the way for traffic, particularly the trams. They march at least ten abreast squeezed between shopfronts on their left and trams slowly queuing one behind the other to their right. The sight of men in overcoats and jackets with every head topped by a flat cap extends as far as the eye can see. There isn't an inch of pavement or road remaining for anyone going about their daily business.[43]

A band leads their march. Above the noise of men and instruments, Constable Gallagher hears Hopkins instruct them not to allow their ranks to be broken.[44] That sounds different from Shinwell's advice earlier to be peaceful. Perhaps seeing someone at the head of the procession carrying an unfurled red flag colours the constable's perception of the crowd's mood. Whether wilful or not, by the time the processions reach Renfield Street, they hold up the traffic for fifteen minutes by Lieutenant Gray's estimate. He perceives their behaviour as deliberate, especially as they have stopped a van carrying funeral wreathes from proceeding on its way. This disrespect influences his observations of the crowd's intentions, although it is difficult to view their actions otherwise when next he sees them threaten the driver of a private vehicle in Buchanan Street.[45] Near St Enoch Square, Chief Detective Inspector Keith witnesses a lady tram driver being assaulted by a young man. He arrests the youth and two days later Alexander Wallace will receive either a fine of £8 8s or twenty-one days in prison from the Central Police Court if he cannot afford it.[46] However, this is not an isolated incident. As the strikers process through the city centre, they shout 'blackleg' and other abuse at passing tram drivers and conductors.

Just after midday, the marchers reach George Square and, as usual with Glasgow crowds, Shinwell, Gallacher and Hopkins head for the front of the City Chambers. They are joined by Neil Maclean MP. Clambering up onto the stone plinth of the building to be seen and heard, according to Lieutenant Gray they address 6,000 men.[47] The strikers continue in good spirits as someone raises a red flag on the council's flagpole opposite the Buildings. Although disapproving hissing can be heard from some of the crowd, more enthusiastic singing of the international workers' song, the 'Red Flag' follows.[48] Is the crowd in a jocular mood or is this a serious political gesture? Shinwell and the other strike leaders will deny any political aspirations for the strike and distance themselves from those raising the red flag. It is not an emblem they wish to be associated with, although the photographer who captures the moment recognizes its symbolism.[49] Gallacher's talk of there being more Bolsheviks within Glasgow's police force than anywhere else catches the attention of Chief Detective Inspector Weir.[50] The police's anxiety is not helped on hearing Shinwell, some think Gallacher, announce they have not come to take the Municipal Buildings today.[51] Sergeant Steele observes Shinwell point towards the City Chambers as he declares they will save possession for a future date.[52] Neil Maclean is speaking, although no one will remark on it, when Gallacher is approached by a young boy in uniform.[53] He has emerged from the nearby North British Hotel with news that inside 'oily magnates' feast on the best food and drink while the staff are starved. It is too good not to be repeated to the crowd so up Gallacher climbs again to inform the strikers that once they have taken control of the City Chambers, they will take the hotel next. Is it incitement to violence or an over-exuberant jest? Constable Andrew Gallagher believes this is the point the red flag is raised on the Square's flagpole, but one thing the police watching all agree on is a member of the crowd now shouting, 'Salute the flag'. Gravely, men remove their caps and with bared heads sing another rendition of the 'Red Flag' in the cold Square.[54] Such incitement to violence followed by the international anthem of the socialist working class, Constable Andrew Gallagher can interpret no other way and anticipates the crowd will imminently conduct themselves unlawfully. Constable Turner agrees.[55]

Inside the Municipal Buildings, Chief Constable James Verdier Stevenson re-assures himself his assessment of the strike has proved correct. So far, the strike is only partial, and the gas and tram workers have not joined in, although his prediction that the strikers would attempt to stop the trams appears to be correct: he is receiving too many reports concerning delays to the tram network as the strikers have advanced on George Square to believe otherwise.[56] He gave orders only yesterday for processions through the city to be accompanied by police prepared to deal immediately with any evidence of disorder and that includes obstruction of the traffic. If possible, they should arrest the ringleaders. In anticipation of a difficult week ahead, he has arranged for the provision of meals to constables detained after midday and further meals and overtime to those still on duty beyond 5.00 pm. Meal allowances of 2s 6d could become very expensive the way things are looking from his position inside the Buildings.[57]

Stevenson is worried as he surveys the swelling crowd below. The crowd is now pressed against the front of the City Chambers and spread across the steps. He makes a mental note to give another instruction: the crowd must not be allowed to position itself so close to the Buildings on future occasions. Indeed, this is going to be a long week by his estimation and the centre of city government must not be threatened.[58]

Addressing the crowd in George Square, Gallacher views himself as a successful leader of the working class and, although a passionate socialist, he and other leaders, he will maintain, have hardly had time to form a plan to challenge the capitalist employers; it has been enough of a trial to organize the strike and persuade sufficient numbers to come out today. He has heard that sections of the army have mutinied in France and at several places in England.[59] Now if they joined Glasgow's strikers that would be something, but this morning he is intent on guiding the men gathered in front of him, not leading a nationwide revolution.[60] Standing beside him, the leader of the Discharged Soldiers' Association adds his organization's backing to the strike and charges the strikers to support them; having fought for their country they now intend to own it.[61] A challenge to the establishment like this and language that a nervous city can only interpret as threatening has landed these strike leaders in trouble before. That was at the height of the war and they understand just how quickly the authorities can move.

On 17 March 1916 the Parkhead engineers came out on strike because David Kirkwood, identified as the key ringleader in the Christmas fiasco, had been forced from his role as Parkhead Forge's spokesman. But it was not just his involvement in the dilution debate that had damaged Kirkwood's reputation with Beardmore's management. He had also been instrumental throughout 1915 in organizing and encouraging the unionization of women workers across the Clyde, but most particularly at Beardmore's Parkhead and East Hope Street sites. After Christmas 1915, Kirkwood had negotiated with the government commission established to implement the Munitions Act on the Clyde at the pivotal moment of a shell crisis at the front. Whether intentional or not, Kirkwood had effectively signed away his right to enter any department at Parkhead Forge to calm trouble, and by also supporting a strike by the women working at Beardmore's for fairer pay his established role as trouble-shooter had become untenable. On 3 March 1916 he resigned. Illegal under the Defence of the Realm Act – legislation brought in to deal with wartime conditions – his fellow workers risked striking to have him re-instated; among them was Gallacher.[62] Reporting to the House of Commons, Dr Christopher Addison, one of the dilution commission committee members, raised his concern that Gallacher's strike intended to stop the manufacture of munitions at a time when heavy gun materiél was in high demand at the front.[63]

It had been easy to arrest Kirkwood under DORA, taking him from his bed in the early hours, escorted by four policemen with sidearms, court-martialling him in his absence and depositing him in Glasgow's Central Police Office before transporting him along with others to Edinburgh. It was certainly a better result than the alternative suggestions: in Westminster questions were asked why the Clyde men had not been sent to fight or tried for high treason. The expedient of a court martial avoided a lengthy criminal trial during which public opinion might have had time to shift in favour of the strike leaders.[64] They had been sent into internal exile, forbidden to travel within the Clyde munitions area. Soon to join Kirkwood and his co-arrestees was democratic socialist and militant pacifist James Maxton, a teacher dismissed from his profession due to his politics. The day after the deportations, Maxton had taken to the stand at Glasgow Green urging workers to strike, to forget to wind up their alarm clocks for tomorrow morning, to down tools. Emanuel Shinwell had also been billed to speak, but as the policeman observing today's meeting, Chief Detective Inspector Keith thinks Shinwell has always been careful what he says and where.[65] Maxton was charged with sedition for inciting valuable munitions workers to strike. Calling Maxton's actions dastardly and cowardly, the Lord Justice-General sentenced him to twelve months in Calton Jail.[66] Gallacher arrived in the same prison within days along with the editors, John Muir and Tom Bell, of the recently established newspaper *The Worker* and John

Maclean for an article misinterpreted by the authorities as an incitement to use force.

Kirkwood remained at liberty in Edinburgh as long as he did not wander further than a five-mile radius of the city. He was free to attend pacifist meetings and to visit his friends at Calton Jail, waving to them when they were allowed into the yard to exercise. By the end of March 1916 the cast of Clydeside leaders was all behind bars in Edinburgh or restricted to the city's limits, but resolve was waning and some had accepted positions working at munitions factories in England in return for their freedom. Kirkwood refused and, after a trip to speak at the Labour Party Conference in Manchester in January 1917, he was re-arrested and unceremoniously re-deported to Edinburgh Castle. Here he befriended his jailer, Colonel Levita, who finally released Kirkwood when his wife was due to give birth at home in Glasgow.

Throughout their ordeal, most of the men court-martialled or convicted of sedition stuck to their principles. After fourteen months trying to persuade Kirkwood to sign away his labour rights, hard-won rights he told them he must defend, it was the Government that quietly let the matter slide. Kirkwood's victory was enshrined in a telegram from Scottish Command on 30 May 1917 rescinding his deportation order.[67]

Despite their temporary removal from the crucible of wartime labour agitation on the Clyde, Kirkwood and Gallacher had returned as heroes. Kirkwood's star had risen so high among his colleagues that he decided to stand for Parliament in the December 1918 'Coupon' elections. He had won the most votes ever cast for a socialist candidate in Scotland, but still had lost his ticket and, on the whole, Glasgow's left-wing election candidates had fared poorly.[68] But surely his individual success is an indication of the support the leaders can expect from the men, a sign of their belief in today's strike?

In 1916 their demands had largely been met and the employers emasculated under wartime restrictions. The Government had listened because they needed the Clyde's workforce on their side, but the war is now over. Prime Minister Lloyd George has worked his magic again. The country is behind him clamouring to make the Germans pay for their barbarity. Can Shinwell, Gallacher and Kirkwood have failed to realize the influence Lloyd George wields? The power of the country's victory to erase the collective memory of pre-war conditions? This morning's pressing question is: will the Government continue to value the Clyde's contribution to the Empire now the war is over?

Standing alongside each other on the City Chambers' plinth in George Square calling unanimously for an all-out strike, it would be easy to forget that, during the war, Gallacher had railed against Kirkwood's conciliatory acceptance of dilution. Both men had realized the animosity Lloyd George felt for the trade unions, but while Kirkwood was a sectional union man concerned with the balance of power between men and management, Gallacher sought a wider solidarity of workers pitched against the establishment; both socialists but one locally minded, the other with an internationalist ambition.[69] It was said the unions' power before the war was so great that, if it had not started when it did, there would likely have been an enormous industrial disturbance.[70] But the war had intervened and the workers' confidence grew further.[71] They had come out on strike on May Day 1917 with an estimated 90,000 thronging Glasgow's streets, accompanied by uniformed police, and again in autumn 1918 there had been further unofficial militancy just before the Armistice.[72] But are some of the most highly skilled shipbuilders in the world sorely conceited? Regionally, they possess limited strike funds and nationally they do not have the support of their trade-union executive or the unskilled workers, yet Shinwell stands before them today declaring there is no German gold underwriting their strike and the pockets of their trade unions will fund them.[73] The former is an allusion to claims the strike is a ruse created by German socialists to provoke havoc across Europe and the latter is pure Shinwell propaganda.

Hopes that the miners will join them are diminishing; the executive of the National Union of Scottish Mine Workers has dissociated itself from the strike and recommends their workers to remain at the coal face until their own demands for a six-hour day are met. For every day the miners continue to work, there is a greater chance of their national British organization negotiating with the Government and removing their sting from Clydeside's strike.[74] This will have to be a short, sharp strike, thrusting to the heart of the city to make itself felt. They have come so far, why would they allow their position to slip back to one of exploitation and grinding unemployment?

From his position on the front of the Municipal Buildings, Gallacher encourages the crowd to disperse quietly and form sectional committees in their various districts, it is the quickest way to spread the message to men who have not joined them yet. Tomorrow, they can picket yards and shops that remain at work, thus removing them from the evil presence of their masters. He jests again. But there is no humour in the telegram the CWC, Shinwell and Kirkwood send to Westminster this afternoon. They exhort the Minister of Labour, Sir Robert Horne, to intervene on their behalf. They anticipate he will understand the gravity of their actions and will desire a smooth return to work rather than an all-out confrontation. The telegram surprises Neil Maclean who will later claim they had decided not to ask for Government intervention.[75] But how can a government minister negotiate with unofficial leaders, in a strike without their unions' sanction and at a time when those union leaders have pledged to the employers' associations their efforts to prevent, or at least suppress, the strikes?[76] Sir Robert decides this situation must be dealt with by the official unions.

Chapter 3

Tuesday, 28 January 1919

The Women

Dressed in robust overalls, with khaki cotton caps keeping their hair in place, in spring 1915 Glasgow's women had joined the war effort working in munitions manufacture at numerous sites around Clydeside. They were single women doing their bit, wives and mothers. A journalist excited by the novelty of the women's contribution to the war effort identified one of them as the spouse of a soldier recently wounded in Flanders.[1] They were working hard, making shells to send to the front. They began work at 6.00 am and twelve hours later could remove their dirty overalls and return home. They rose in the dark and returned home after sunset, and the wives among them then took up their household duties, cooking meals, cleaning and retrieving young children from neighbours who had minded them during the day. It was all in a day's work and if they complained it was rarely heard beyond the family home.

Working wives were largely either the spouses of the lowest paid men, working to supplement the household income, or they were the partners of soldiers, or widows struggling to maintain the family with their husbands temporarily, or permanently, absent. Munitions work offered them new freedoms beyond the home; it was well paid and was one way for women to join the fight if they were not trained nurses or Voluntary Aid Detachment auxiliaries, the only other options available to them. Other women filled roles vacated by men who had volunteered for the front. Some became tram drivers and conductresses for Glasgow Corporation's tramways, like Margaret Buchanan and Mary Beattie, fitted out in practical Black Watch tartan ankle-length skirts and dark military-styled jackets.[2] But of all the hard and dirty work available to Glasgow's women, munitions manufacture at Beardmore's was arguably the best.

Early in the war, Sir William Beardmore had realized that for his company to benefit from this new and potentially cheap workforce, better facilities than the men were used to were needed to entice women workers. Cocoa on arrival in the morning and provided again as the night shift arrived at 6.00 pm, as well as a recreation room made tolerable the arduous work of producing shells, the heavy lifting and precision operation of machinery. Although many of the women had never set foot inside a machine room, it was considered they coped well. But not all the women working in munitions were local Glaswegians returning home to their families nightly; many had travelled from around the country to be here, and it was felt they required guidance to manage their new lives and to keep out of trouble. Therefore, lady superintendents offering welfare and motherly advice were engaged, a work-place benefit free to all women working on Clydeside, not just those far from home.[3] It seemed a considerate provision for young women who were newly arrived in Glasgow, but, for local lasses and married women having a middle-class woman meddling in their lives and asking personal questions, it was provoking. These ladies did not work alongside them on the boring machines or carrying shell cases from one end of the shop to another. It provoked a particular variety of class conflict – that of quiet grudging and individual resistance – which had been the catalyst for the strikes in March 1916, and which had ended in Kirkwood's and the men's deportations to Edinburgh.

One of the dilution commission members, Dr Addison, identified the spark for the March 1916 strike at Beardmore's Parkhead Forge in the machine room. It was here that Kirkwood spoke to a lady superintendent in a manner she was unaccustomed to. She had complained to the manager, Mr Chisholm.[4] It was the last straw for Chisholm, who had already been given a dressing-down in early 1915 by Sir William over a previous strike. Chisholm felt it had undermined his abilities to manage the men in favour of Kirkwood. Sir William, unwilling to allow labour relations to disintegrate further, particularly after events at Christmas 1915, favoured his manager this time, which meant Kirkwood had to leave.[5] Kirkwood resigned.

But Glasgow's women do not need the men to lead them out on strike. They have readily done that for themselves in the past, and they are with the men on the Forty-Hours campaign today. It is Tuesday 28 January 1919 and yesterday's instruction from the plinth of the City Chambers to take the workers by the hand and lead them out is being put into effect. It is proving to be a struggle to make this the strike of the century to which Shinwell aspired yesterday and those 'other means' he and Gallacher mentioned are being put into practice today. So far, the patchwork of stoppages across the city has persuaded the men that they must start picketing if more sites are to join them. Unusually the pickets include women, a sign of their militancy and solidarity in a cause that may affect their own futures, not just those of their men.[6]

Picketing is coercive and often intimidating. The pickets – sometimes in their thousands – gather outside the gates before lunchtime. As the men exit the works to take their rest break and eat, they must pass through the narrow funnel left by the pickets. They form a living barrier of bodies, where there is opportunity to discuss the strike, explain their motives and induce them not to return after their meal.[7] The sheer numbers involved in the picket are intimidation enough for many who disappear home. However, if they do not take the hint, there is another chance to dissuade them as they return to the yards for the afternoon session. Clearly more work is required to spread the message, not least because of the confusion between the Forty-Hour campaign which Glasgow's labour leaders are promoting and with men striking to get higher piece rates for their individual shops.[8] The former serves everyone, getting demobilizing soldiers back into employment and reducing the number of hours worked, creating more leisure time, but the latter only benefits men who are already employed.

For those still in two minds whether to strike, passing the picket line proves too much. Although there are as yet no reports of violence, there has been some physical intimidation, particularly at the North British Locomotive Works where manager Thomas Johnston reports jostling and shouting.[9] Do intimidated men count as strikers sympathetic to the cause or rather are they simply men frightened into stopping work? There is no way to make the distinction. There are definitely more men out today than yesterday, although it is impossible to estimate numbers with any accuracy.[10] The strike's success is causing Government concern: public opinion against picketing and intimidation may leave them no other option but to become involved. To add to their concerns, yesterday saw the Spartacists in Wilhelmshaven in Germany take control of the imperial bank and stop all rail traffic.[11]

Across the Irish Sea, the strike has plunged Belfast into darkness for another day with the post office operating by candlelight and there are calls for the city's lord mayor to intervene, while in Glasgow no one has yet appealed to James Stewart, the Lord Provost, for whatever help he may be able to offer. The carters have voted to come out on strike which will upset the public. Their actions will disrupt food supplies and it is a brave man willing to face Glasgow's angry, desperate womenfolk with families to feed. Yet food shortages, which always hit the working classes hardest, may play out differently with wives hot on their husbands' heels forcing them back to work, particularly as not all unions are prepared to offer strike pay. The Co-operative Wholesale Society has 800 horses idle today around Glasgow, so supplies of potatoes, flour and maize meal at the city's shops will surely become scant in the coming days, and although the bakers have flour sacks piled up in their bakeries, they are running low on coal: no coal, no ovens, no bread.[12]

Glasgow's women's most recent experience of food shortages has been during the war, when families were prepared to make personal sacrifices, but now the mood has altered. Yesterday's marches through the city prove the change in temper. Previously women have made do struggling with dearth and rising domestic costs. If you don't have much in the first place, there is little to lose. And Glasgow's women have a reputation for ingenuity when prices rise; they would rather huddle together to save money on household bills like rent than starve, which they did in 1915 when the men were agitating against dilution. What the women of Glasgow did to reverse spiralling rents in the midst of the war was arguably more important for the entire nation than any labour strike by their men.

Since the late nineteenth century, much working-class housing in Glasgow has resembled a sprawling slum rather than habitation fit for human beings. There has been a slow decline as the middle classes moved out and the working classes became packed tight into areas such as the Gorbals and Glasgow's Southside.[13] By the middle of the war in the Anderston district, Government investigators were reporting on the foetid privies running through tenement back closes with often eleven people living in one two-roomed apartment.[14] A situation already dire as Queen Victoria expired had not changed as her grandson King George V assumed the throne, but throughout the war conditions had been exacerbated by the influx of munitions workers seeking accommodation across the Clyde. Glaswegian working-class wives had always supplemented the family income by taking in occasional lodgers when necessary. Since 1900 the city's population has increased at roughly four per cent every year with a quarter of the population living in single-end, one-roomed houses, and one in seven of those homes also housed a lodger.[15] Having another man in the home required only a re-arrangement of beds, with younger sons sharing with the newcomer while mother and daughters crowded into the kitchen bed, often with the father if he was at home.[16] The extra few shillings every week outweighed the discomfort and disruption and helped to put food on the table. But then rents began to rise and there was no more room into which another lodger could be squeezed. Huddling together to make ends meet had reached its limit by autumn 1915 and so had Mrs Mary Barbour's temper.

Mary Barbour had married an engineer before the turn of the century, so she knew a thing or two about having a husband out on strike and how one was organized. She was acutely aware of the unfair practices perpetrated by landlords around her in Govan where she now lived among very poor families. Since the start of the war, working-class rents in Govan had risen up to 23 per cent and were now an average of £14 6s 8d annually, and although there was enough work for everyone for now, wages had not increased at the same rate, if at all.[17] Some wives suffered in silence, scrimping to find the extra shillings every week to hand over to the landlord's rent-collector, but moral outrage at asking for higher rents from soldiers' wives, Belgian refugees and those on welfare was too much. Agitation began locally in June 1915 and quickly the link was forged between the men's voices calling for non-reduction of their wages and increases in rent; if the latter went up, effectively the former came down.[18]

By early October 1915 it was clear many working families sided with Mrs Barbour. Even the shipyard employers agreed because, although they controlled wages for the present, they had no leverage over landlords' rents, and higher rents would inevitably result in a demand for higher wages perhaps leading to strikes.[19] With women and employers on the same side, David Kirkwood invoked the power of the Glasgow Corporation to act on their behalf, warning this attack on the working class could only have a ruinous outcome.[20] The implication was a munitions workers' strike just when the factories were struggling to keep pace with supply to the front.

Whereas the men preferred their meetings in lofty city-centre halls, Mrs Barbour held back-court meetings away from prying eyes with women gathered on tenement stairs to discuss their plans. The Barbours' home at 43 Ure Street (today's Uist Street) was in the centre of Govan, south of the Clyde and close enough to the engineering works lining the river's banks for Mr Barbour to walk to work. The Barbours occupied an apartment in this four-storey red sandstone tenement, rented for themselves and their son. As an engineer, Mr Barbour could afford a more spacious house for his family, but Mrs Barbour was surrounded by families in less comfortable circumstances and feeling the pinch. Of all the districts identified with the highest rent increases, Govan and neighbouring Fairfield were the worst hit.[21] Such scurrilous tactics by the landlords required peaceful but full scale retaliation. Knocking at a young wife's door demanding the week's rent, telling her that Mrs So-and-So next door had already paid up and eviction was the other option available, was poor behaviour by the factors collecting on behalf of their employers. From the moment word got out about their tricks, the rent factors were confronted with window after window displaying the same, red-painted placards: RENT STRIKE, WE ARE NOT REMOVING. Wherever they went across Govan, Mrs Barbour's army sniffed them out at a distance; bells rang, kettles were banged, doors remained unanswered and rents uncollected, even eviction notices were ignored. A factor or sheriff's officer brave enough to enter the dark closes with middens brimming with handy putrid missiles and a single means of exit back the way they had come was quickly surrounded by tens of angry women, doused with flour, deluged with water and bombarded with heated words. The strategy worked and attempts to evict families while their men were at work dwindled because every time the landlords tried it the men downed tools and left their workshops to protect their homes.[22]

The momentum born of Mrs Barbour's actions spread across Glasgow and caught the Government's attention. It was forced to instigate a public inquiry held on 27 October 1915 in Glasgow's Burgh Court Hall, a dark panelled room, solemn and incongruously sized for the subject under investigation. The meeting was sparsely attended by Glasgow's working-class rent payers.[23] Either they could not afford the time off work or they were disinclined to listen to the city's officials delivering dry statistics and debating the reasons for the squalor they experienced. The inquiry established that Clydebank and Renfrew were overflowing, and the current housing stock could not be augmented quickly enough; it might take years to achieve. Essentially, Glasgow's rented housing stock had stagnated long before the war had started. The problem was a matter of ownership: myriad small landlords owned the working-class housing stock and these same people controlled the city council. It was not in their interests to promote council-funded housing. Also, Lloyd George's 1909-10 budget had placed a 20 per cent tax increase on all heritable property, thus stalling speculative housing construction; investing in bricks and mortar was no longer so enticing.[24] Having been raised in a single-end, Councillor John Wheatley had personal experience of the debilitation overcrowding caused, but his campaign for £8 affordable cottages had found little traction at the City Chambers when first mooted some years before the war. No one wished to use the profits from the Corporation Tramways to pay for cheap working-class housing on the city's outskirts and councillors argued that it would have a limited impact on the enormous problem they faced.[25] The municipal authorities had failed to act, and private landlords proved unwilling to invest in new developments while wages and construction costs were high.[26] It was a fair point, but five years later, why take advantage of the war to increase rents when demand was acute and munitions workers had no other choice? This was rack-renting when the nation's back was against the wall. Glaswegians prided themselves on having a sense of fair play combined with a fair price for everything supported by burgeoning concepts of social welfare.[27] If nothing was done soon, the situation could only spread to other munitions centres. Despite circumstances being abnormal, artificial and temporary, the Minister of Munitions, David Lloyd George, took decisive action.

By the autumn of 1915, 15,000 households had withheld their rent; by November that had increased to 20,000 and, as Mrs Barbour's movement spread across Glasgow's working-class districts, the landlords made one last attempt to get their rent money.[28] Since eviction notices threatened rent and labour strikes, the landlords decided to sue rent with-holders at the small debt court. Strangely, they did not summon the women refusing to pay the rent from their husbands' wages, instead they sued eighteen male munitions workers. What had been a women's movement spreading street by street was now a Clyde-wide protest. Workshops across the city sent delegations to the court, which both Gallacher and Kirkwood helped to orchestrate, and Mrs Barbour's army marched to the city centre from Govan. They waited most of the day while the sheriff contacted London where the Secretary for Scotland advised caution. Ultimately, the threat of a strike, which the workers' delegates declared was beyond their control, swayed the sheriff's decision. In wartime striking was illegal, but the Govan Trades Council led by Harry Hopkins had the support of the workers and ignored what the official trade unions advised; they threatened a general strike across Clydeside.[29] The sheriff dropped all eighteen suits and everyone marched home triumphantly.[30] This had been a local victory, but it bore two fruits. At Westminster, the Rent Restriction Act, already under discussion, was rushed through Parliament with Lloyd George's unswerving support and was passed a week later. The Act declared that rents would remain at August 1914 rates for the duration.[31] To anyone intending in any way to profiteer from the war, this was a clear message that the production of munitions to support the efforts at the front was to be prioritized over private interests. And in the west of Scotland, the Withdrawal of Labour Committee was transformed into the Clyde Workers' Committee with Gallacher at its helm. Clydeside's working-class men and women had scored two victories, and Lloyd George's next engagement with the newly-formed CWC was only a matter of weeks away at Christmas.

The success of Mrs Barbour's rent strikes was not the first time Glasgow's men and women had joined together to agitate for the same purpose. Enough of those involved in the rent strikes recalled the Singers' strike of 1911 when the women polishers finishing the famous sewing machines walked out, followed by the men, but every department that stopped work back then had had its own different grievances.[32] Mrs Barbour's rent strikes were not one trade or craft attempting to protect its superiority from encroachment by semi-skilled and unskilled workers, neither was it a gender conflict to keep lower-paid women out of men's roles for fear of skilled men's pay rates being eroded, nor was it a unionized protest. The rent strikes were a spontaneous response to grossly unfair opportunistic profiteering, and Glasgow's women and men responded with working-class cohesion district by district stretching from the skilled tradesman to the unskilled labourer, because rising rents affected everyone's standard of living.

Solidarity had proved successful, and it would not be the last occurrence before the war was over, but today on the second day of the strike, there is a national conference at St Andrew's Hall in the city centre where the strike's leaders have forgotten the moral authority that including the women might bring to their protest in the nation's eyes. Even Edith Hughes, a prominent woman of Glasgow's left, member of the Scottish Labour Party's administrative council and honorary treasurer to the Glasgow Trades Council, goes unmentioned by news reporters. Aged 29, she is an accomplished and committed socialist and if there is a woman who should be visible among the assembly, it's Edith. But today, like any other women who may be in the hall, she is invisible.

The strike leaders wish to ascertain how far the rest of the country's men will support the Clyde. Since early this morning, messengers have been arriving from all the city's districts bringing news from which the Joint Committee compiles reports to be distributed back to district offices. Everyone is in touch with one another with the most up-to-date information speeding back and forth across Glasgow.[33] They are hearing too of stoppages at Grangemouth and Leith shipyards where very few men are at work, with the jute weavers in Dundee also coming out in favour of the forty-hour week.[34] But is it sufficient support to claim a nationwide general strike? And are they all adopting the same aims?

Today's meeting is attended by representatives from most of Scotland's main industrial cities and towns, and delegates have arrived from Grimsby and Rugby, as well as a presence from London's ship-repairers. Emanuel Shinwell is in the chair again. The representatives gathered before him agree on one thing: the strike will be prosecuted until the Government opens negotiations with the Joint Committee and, once they have received their set of proposals, only then will the committee submit them to the men for approval. They are adamant it is forty hours without a reduction in wages for all workers.[35] Shinwell will only deal directly with the Government. Is this a legacy of the dilution negotiations at Christmas 1915, of Kirkwood speaking directly to Lloyd George and taking tea with Churchill? They have made no approach to the shipyard owners, their employers. Are they leap-frogging them to reach the men at Westminster whom they consider the real decision-makers? It would seem so, because only in late December 1918 has the Scottish Trades Union Council agreed to industrial action if the Government declines to act on the forty-hours issue.[36]

Yesterday they sent a telegram to the Minister of Labour asking for his personal intervention in the dispute and today the minister's permanent secretary has responded. He requests an immediate resumption of work in return for expediting an answer to their question.[37] Plainly, Sir Robert Horne has no intention of intervening at the request of an unofficial movement. For the moment Shinwell and the Joint Committee are stumped; they turn their attention to the issue of food shortages. This matter will become urgent if they are forced to dial up the pressure on the city's leaders and central government. The Joint Committee instructs that all questions concerning food supplies should come through them.[38] Perhaps there is concern that if districts decide to cope with food shortages individually, rivalries will develop which may break the strikers' resolve as they compete with one another for supplies. After all, this is not a dilution issue where skilled men were threatened by the unskilled and women replacing them. The Forty-Hours strike has been started by a skilled workers' union, the Amalgamated Society of Engineers, but for the strike committee to succeed in its aims for its skilled members, it needs a nationwide stoppage of all workers. The old fracture lines of skilled versus unskilled labour interests will not help the Forty-Hours campaign this week; otherwise, it could be a repeat of what happened three years ago.

In March 1916, when Kirkwood, Gallacher and their colleagues were transported to Edinburgh going into internal exile and jail, a special meeting of Clydeside's Association of Shipbuilders sat down to discuss how they would deal with dilution now the strikes were over and the leaders removed. The engineering shops had been dealt with and now it was time to turn the spotlight on the shipyards themselves. The shipyard owners were not prepared to remain unconsulted as they considered they had been over the implementation of the munitions legislation.[39] Having established a government commission to investigate the matter, the First Lord of the Admiralty, A.J. Balfour, wished to push production to the utmost and, being fully aware of the issues experienced before Christmas, he appealed to the employers for their advice. He explained that in Scotland's north-east coast shipyards there had already been widescale employment of women undertaking tasks such as punching machines and pneumatic riveting. First, the Association desired to know the commission's powers because they did not want to experience strikes the way Beardmore had. Lynden Macassey KC was His Majesty's commissioner on this matter, and he assured the Association that the legislation of the Munitions Act regarding the restriction of output would be invoked if there was any opposition from the workforce. Macassey had been no friend of the workers in the autumn and boasted that he had played off the engineers' union against the CWC on the introduction of dilution.[40] Second, they wished to understand how the Admiralty intended to enforce better timekeeping. They did not want to see women employed when the men were not working the full number of hours expected every week and then were claiming overtime. Mr Macassey promised to bring the matter to the First Lord's attention. The meeting was held behind closed doors without union or workshop representatives, yet the employers agreed they would prefer a general scheme rather than individual arrangements for each shipyard.[41] It made sense to have an area-wide shipyard policy for ease of implementation, but it also created a solid block of employers and the Admiralty to oppose any potential disagreement coming from the shop floor. The Clyde shipbuilders were not going to entertain the difficulties experienced in late 1915 and early 1916 among the engineers where individual workshops struck their own agreements with their employers. If workshop representatives like Kirkwood retained their direct relationship with the workforce and spoke for them in front of the yard's management, it could only lead to the same problem as Sir William Beardmore had experienced the previous week. However, whether engineering works or shipyard owners, the employers had not bargained on the unionization of the women munition workers. It had been expected they would form a cheap labour force, grateful for the work and inclusion in the war effort; the vociferous involvement of the National Federation of Women Workers had not been anticipated.

Established in 1906, the NFWW represented low-paid and under-paid working women who were excluded from the men's craft unions. Unionization had become important if women's wages were to approach men's for the same or similar jobs. They were not skilled roles but, working alongside unskilled men fulfilling the same monotonous tasks, they ought to have been paid the same, but the concept of a family wage did not apply to women. Men were the breadwinners, and even if they were single men without a family to support, they still received higher piece-rate wages than working widows with a family.[42] As he was at pains to explain, David Kirkwood was not against dilution; in fact, he understood the need for an expanded workforce and, with so many men away at the front, there remained only the women to call on to plug the gap. In agreeing to a set of hastily formulated terms created by John Wheatley and put to the Dilution Commissioners at Christmas 1915, Kirkwood had intended to secure equal rates of pay for men and women doing the same job and a system of binding arbitration with the employers. However, in Gallacher's eyes, Kirkwood had effectively signed up to dilution on behalf of Beardmore's Parkhead employees without consulting the CWC. Gallacher was incensed. He preferred individual shop stewards to negotiate with their employers and interpreted Kirkwood's proposals as removing the shop steward's supervising responsibilities on the shop floor.[43] That he might have done, but Kirkwood had ensured that cheap labour could not be introduced and working practices could not be eroded; he had also cemented his alliance with the women of the NFWW. Women could now expect £1 per week, not the 15 shillings Sir William Beardmore had tried to pay them in October 1915, but collaboration with Kirkwood had come at a price. The NFWW leadership had agreed to the restoration of trade union practices and to the return of men to their rightful jobs after the war.[44] No one knew how far in the future that might be or what might change in the meantime. Sir William was a man charged with dealing with the present and no one wanted trouble with the lassies at the shells, particularly if they had the support of the men in their shops.[45]

Having conceded a fairer wage to women workers by spring 1916, the situation settled down on the Clyde, at least for the women. The labour movement's key leaders remained in prison or exile, and everyone knuckled down to producing ordnance and munitions for the war's next great battle. The Somme was a matter of months away but, before that, the city marked another auspicious date for working-class solidarity. Glasgow's women were always highly visible at the May Day demonstrations, parading to Glasgow Green decked out in red sashes. It was a family event with lorries transporting children from all the city's wards, banners fluttering above their heads and their voices ringing out to spend the day in the city's large central park situated on the north bank of the Clyde. May Day was a social as well as socialist family day out. Harry Hopkins of the Independent Labour Party was the May Day secretary, and his treasurer was a member of the Socialist Democratic Party.[46] This was no may pole and summer fete affair, but rather a joyful gathering to celebrate international workers' day. In 1917 May Day assumed a redder than usual hue.

The first Russian Revolution in February may have increased passions on May Day in the third year of the war but, closer to home, a shortage of bread and potatoes fuelled Clydeside's female tempers. Since March the Government had attempted to control foodstuffs through voluntary rationing and limited legislation. While milk supplies and maximum prices for everyday groceries were negotiated in London and applied nationally, government-controlled tea supplies had failed to reach Glasgow. Promised at no more than 2s 4d per pound, some grocers were selling their dwindling supplies at higher prices. Peas and beans imported from Burma were also sold at a fixed price so that everyone could purchase their share, but in Glasgow the most pressing issue was bread. Like tea and oats, it was a staple of the working class. Bread consumption had gone through the roof, exceeding government estimates and causing panic at Westminster. If such consumption continued, then flour supplies would rapidly be depleted and there would be nothing to eat. On Scotland's west coast, increased bread consumption was blamed on the shortage of porridge. The Government was only now alive to this issue and it was too late. They had restricted oatmeal supplies intended for the population diverting oats to feed military horses. Horses at the front needed fodder, but the situation was also aggravated by military requirements at home and, without porridge, the Clyde's housewives had opted for the other Scottish staple – bread. Having forecast dwindling flour supplies based on four pounds (4lbs) of bread per person per week, some areas of the country – no fingers pointed – were munching their way through 6lbs instead.

It was suggested that personal rations be reduced from four slices to three per day, thus saving a slice a day, seven slices a week and fourteen in a fortnight, or one 2lb loaf every two weeks. If non-manual workers could take porridge for breakfast, then they should consider a slice of bread later in the morning with two slices for tea; there was no consideration whether they had access to meat or fish or eggs to provide necessary protein. Already the sale of 'smalls' such as bread rolls had been delayed so that none could be sold until at least twelve hours old and going stale. This had been intended to promote home breadmaking, and there was a 'Cake and Pastries' order, as well as an instruction to stop serving a bread roll with soup in the city's hotels and restaurants, with guidance on refraining from afternoon tea. The Government recognized the greater need of miners, steelworkers and others in heavy industries, but they had failed to consider that these last, more genteel, measures would have little impact in districts such as Govan, Gorbals and Partick where food shortages would soon culminate in violence.[47]

By May Day 1917 queuing for food was consuming valuable time in the day for Glasgow's women. Those who worked could not take time out to queue and neither could their husbands or sons. This year the crowds marching on Glasgow Green numbered 100,000. They were celebrating their workers' day off, protesting against the war and demonstrating about the shortage of the very foods their families relied on to keep body and soul together.

The early potato harvest expected from Ayrshire within weeks was delayed with neither sufficient good weather for them to be ready yet nor men to lift them when they were. Relief supplies from England had failed to materialize. However, as a lone lorry passed through Partick piled high with sacks of potatoes, five desperate married women waylaid the driver and removed the sacks from his vehicle. They were joined by nearly 500 other women, armed with shopping baskets and net bags swarming round the lorry. Taking scissors and knives from their pockets, they made short work of the sacks and redistributed their contents among themselves. The driver made his escape with some sacks remaining, but a woman with a hand bell led the crowd after him and they finished off the job.[48] Nearly two years since the rent strikes, Glasgow's wives and mothers had taken matters into their own hands again. It had been another surprise for the city's law officers who could only respond with appearances for the perpetrators before the Sheriff Court. Unable to solve their food problems and equally powerless to hand down convictions to teach a lesson to any women wishing to protest similarly, the situation worsened until the tinder of discontent was sufficiently dry to combust at the slightest provocation.

By autumn 1917 the situation at Beardmore's East Hope Street works had become untenable. Effectively, Sir William had accused the women workers of shirking, of restricting output, and he had failed to uphold an increase in time and piece rates negotiated by a special tribunal. Simultaneously, Sir William had not bargained on Gallacher's release from prison and his resumption of CWC activities, nor the return of Kirkwood.

Under the experienced leadership of Mary McArthur, who had founded the National Federation of Women Workers eleven years earlier, the NFWW was not shy of calling its own strike. McArthur had excelled in unionizing Clydeside's women before the war, but her efforts had seen the most success in the textile industries.[49] Having Gallacher's and Kirkwood's support for women employed in engineering and shipbuilding placed the NFWW on surer footings. Gallacher had returned to Glasgow in fighting form, calling a strike over wages in September 1917. It lasted only a few days, but the Government responded with a 12.5 per cent increase in the weekly wage to skilled time workers.[50] This did not extend to Beardmore's East Hope Street works, where Sir William's hostile attitude towards women munitions workers and their unions blocked increases which would benefit them and their families as household prices continued to rise. Accusing women working on heavy gun manufacture of going slow was not in the spirit of all that Clydeside was contributing towards the war effort and it could only be taken as an attack on the NFWW. Beardmore picked four night-shift workers, all of whom were members of the NFWW, and accused them of reduced output which he said had been ordered by their union. It was too much, especially when the night shift was less unionized than the day shift, yet more productive. Immediately, over fifty women walked out, followed by five times that number during the following week. It was a poor show to sack a woman with a reputation for being the best borer the company had seen and to whom the management had awarded the highest bonus for over two months in succession. One of the four women had recently been widowed and was supporting her children on a single-woman's wage, but no quarter was given for presumed reduced output. It did not make sense unless it was a warning to the NFWW not to collaborate with the men's unions.

To show their solidarity, Kirkwood's Amalgamated Society of Engineers stopped setting tools for women workers who had not come out on strike, which both slowed production and persuaded the women to join the campaign. It was a tactic the men had employed before the war, a strategy used to encourage all crafts to come out together. But not all the night shift was in the NFWW and some women were compelled by need to continue working. By late November the CWC was threatening a total walk-out if Sir William did not yield. He did and was forced to agree to arbitration. Yet, he had one more card to play. Between Friday 7 December and 11 December, he closed the works for the weekend, re-opening on Tuesday when he advertised he would be engaging new staff. He did not necessarily require more workers, but he did need to replace the 200 troublemakers he refused to re-instate. And then he rejected the invitation to arbitration with the Government's representative.[51] As owner of the works with a business to run and as a patriot with a war to help win, Sir William had played a hard game which, ultimately, he was forced to cede. It was another Christmas of intense negotiation, flat refusals to talk and strike threats. But when it was finally resolved in January 1918 further fracture lines had developed.

The 12.5 per cent increase for time workers equated to a weekly rise of 7s 6d, but the Government had only offered piece-workers an increase of 6s 9d.[52] In their dispute over the unfair treatment of the women's night shift, the NFWW had stuck together; their message to Sir William was 'treat us all the same'. In their fight for fairness, they had won the men's support but, in the matter of bonuses and who should and should not receive them, the men had displayed a deep-rooted craft conservatism. Alongside its report on the parlous state of labour relations on the Clyde, the *Glasgow Herald* appealed for men neither fighting nor building ships to lend their money in War Bonds because the soldiers and shipbuilders were splendid men indeed. Were these men with surplus cash lending to their utmost capacity?[53] East Hope Street's munitions women had proved they were working at maximum capacity and were now being paid for it, but increased wages meant little in the face of increasing prices and further shortages.

Meat was scarce, there was no butter and now government consignments of cheese were delayed by terrible weather. But no matter how severe the gales or heavy the rain, Glasgow's women queued for what they could get: government-issue margarine and a new product on which to spread it, bread supplemented by potato flour, had appeared in bakers' windows.[54] And to prove their forbearance while working long hours, managing at home, queuing at shops and continuing to raise their families, Glasgow's women found spare pennies to contribute to the city's staggering £2,076,263 in War Bond sales in 'Tank Week' which ran from 13 to 19 January 1918. Despite pockets of anti-war agitation, Glasgow's citizens were leading the nation in their financial generosity to the war effort and coming out in their droves to walk beside the 'Julian' tank as it paraded the city's streets. The enthusiasm for 'Julian' put Glasgow in the competition for contributing £10 million in War Bonds which would put it beyond every other city in the country. Pictures of 'Julian' surrounded by smiling Glaswegians appeared in *The Times* newspaper for the whole nation to see.[55] No one knew how long the war would continue; would there be a need to dig deeper into their pockets for a tank to parade in Glasgow again next year?

Tuesday has been a quiet day in Glasgow while the strike's leadership tries to build momentum, but in London anxiety is increasing. This morning at Westminster, the Minister of Labour Sir Robert Horne acknowledged receipt of the strike committee's telegram from yesterday but repeats he is unable to go over the heads of the union executives. Horne believes reports in the news are alarmist and he has interviewed a number of men of the press impressing upon them the need for calm.[56] At the War Cabinet meeting at 3.00 pm at Downing Street, the Home Secretary circulates his fortnightly report on the situation across the United Kingdom. It is another alarming Special Branch dossier. No one reading it doubts these are troubling times, but is the analysis correct that John Maclean's speeches in the north of the country are so fiery that 1919 will be the year of social revolution with the government of the country transferred to the workers, either by peaceful means or otherwise? Maclean is described as unstable, but he attracts a large following. The situation in France is also worrying.

The tram and Metro workers are on strike and it appears Prime Minister Clemenceau is dangerously indifferent to the unemployment situation as soldiers demobilize. The British Home Secretary is not so complacent; his report leaves its Cabinet readers able to relax into their well-used leather armchairs because, unlike the analysis on the French situation and the position Clemenceau finds himself in, they are told they are not sitting on a volcano.[57]

Yet, there is always calm before the storm and today there has been no communication from Glasgow's strike leadership. Men out on strike have spent the morning meeting in halls to listen to their local leaders. They spread the word from the Joint Strike Committee and rally the men for tomorrow's planned protests. Those with the remains of Saturday's wage packet still in their pockets linger in the city's bars, but there is a need to conserve their earnings because they are in this for the long haul. Wives have taken their portion of the wages to see the family through the week ahead. The Government continues to control oat and bread prices, and their few shillings must be eked out. The children are herded to the shared lavatory on the stairs queuing for their turn in the damp, reeking cubicle, then nestle into shared beds under spare blankets in Anderston, Govan, Partick and elsewhere. Fathers not usually home so early have spent a penny to purchase the latest newspaper. It is slow news but will pass the time in the bustle of crowded single-ends. The dishes are washed, children settled if not properly asleep, a clean chamber pot positioned in its usual place in the kitchen so everyone can find it during the night. This has always been women's work, to support the men in the family. But now the war is over that relationship has changed, because the men still have their support at home, but Glasgow's women have had their eyes opened. Many have experienced work and their own wages, and there is a looming threat to their new-found freedom. While the news reports there are more men in employment in the past week than earlier in January, the number of employed women has fallen.[58] As men return from the front, fewer women will be heading in the dark mornings to Glasgow's factories and workshops. Instead, they are likely to remain at home, returned to their pre-war status. Some will do so quietly, others may not like it, but they have no means to fight their corner. Few intend to turn this into a women-versus-men conflict with the battlefront stretching from the home to the workplace. They have continued to cook and clean and chivvy and care for children throughout the war; now there is only one way for emancipation to continue for those who want it and a return to domesticity for those who would prefer a husband in work. They must stand beside and behind their men as one union.

Chapter 4

Wednesday, 29 January 1919

The Men

Since long before dawn miners have been picketing the Cambuslang colliery standing shoulder to shoulder in the early morning darkness and grim chill. Their aim is to get the entire shift out with them, a goal everyone involved in day three of the strike is striving for this morning. At 10.00 am in Partick William Gallacher speaks to a crowd gathered at the Orchard Street picture house, a brick-built modern cinema which can take 1,300 seated, but more have squeezed in to listen to what Gallacher has to say. He encourages the crowd to march to St Andrew's Hall in the city centre from where they will continue to the power stations at Port Dundas and Pinkston, not far away, and which are still in full operation. He urges the crowd to stick together if they are to defeat the master classes. It sounds like revolutionary talk to Detective Sergeant George Ross who listens among the crowd; no wonder police protection has been requested as a few miners are anticipated at work at the colliery this morning.[1]

Of all the Clyde Workers' Committee and strike committee leaders, Gallacher is arguably the most committed socialist and syndicalist. He wants the workers to take control of industry, wresting power from the capitalists, which can only be achieved if large numbers join the struggle to sever the working class from the tether of capitalism, government and employers.[2] He would like to see the pyramid of class relationships turned upside-down with the men on the shop floor taking control. The shop stewards have been instrumental throughout the war in spreading socialist ideas inside the workplace and from street corners.[3] Since the rent strikes, the CWC has been quieter but far from silent and its members' activities have made evident the power they might wield on Clydeside if greater cohesion can be fostered. The numbers striking in the agitation of 1915 are nothing compared with the strikes of early 1918. If all goes well this week, the Clyde might show Westminster its true mettle because they will win decent hours, fair wages and make unemployment a pre-war memory.[4] Everyone was committed to the war effort until eleven weeks ago and the re-introduction of employers' practices like the perverse blacklisting of strikers or issuing of character notes will not be tolerated simply because the war is over.[5] They consider it unacceptable that an employer's opinion on a man's character might prevent him from seeking and gaining a job wherever he can. So far this week, the strikers have largely come from the shipbuilding industry, and Gallacher is keen to bring out the coalminers too. His motivation for striking and his choice of words may sound revolutionary, but his heart is with the men, the workers and soldiers who recently won the war and, more recently still, the right to vote. And here they are again having to strike to be heard.

After a quiet day yesterday, this morning the mood of the Forty-Hours campaign appears to have changed. They need the authorities to pay attention and so protests have been organized. It is a short walk through the city's parks from Partick to St Andrew's Hall and it has now become a pleasant enough morning for a stroll. They are keen to hear what the plan is as Gallacher and the other strike leaders organize for what they expect will be a pivotal third day for the strike. Yet anyone enjoying a more leisurely and warmer start to the day sitting at a late breakfast reading their copy of the *Glasgow Herald* is awake to the news that the carters have crept back to work in secrecy despite worrying the city to its core that if they remained out food would not be distributed. The carters' leader and CWC member, Hugh Lyon, supported the Forty-Hour campaign last week, although not the strike. Now he has treacherously accepted a deal behind their backs for a forty-eight-hour working week and has sent his men back to work.[6] If anyone requires police protection this morning, it is Mr Lyon.

The alarmist fears that Clydeside is assuming the mantle of Britain's very own Petrograd are being fuelled by the broadsheet press.[7] The CWC's message aims to force a re-balancing of power and influence in their places of work so that the unit of production becomes the unit of representation. The shop stewards' movement is tired of national union politicking, they want to control the process at their own pace.[8] Arguably that is all Gallacher and Kirkwood have been attempting to achieve since the rent strikes – to make the employers listen, negotiate and improve pay and conditions – and today it has come to this, threats to stop every tram, switch off the lights and paralyze the city; they will not hesitate if the strike is not settled by Friday. To those reading at home, this is revolutionary language indeed intended to reduce the country to anarchy; fighting talk and a chance to improve their lot to those listening in the streets.[9]

The procession of strikers snaking its way to St Andrew's Hall is almost a mile long with a brass band escorting them. They arrive shortly after 10.00 am to find their next meeting in full swing and the building filled to overflowing.[10] For anyone teetering on the last remaining inches of pavement, it is an impressive spectacle with as many men outside the Hall as are pressed inside.[11] Again, Emanuel Shinwell is on stage conveying two very important messages. First, they are going to take an orderly walk to the power stations where further meetings will be held, and at no point are they to allow their ranks to be broken. Before he can continue, he is forced to pause for the uproarious applause to quieten. Then he explains permits have been granted to seven motors driving coal to the city's schools and to workers at Yarrow's workshop who manufacture artificial limbs for soldiers.[12] Listening intently, Partick strike leader and shop steward, Herbert Highton does not construe the doling out of permits as revolutionary talk or behaviour because Shinwell follows it up immediately by explaining that those who raised the red flag on Monday must not be confused with the Forty-Hours strike.[13] He reiterates strongly what they have said since the strike started: it is not political, they are not political. Shinwell informs the journalists in the crowd of his opinion on their responsibility for raising the heat, creating fear where there is nothing other than workers striking for the right to a job; he warns them they risk expanding the campaign beyond its definite and declared objective.[14] John Angus, a sheet metalworker and member of his union participated in Monday's procession to the City Chambers and he has returned today to do likewise. He hears Shinwell declare this an official strike that has nothing to do with politics and that he wants no disorderly conduct from the men, but he urges them to do all they can to bring out the municipal employees.[15] Which is why they urgently want the tram and power station workers to join them – their collaboration will literally stop the city in its tracks within hours, forcing someone in authority to listen.

Crowds have been gathering at St Andrew's Hall throughout Shinwell's speech and there are now two overspill meetings. One organizes itself to head the two miles to Pinkston Power Station, led by Harry Hopkins who, since his involvement in the rent strikes, is no stranger to demonstrations like this. He is accompanied by a colleague, Ogilvie, as they head along North Street to Keppochill Road and onwards to Pinkston Power Station which generates power for the tram network. As they depart, the brass band strikes up again, but marshalling thousands of men spread four sometimes ten deep across the road is impossible for Constable Ritchie and Sergeant Steele who accompany them.[16] Inevitably, the crowd creates havoc with the trams running along their route north to Pinkston, which is not helped when Hopkins holds up his hands to signal to them to deliberately stop the trams. This is not what Shinwell instructed and progress to the power station is slow. Sergeant Steele observes it is approximately midday when the crowd reaches their destination.[17] The throng has become so dense they block any available exits from the building for those who might wish to leave.

Inside the station the 62-year-old manager, David Baillie, is informed at 12.15 pm of a crowd of strikers approaching. He listens for a while as outside the speeches start again. Hopkins addresses the crowd and what he says truly rattles Sergeant Steele. If Glaswegians were as united as Dubliners had been at Easter 1916, then the same could happen here. Whether that is what he truly means, Steele interprets Hopkins' words as incitement to rebellion, and then Ogilvie takes the stand. Everyone looking up at him knows who he means when he refers to 'Tzar Dalrymple'. The Corporation general manager of tramways is well-known across Glasgow, the man who proudly recruited an entire Highland Light Infantry battalion from tram staff at the outset of the war, short tough Glaswegians ready to fight for the cause; only now it is hoped they have a new one.[18] Ogilvie points to a rope dangling on the building opposite him. Evidently, he has different ideas from Shinwell because, not satisfied with a hanging rope, he suggests a good square brick might have more persuading power than peaceful picketing. Ogilvie's speech has been so distracting that Sergeant Steele fails to notice Hopkins emerge from the power station where he has slipped inside to speak to the firemen who stoke the coal burners. They have promised to come out when their shift changes at 3.00 pm and, until they do, the crowd must close ranks to allow absolutely no one else to enter. They are not to worry about the police, they are powerless, why else would the authorities have sat on copies of incendiary speeches delivered by John Maclean and Gallacher for the past four years at the Central Police office and not acted? There is no reason to be afraid; he predicts they are unlikely to behave any differently today.

Inside the power station, manager Baillie makes his own offer to the men gathered in the engine room. In return for being well paid, ample food, bedding, tobacco and general comfort, he asks them to remain faithful and stay to keep the station operating. He leaves them while they consider his request. He does not have long to wait for their reply: they will remain until 5.00 pm. However, of the men who promise to stay, already their number is diminished because eleven have not made it back at 2.00 pm after their dinner hour due to the pickets outside and throughout the afternoon more men fail to arrive for their shifts. The foreman engineer is unsure whether they have decided to strike or simply cannot get through the picket.[19]

The tactic is for the pickets to line up on both sides of the road by the plant's exit gates so that men leaving work must walk through the narrow gap left for them while being deafened by hundreds of jeering onlookers and running the risk of being jostled or assaulted as they go. Rather than suffer the ordeal of the flying picket, which has been gathering momentum since Monday morning, moving from shop to shop, no wonder some men have failed to appear for work.[20] The *Manchester Guardian*'s journalist reports the strikers' aim is to upset the public, thus forcing government intervention because it appears their numbers are only moderate so far; and so action verging on intimidation is spreading.[21] There has been little overt violence yet, but they cannot be sure that a length of lead pipe hidden under an overcoat will not be employed to convince them to join the strike, because that is what happened during the strikes a few years ago.[22]

By 4.30 pm Sergeant Steele has heard enough. During the entire afternoon, he has not taken any notes, but what he has heard is so fiery hopefully it will remain with him until he can report to a superior.[23] Standing nearby is Constable Ritchie who, despite the tumult of the crowd, hears the same speeches and later will repeat Steele's account verbatim. On duty with them is Detective Sergeant James Wilson, who is also disturbed by talk of actions being different tomorrow if supposedly peaceful picketing is unsuccessful today. With eighteen years' service, he is sufficiently experienced to understand how quick to violence this heated crowd may be. It might be tomorrow, or it might take until Friday to boil over.[24]

There are similar scenes at Port Dundas Power Station which is responsible for supplying the city's street lighting and public buildings as well as selling electricity to industry. If this station comes out, there will be more disruption than would be caused by just closing the tram network. The men at Port Dundas have yet to join the strike, presumably because they already enjoy a recently negotiated forty-eight-hour week.[25] Getting here has been a dangerous affair with the procession spreading across the entire street, bringing the trams to a halt. Gallacher will later claim he darted here and there smoothing altercations with motorists and troubles with the police.[26] Their mood appears less festive given the placard they carry with a legend underneath explaining what happens to civilians who do not support their industrial comrades – they are hanged.[27]

Shinwell and Kirkwood have accompanied the strikers all the way and, on arrival at the power station, Shinwell prepares to speak first. Someone erects a low form for him to stand on so he can be seen, but only those at the front of the procession can hear him because the crowd is so extensive.[28] His speech earlier this morning requested calm, but the police who are near the front of the crowd hear only fiery words now. Shinwell urges those inside the power station to join them, but if they are not prepared to listen then the strikers will burst open the gates and drag them out, and he cannot rule out blood being spilt. Inspector John Florence of the Northern District police hears Shinwell address the crowd as comrades who will drag the workers out by the back of the neck if he asks them to and worryingly, like Hopkins at nearby Pinkston Power Station, Shinwell tells them to disregard the police presence, both those officers among the crowd and the handful on duty behind the gates. He is intent on bringing the capitalists to their knees and his disappointment at the reluctance of the municipal employees to join their ranks is palpable. After all, if they had come out on Monday, the city would by now have ground to a halt and the authorities would have been forced to negotiate. He regards their behaviour as despicable. Inspector Florence is not re-assured by the mention of the newly-formed police union and Shinwell's avowal they are all brothers now.[29]

Kirkwood is up next, directing his speech to the 'scabs' still working inside the power station. He is also heard to mention blood being spilt, but this time it is the workers' blood in their struggle to force out the municipal workers. He entreats them to trust their leaders to see them through this protest. His calmer approach suggests they will not need to rush the gates or resort to violence when those inside realize there are 100,000 men and their families outside encouraging them to do the right thing. The *Glasgow Herald*'s journalist listening alongside the police does not report any of the incendiary remarks by Shinwell and Kirkwood that the police claim they hear.[30] The two speeches take less than an hour, and then the crowd re-forms into a wide procession heading to the City Chambers in George Square, zig-zagging their way through the streets preventing the trams from running to time.[31]

Unusually, the procession does not head directly to George Square. Instead, Constable Donald McDonald sees them approaching him where he is on duty at the junction of Argyle, Union and Jamaica Streets, reputedly the busiest tram intersection in the city. If a tram is held up here for even five minutes, then the entire network will suffer delays. McDonald has stood on duty at this spot for the past nine years; he is an expert on the smooth running of the trams and is concerned by the complete blockage now caused by the mob. He becomes alarmed when a stationary tram is boarded by Shinwell and Kirkwood, from which they address the crowd. Evidently, the strikers remain jovial because someone among them calls out to Kirkwood to mind the live wire above him to which he retorts jokingly he's a live wire himself. He speaks for ten minutes during which time he reminds the crowd the trams belong to them.[32] He has a point.

Municipal socialism has been a cornerstone of Glaswegian endeavour since before the turn of the century. It is a complex system of citizen representation on the city council which somewhat dilutes the overriding influence of merchants, manufacturers and professionals, and its aims have been to improve the fabric of the city for the benefit of all its residents through the formation of a corporation. The City of Glasgow Corporation employs over 32,000 men and women on the tramways and in the power stations; in tailors' workshops and saddleries; with departments handling everything from printing to bricklaying, as well as blacksmiths at Coplawhill. Since its inception in the last years of the nineteenth century, the Corporation's employees have enjoyed a maximum working week of forty-eight hours and the freedom to combine in trade unions or friendly societies with their representatives negotiating on their behalf. The city rates have supplied a Common Good Fund to relieve distress during periods of industrial depression, even millions of gallons of drinking water wending its way from Loch Katrine is owned, cleaned and provided by the city council. Frankly, the Corporation is the life blood of the city, making Glasgow a world leader in municipal enterprise; its tram system is seen as a model for tram systems in the United States.[33] Therefore, if the power station and tram workers strike, they are protesting against a perceived unfairness in an organization which both employs them and which they own through payment of their rates. If workers are privately employed by the Clyde's shipbuilding magnates, then at the minimum they own a share of the city's transport, power and water systems. So, when their temperatures are raised and someone with the skilled emotional and excitable oratory of Kirkwood puts it so simply, then yes, they own their means of transport and if they wish to disrupt the trams, they will.[34]

The woman conductor stopped beside Constable McDonald at the busy junction is desperate to keep her tram moving and she struggles to replace the trolley on the wire, but at every attempt she is prevented until eventually one of the strikers ties the trolley rope to the car's railings on the top deck putting it out of reach. Constable McDonald is most concerned for passengers wishing to get home for their lunch because all this speechifying has already taken half an hour, which means the tram network is going to be backed up for hours. Passengers and pedestrians alike appeal to him to intervene, but alone he is powerless. It is the busiest time of the day and he estimates there are 300 tram cars stacked behind as Kirkwood climbs down and heads to the Square; the mob has practically paralyzed the city for the rest of the afternoon and they have done so without threat or demand.[35] Caught up in the traffic is a horse-drawn lorry transporting empty bottles.

Some of the strikers hold the horse's head while others grab bottles, and one over-enthusiastic man throws his missile, striking a pedestrian.[36] It could be the start of something but, for now, mob violence is avoided, although it takes the persuasion of Constables McDonald's and Clark's batons to disperse the standers-by slowly towards George Square.[37] Nearby, their colleague, Constable Andrew Gallagher, leaves the procession which he has followed from Port Dundas. It is 1.20 pm as he departs along Sauchiehall Street just short of reaching the Square.[38]

The crowds converge on George Square from all directions. Lieutenant Lawrence Gray is waiting for them with a group of policemen by the ornamental stonework in front of the Municipal Buildings. His superiors do not want a repeat of Monday's actions and so his instructions are to prevent anyone addressing the masses from this position, so far with success. He watches across the short distance from the steps as Shinwell, Gallacher and the MP for Govan, Neil Maclean, mount the plinth of the Gladstone statue.[39] But the noise and constant motion from the swirling and increasing crowd create confusion. Gray's colleagues will later recall spotting Maclean and Kirkwood on the plinth and Detective Inspector Louis Noble is one of a small handful of officers who sees an attempt to hoist the red flag foiled by a constable who cuts the rope. Noble hears Shinwell tell the men to leave the policeman alone because he is a worker like themselves. Only Sergeant Beaton claims to hear Shinwell proclaim their goal now they have reached the Square: they intend to interview the Lord Provost to request the trams are removed from the streets.[40]

From the Gladstone plinth, Shinwell can see the ranks of police in front of the Municipal Buildings and he acknowledges their presence by claiming he has done more for them than any of the members of the town council. But this is not the beginning of another lengthy speech. Either Shinwell asks the crowd to appoint a deputation to speak to the Lord Provost or he agrees to a suggestion from one of the crowd. But a deputation is appointed. Apparently, the deputation has no formulated plan nor does it know what the meeting is about, although Detective Inspector Noble will retrospectively claim that their intention is to ask the Lord Provost to send a message to the authorities in London, which will become Shinwell's own version in the years to come.[41] Quickly, six men are selected while others attach themselves to the delegation including an unnamed woman and a seventh man who will later be blamed for much of the confusion in the discussion with the Lord Provost. They head into the throng but still they have no agenda despite claims later by two members that they had a defined mission: Isaac Sim, an engineer and the only named discharged soldier among the group, claims his intention is to ask the Lord Provost to use his influence with the Government, although his evidence is generally unreliable; and Ayrshire miner Donald Kennedy's mission is divinely ordained because he will later claim that, this afternoon, he is representing the trade unionists and followers of Christ.[42]

A news reporter describes the Square thick with excited bodies, jostling and rubbing shoulders. The crowd parts to allow the chosen six and their two hangers-on to move towards the Municipal Buildings. Isaac Sim leads the delegation to the entrance, where they pass Lieutenant Gray and his men but are halted by the inspector of police, who informs the doorkeeper who they are. Deep in the Square, the confusion when they reach the steps to the Buildings is witnessed and the crowd becomes menacing at the delay.[43] Shinwell steps forward; as a councillor he may be able to help and his presence does appear quite literally to open doors. Following him are Kirkwood and Maclean, who claims he is only involved because he wanted to help sort out the hold-up at the City Chambers' door.[44] Has the suggestion and selection of the delegation been spontaneous? Or as some accounts will suggest, has the process simply been a veneer to allow Shinwell to force the Lord Provost to ask the Government to intervene? On Monday they sent a telegram to the Minister of Labour who demurred to intervene in the strike and yesterday, a national conference in St Andrew's Hall instructed no further approach to the Government.[45] What is Shinwell's purpose in disobeying?

So far this week, James Stewart has not had any involvement in the strike; it is a matter between the men and their employers. He has remained sequestered in the City Chambers at endless meetings, another of which detains him this afternoon. Everything has happened in such haste that, as the delegation walks through the imposing doors of the Municipal Buildings, no one can truly say how long the whole affair has taken. One minute they were at the plinth, the next at the door asking to see the Lord Provost, and before they know it, they are inside: six delegates, the seventh man and a lone woman accompanied by Shinwell, Kirkwood and Maclean. The Town Clerk, Sir John Lindsay, is with the Lord Provost in his personal office overlooking the south-east of the Square when the Chamber Keeper knocks to inform them a delegation wishes to see them. James Stewart senses the urgency required to avert disorder in the Square.[46] He indicates he will speak to the group once he is disengaged.[47] Downstairs, the delegation remains in the hallway, still apparently without an agenda and yet they are moments away from having to formulate their demands. Finally, they are shown up to the library but, as the woman attempts to follow, she is turned away. She mentions something to do with being on the Lord's work and impatiently Kirkwood replies this is no place for that kind of talk.[48] The delegation is reduced to six plus the seventh man and Shinwell, Kirkwood and Maclean, who later claims to have taken no formal part in the delegation at all despite doing a lot of the talking. The Lord Provost meets them in the library accompanied by Sir John. It is just after 2.00 pm.[49] Now they must state their purpose.

Because he is the only delegate the Lord Provost knows personally, Councillor Shinwell introduces Maclean and Kirkwood but is lost for names when the other seven men shake hands with him, one of whom offers a masonic grip.[50] The Lord Provost indicates a half circle of chairs for the men to sit and then, because there has still been no agreement on their purpose, after the first few speakers have their say, everyone chips in at once.[51] At some point in the ensuing hour, someone declares that if they are not listened to then unconstitutional methods will be employed, most particularly if the tram cars are not removed from the streets. Is the demand a repeat of what has happened in Belfast where stopping the trams got the authorities' full attention? With everyone talking over each other, later the delegation's demand that the trams be removed from the streets will be attributed to Shinwell, Kirkwood and the elusive yet blameworthy seventh man.[52] The motive for the request will remain contested: to protect the processions, or to shut down the whole system and pressure the Government into intervention?

As the meeting progresses, Shinwell, Kirkwood and Maclean emerge as the prominent speakers, perhaps with a coherent proposition they have concocted themselves over the last few days. It will be denied later, but it seems they want the trams removed by the following morning to compel the Government at Westminster to intervene to resolve the forty-hour week issue. If that is not promised, then they will create havoc for every business and industry, ultimately paralyzing the city. Whether Shinwell and Kirkwood intend to use the issue of the trams as an ultimatum, or if they simply want them stopped while the processions fill the streets remains ambiguous, but to a town clerk anxious about events occurring outside his window, he assumes the former, as does the Lord Provost. James Stewart cannot see how he can stop the trams; it is a matter for the Tramway Committee. But he is the Lord Provost with overall charge of the Corporation, and if he cannot influence the Tramway Committee, then who is governing this city? Perhaps realizing they have overstepped their remit, Shinwell and Kirkwood backtrack and repeat they only wish to stop the trams while the processions continue. But James Stewart responds that he would have a delegation of tram passengers in here tomorrow requiring an explanation for stopping the trams. Approximately 70,000 strikers each with an estimated family of five are asking him to stop the trams and so inconvenience the remaining 'one and a quarter million' Glaswegians.[53] As Lord Provost, he explains, his responsibilities lie with Glasgow's entire citizenry, not just its disgruntled strikers, however much those in front of him might disagree. Shinwell invites the Lord Provost to risk telling this to the crowd downstairs himself before Kirkwood reminds him the Lord Mayor of Belfast has recently complained he received no notice of the tram stoppage but if he had, then the problems that ensued could have been avoided. Kirkwood does not wish the Lord Provost to be able to plead the same excuse in the future that he was not given sufficient notice to stop the trams.[54] And look what happened in Belfast. Is that what he wants in Glasgow? Shinwell will describe Kirkwood as excited and voluble, someone who leaves little room for anyone else to express their opinion on this matter, but this version is different from all other witnesses'.[55] They are giving the Lord Provost every notice of their request; he has only to act appropriately.

As the meeting becomes more heated, the issue of the trams dominates. There appears to be little discussion of the strike, whether forty-seven, forty or thirty hours can be achieved, or indeed how to resolve the strike and get the men back to work, none of which is in the Lord Provost's gift. In fact, tempers are so heated threats are issued. Does the Lord Provost want the strikers to resort to unconstitutional means if their request to stop the trams is denied? What does he think direct and drastic action will entail if he does not heed their demand? James Stewart and Sir John Lindsay listen with increasing alarm. Can the delegation really be threatening to remove the trams from the rails with their own hands, that they will force the Corporation workers to shut down the power stations and join the strike? Or is there some arcane, narrower meaning implied in their choice of words? So far, the CWC's calling of the strike has been 'unconstitutional' because it is against the trades unions' joint decision, which amounts to taking 'direct action', but cannot be considered drastic action, yet. But, the Lord Provost and town clerk either do not understand, or are not told, the meaning of these alternative definitions. Ten increasingly angry men sit before them in the library and pulsing through the windows is the cacophony of thousands of protesters in George Square. The tensions get the better of the seventh man who bursts out that all the trams should be removed from the streets.[56] Isaac Sim disagrees. His recollection of what he says requires only the removal of trams where the processions might coincide and become dangerous.[57] Afterwards, depending on who is listening, every one of the delegation, and none of the delegation, will admit to demanding the stoppage of the trams for safety reasons in the Square and, across the entire city, as a threat.

Glasgow has previous experience with trams and protesters. The tram strike of 1911 saw violence between striking and non-striking tram workers: motor handles snatched from drivers, windows smashed and bolts and wooden wedges inserted in the rails with the obvious intention to derail the cars and cause crashes. That strike was by tram workers for better conditions for themselves and involved picketing and sabotage, but they do not seem inclined to join the Forty-Hours campaign this week.[58] Shinwell reminds everyone that, outside, the men's blood is boiling and they need to address their concerns.[59] If left unchecked, without word from their leaders or solutions to their demands, 1911 might be repeated.

The key players have recognized the problem they face; the meeting began with no explicit purpose and has descended into an argument about trams. To move matters along, and perhaps it was Shinwell's plan from the start, it is decided to appeal to a higher authority. Later, several of those in the room will claim it is their idea, but the outcome is that the Lord Provost suggests contacting the Minister of Labour: Sir Robert Horne may be able to resolve their matter. Shinwell shrugs off the idea, they have already sent him a telegram on Monday but to no avail.[60] Member of Parliament for Govan Neil Maclean aims one higher and will claim he suggests invoking the Prime Minister. With considered charm, the Lord Provost puts the idea to the rest of the delegation. Is this what they all want him to do?[61] But isn't the Prime Minister still in Paris negotiating the terms of German reparations? One of the delegation has read the morning papers which he has incorrectly interpreted to confirm the Prime Minister's return to London, so there will be no issue in getting the telegram to him or anticipating his response within the next twenty-four hours, will there?[62] James Stewart agrees to send a telegram to both senior authorities. Now the serious business begins: drafting the telegram and prioritizing its contents. A great deal of discussion ensues in which Kirkwood takes a leading role while the Lord Provost jots down his notes in pencil.[63] Finally, he has a draft ready to read at which more discussion breaks out. The first sentence is particularly irksome to the delegation.

The Lord Provost begins by referring to the threat of forcible removal of the trams; after all it has been the main topic of discussion. The delegates object. Neil Maclean suggests the sentence's removal and replacement with something less inflammatory, along the lines of dislocation of the city's businesses and industry by any methods they think fit.[64] The ambiguity means the connection with recent events in Belfast may not be so readily made and it leaves the strikers with a lot more scope to disrupt the city beyond taking the trams off their tracks or shutting down the power stations.

70

But it also perplexes Sir John because what he has mostly heard discussed since the delegation entered the library is the shutting down of the tram system; now it appears they do not wish to include it at all, which is odd. He has assumed their reasoning connects the tram stoppage to Government intervention in the strike.[65] Kirkwood does not want there to be any trouble with the Government and adds his voice to the growing consensus from the delegation that the issue of the trams should be omitted.

If only the delegation had had more time downstairs in the hallway to formulate an agenda and some agreement on their requests, better still to have had a plan before they left the Gladstone plinth because now they cannot agree whether they want to hear the Government's response by the morning or if they can wait until Friday. Tomorrow morning is impossible according to James Stewart.[66] Not only has the telegram, once agreed upon, got to be typed and sent, but the ministers involved must be allowed time to consider their options. The delegation looks from one to another and agrees Friday noon will suffice.[67] Then the Lord Provost reads out the draft telegram, the contents he has managed to construct so far.

> I have been waited upon by a deputation appointed by a largely attended meeting of those who are dissatisfied with the present working conditions, and which was held in front of the City Chambers. The deputation consisted of eleven (actually ten) members including Messrs Shinwell, Kirkwood and Maclean, M.P. for Govan, and they requested me to represent to the Prime Minister and also to the Minister of Labour that they wished the Government to intervene with the employers in order to secure a reduction of the working hours to forty per week with no reduction in wages so as to provide those who had been demobilised and are without employment. It was further stated that they had hitherto adopted constitutional methods in urging their demand, but that, failing consideration being given to their request by the Government, they would adopt any other methods which they might consider would be likely to advance their cause. They have, however, agreed to delay taking any such action until Friday in order that I may be able to communicate your reply.[68]

James Stewart's telegram conveys to the Government that the matter is beyond his remit; he is merely an intermediary because plainly the delegation does not require his personal intervention, otherwise they

71

might have said so before now.[69] Instead he is the conduit for shaping their demands into language that will be familiar to Westminster, and to present the matter as agreeably as possible to the delegation. The inclusion of 'other methods' will send coded signals of alarm to anyone reading the telegram in London but has allayed fears here in his library of any indication of violence anticipated on Friday from the strikers. He has bought himself and the Government a reprieve of forty-eight hours. The irony of the number of hours they have agreed goes un-noted by the delegation as they depart the library headed for the Gladstone statue to report to the patient crowd awaiting them.

In his office the Lord Provost continues with his general business after the delegation's interlude, when he is presented with a communication just in from the power stations: the city's electrical department workers have been prevented from returning to work and have been compelled to join the strike. Only a skeleton staff remains to maintain power to hospitals and, hopefully, the city's homes. The street lighting will be affected. He hesitates before handing his pencil-scrawled draft telegram to his secretary and then adds a final sentence.

> I have just learned from the manager of the electricity department that all the men in the generating stations have been compelled to-day to join the strike, and that only sufficient men will be allowed to run the plant necessary to provide lighting and power for hospitals and infirmaries and possibly lighting of private dwelling-houses.[70]

The delegation has not only not received this news themselves, but has not agreed this addition to the telegram, which will surely raise concern when delivered to the Government.[71] The distinction between the tramway's power station at Pinkston and the city's power generated at Port Dundas may be lost on Westminster. The engineering workers at the Coplawhill car works have come out entirely, but they number just twenty men, and their female colleagues remain at work.[72] The ambiguity may lead the Government to anticipate another Belfast is brewing. The draft telegram is taken away to be transmitted to London during the remainder of the working day, one copy despatched to the minister and a second to the Prime Minister.[73] Whether it is read tonight or tomorrow morning, the Lord Provost has at least the strike leaders' agreement they will do nothing until Friday.

No one inside concentrating on the precise wording of the telegram has had a moment to consider what is occurring outside in the Square where

Gallacher entertains the massed strikers. Chief Detective Inspector Weir with his colleague Louis Noble listen intently to what they will later claim is an incendiary speech. Gallacher promises the crowd that the miners who have joined the strike so far will see them right for free coal to heat their homes if the strike goes on much longer. And if it is not over by the weekend, then they will stop every tram car and shut off the city's lights and paralyze the entire city.[74] He moves on to more convivial material: he points at the Municipal Buildings and declares the quantities of whisky contained indoors far exceed what is in the public houses where they get their dram. His appeal to the police in the crowd though is no joke. As the sons of Highlanders forced from their islands and glens by rapacious landlords in the last century, surely, they feel some comradeship with them, but if the police touch the strikers, use their batons on them, then by God they will go down because the class betrayal would divide the police from their fellow men. As a friend to the strike leadership and their sometime legal advisor, Rosslyn Mitchell, who is milling in the crowd, is not impressed by Gallacher's references to alcohol and, as he climbs down from the plinth heading for the Buildings, Mitchell tells him not to be so foolish.[75] After an hour inside and not a hint to the protesters outside of what has happened, finally the delegation emerges.

Immediately their leaders head for the Gladstone plinth, the only place where they know they can be seen above the crowd and hope to be heard. Shinwell, Kirkwood and Maclean deliver triumphant speeches. Having moved from the front steps of the City Chambers, Lieutenant Gray makes a special effort to hear what Shinwell says.[76] Reporting on the content of the discussion upstairs in the library, they tell the strikers that unconstitutional methods have been threatened if the authorities will not listen to them. It raises a hearty cheer. Shinwell notes the delegation's discharged soldiers for special mention and effectively shifts the blame for threats of violence onto their shoulders. If their need for work is not heeded, if the forty-hour week is not conceded, then drastic action will follow.[77] Cheers swell again. There is no immediate need for action, he has given the Government until Friday to respond, but of course if the strike is not settled by then, they will not hesitate to grind the city to a darkened standstill. Although Lieutenant Gray is not close enough to hear anyone else deliver their words from the plinth, what he will later recall is supported almost verbatim by the journalist nearby scribbling notes which will be published by the morning.[78] With the delegation now safely outside, the City Chambers' doors are locked and bolted and it will be reported that a detachment of mounted police remains poised in the Building's quadrangle should there be any further disturbances.[79] They will require more men than that if Shinwell's last entreaty to the strikers to come in their thousands on Friday comes to fruition.[80]

Until today the Lord Provost has not actively engaged with the strike leaders or the men, but working in the background since the Armistice, planning for the post-war industrial environment and a possible return to pre-war conditions, the Clyde Engineers' and Shipbuilders' respective Associations have been busy. They do not intend to accept the Forty-Hours campaign without a fight. They have trod cautiously enough during the war careful not to incite anger amongst the men on matters of pay and trade practices, ceding to Government decisions they may not have countenanced if it had not been for the drive to win the war at all costs.[81] Bringing in non-union men, naming and shaming strikers and threatening lockouts were pre-war tactics, but they remain weapons in the employers' armoury if the Clyde does not settle down soon.[82] They have watched the unions' influence grow in recent years, but this strike is different. The Government appears no longer inclined to arbitrate and the teeth have fallen out of the apparatus erected during the war to manage labour disputes.[83] They have owned the shipyards and heavy industries of the Clyde for decades and understand the impact of major international events on their business, the cyclical slumps outside their control. They are now properly into a post-war period with unemployment rising, and, as yet, soldiers returning from the various fronts are not counted in these statistics.[84] Once they are, the picture will become ever more bleak. Getting the Clyde back to work at full capacity is essential if they are to protect their businesses from the encroachment of overseas competition where labour is cheaper and at present hungrier for work than their Clydeside brothers appear to be.

In yesterday's meeting attended by the Associations' several representatives, Mr Hannon, the General Secretary of the British Commonwealth Union, was invited to address them and requested their support. The Union is notably anti-socialist and opposed to trade unions, and Mr Hannon explained that if the Prime Minister had been in London and not Paris earlier in the week, he would likely have opened negotiations with the unofficial strike leaders by now. This would have side-lined the industrialists and without a body of employers represented in the House of Commons there is no obstacle to such direct talks. However, the British Commonwealth Union has fifty-five sympathetic members in the House since December's general election and there are plans for a front-bench man, most probably Sir Edward Carson, Irish unionist and one-time attorney-general, to reply to Government questions from the floor of the House. And they have a press agent in mind to maintain a position in the lobby writing reports on labour questions to be presented to Government. Mr Hannon concluded his speech yesterday entreating the Associations to get a correct grip on the Clyde's complex industrial problems, and that co-operation is the way forward. The Association representatives thanked him for his time. They are aware the current strike is not a protest against the employers but one about working conditions in general.[85] They are prepared to sit and wait to see how this particular strike plays out.

In the meantime, during today's demonstrations, the employers' Associations have despatched Mr Thomas Biggart to investigate. This afternoon Mr Biggart visits the Chief Constable of Glasgow, James Verdier Stevenson, to discuss developments so far. He learns that the chief constable is well aware of the problems with peaceful picketing but, unless the pickets prevent people getting to and from work, he cannot declare it illegal action, and even if he could, he lacks the manpower to police the situation. Stevenson estimates he requires a further 600 men to bring his force up to strength and contend with today's issues. His men are spread so thinly with requests from numerous works to police the pickets he believes his final recourse may be to request military assistance. Mr Biggart leads him to understand that until now the employers have not favoured such a move. He leaves the implication of their possible change of mind hanging in the air.[86] The employers have history in quelling troublemakers and poor timekeepers in the workplace. During the war, they attempted to threaten such men with the withdrawal of their exemption certificates which kept them in Glasgow in trades pivotal to the war effort and away from the front. However, the need for skilled workers during the war was so great the threat could not be implemented.[87] The use of the military is not without precedent when strikes have led to unrest, but they hope it will be unnecessary.

In London Sir Robert Horne contemplates another situation beyond the labour strife affecting the country. There is apparently some unrest among soldiers in Scotland because the body of Private Francis Jones has inexplicably been returned home packed in sawdust.[88] It might not be Sir Robert's responsibility to explain how this has occurred, but loyalty and discipline among the military are essential on the Clyde, especially right now. As he formulates his report on the labour situation across the nation, Sir Robert is clear on certain aspects of the Clyde strike so far. He regards the strike leaders' demands as inchoate and without unanimity. He is right. The campaign goes under the banner of Forty-Hours, but already some have returned to work on a promise of forty-seven hours and Gallacher would still prefer thirty hours, while others have yet to decide whether to strike and, if so, for what. Sir Robert is also correct in his evaluation that there is large scale discontent. He observed this during the war, but the current strike leaders are not addressing their concerns through normal trade union channels, although he appreciates the efforts of the trade union officials who are working hard to persuade men to return to work. This action has met with some success in the Fife coalmines and miners in West Lothian appear to be wavering. There has been no approach for mediation from the Clyde except Monday's telegram sent directly from the strike leadership to himself. If he receives another telegram requesting his intervention, then such direct action can only be viewed as a desire to exploit industrial strife for political ends.[89] Which shall be met with decisive action: there will be no revolution anywhere in the United Kingdom.

It is almost 6.00 pm in Glasgow where George Lingard has continued working since Monday because he believes unfair voting tactics are being employed to bring men out. It is already dark and cold when his wife opens their front door. Three men stand on her doorstep with a crowd beyond them. She knows who they are and immediately closes the door. The men wait for half an hour to see if George will emerge. He hides inside. Intimidation is clearly ramping up to coerce men to join the strike.[90]

Chapter 5

Thursday, 30 January 1919

The Police

Yesterday afternoon's alarm that the power stations had come out in support of the strike is not quite as disrupting as the Lord Provost feared or as true as the strikers might like. Port Dundas is on short supply, only providing electricity generated by a handful of men with the strike committee's permission, and very little power is reaching the city's industrial operations.[1] The streetlights are still on, for the moment. The strike movement's new organ of communication – the *Strike Bulletin* – believes the action of the Corporation workers at the power station will have a great influence on a meeting of municipal employees scheduled for later this evening.[2] This is its first day in print and the *Strike Bulletin* carries the latest enthusiastic update on the progress, and success, of the Forty-Hours campaign. For just a penny, anyone can read the strikers' perspective on the latest news on day four of the strike. However, what the new protest press fails to report is the intimidation suffered by the few men keeping the lights on.

At Pinkston Power Station, the manager, David Baillie, anticipated trouble with Wednesday's night shift and planned ahead. A meeting at 5.00 pm yesterday resulted in five men leaving for the day, having been dissuaded from extending their shift by the sheer numbers of pickets crowding outside. The pickets know the Corporation workers' shift patterns and at 10.15 pm last night a crowd of 700 was still gathered outside the gates, muffled against a chilly force three wind and temperatures hovering around freezing.[3] But Baillie had kept his in-coming shift at home in the warm. He sent runners to everyone's door to tell the men due to arrive for the 11.00 pm shift that there would be a delayed start and to report to the head office. Shortly after midnight, Baillie judged the coast to be sufficiently clear and telephoned for two cars to transport the men from head office to the power station, followed by a further two packed with food. As the vehicles approached the station, their headlights peering ahead, they picked their way through strikers just stirring to life as engine noise and lights heralded their arrival. Swarming out of the darkness, over

300 pickets rushed forward and almost forced the vehicles into the canal. They refused to obey the police's instruction to stand back and so everyone became warmer than expected in the freezing night air as the constables charged the pickets chasing them back to Pinkston Road. Baillie managed to keep the shift together, although another shift due to arrive at 3.00 am was short by five men and, by breakfast, another five failed to arrive for work.[4] Baillie's men will remain under siege in the power station until 6 February. It is just as well they do, because unbeknownst to them, the strike committee has made plans to sabotage key installations if the strike does not succeed.[5]

While not a complete paralysis of the city's industrial sites, the reduced electricity output from Port Dundas has forced many large establishments to close this morning, putting men out of work temporarily. It is feared the strike leaders will use their absence from the workplace to claim greater numbers supporting the strike.[6] Elsewhere in the city, other men still attempting to work have been alarmed by the intimidating tactics of the pickets. William Henderson, a 51-year-old head foreman at the North British Railway Company Works at Cowlairs, has already run the gauntlet of pickets outside his yard yesterday but has remained unmolested by them. His colleague, George Lingard, determines to remain at work, but is so scared by last night's visit to his home he and Henderson instigate a plan for him to avoid molestation by the pickets. They decide to make George's working pattern unpredictable, leaving at unusual hours and by a different exit every time. The pickets get wise to their tactics very quickly because, by tonight, Lingard will ask to be allowed to stop work.[7] So, while the newspapers report over 100,000 now out on strike across Scotland, it would appear they are still not enough to persuade the Government to listen to their demand for a forty-hour working week with no loss of earnings.[8]

While Glaswegians, strikers and those disrupted by the disturbances await a response from London, the police are stretched monitoring the continuing picketing of yards not yet on strike and attending the various meetings planned for today. After yesterday's command to come in their thousands to George Square on Friday, they need to keep their ears to the ground to understand what is afoot, and just how many intend to converge on the Square tomorrow at noon. However, the police in Glasgow are stretched most days. There is a reason why two high court sessions are held in Glasgow when the High Court of Justiciary is on circuit and that is because Glasgow experiences more crime than other Scottish cities in an average week, but the last week of January 1919 is far from average.

Before the war Glasgow was the most intensively policed district in Scotland with one policeman for around every 500 citizens.[9] Yet in December 1918 there were over 700 police vacancies – most of them men who had not yet returned from war service – leaving Glasgow's force significantly undermanned.[10] In any year, they deal with murder, serious assault and sexual violence, crimes which are sent to the High Court for trial by jury. An even greater number of day-to-day crimes such as domestic abuse, theft and lesser assaults is tried more locally by the sheriff or at police courts where justice is summary. Which is where Alexander Wallace appeared yesterday, and his case is plastered all over the press today. He is the culprit arrested for the assault on a woman tram driver during one of Monday's processions and already he has been tried and sentenced at Glasgow's Central Police Court. Apprentice riveter, 17-year-old Wallace has been fined £8 8s or he can opt for the alternative of twenty-one days in prison; either way it amounts to a significant dent in, or loss of, earnings. Whether his actions were the result of over-exuberance or a misogynistic assault on a woman daring still to do a man's job, the *Strike Bulletin* reports it as an 'alleged assault' this morning caused by the tram travelling too quickly and Wallace jumping onto the platform to slow it down.[11]

The summary judgement of the police court shows no empathy with the young striker's cause. Since the Police (Scotland) Act of 1857 Scotland's police forces have always followed an underlying ethos offering a buffer between capital and labour, their role including the provision of welfare as well as crime detection.[12] However, exhausting hours for little pay can only continue for so long. Although many Scottish police have joined the Police Union since its inauguration in 1913 they have not yet used their collective bargaining power to threaten a strike and are unlikely to. Only in the last few weeks the Secretary for Scotland has agreed to a minimum wage for constables of £3 per week and a pension once they have served for twenty-six years.[13] If it was not done on purpose and in haste to guarantee police loyalty during the anticipated disturbances of post-war transition, then the timing of the Scottish police pay agreement has been most fortuitous. Many of the police on duty today reporting on the meetings will benefit from the new pension in the next few years, men like Sergeant John Steele of Western District with twenty years' service. His testimony will later prove to be unreliable, but this morning he is the senior man attending a meeting at Glasgow docks in James Watt Lane. He is accompanied by six colleagues. It is a little before noon and he estimates approximately 200 men are present.[14]

As leader of the Glasgow branch of the British Seafarers' Union, Emanuel Shinwell is addressing sailors and ships' stokers at the docks. He wants them to support the strike committee's proposal for a convention to discuss fuller employment. He hopes to persuade his union's shore workers to join the Forty-Hours strike. What Sergeant Steele and his colleagues hear is hardly a comradely workers-of-the-world-unite sentiment. Shinwell proposes to eject Chinese workers from ships in the Clyde in favour of white seamen. He objects to an employers' policy of entraining Chinese seafarers from Liverpool to Glasgow who are prepared to work for lower wages while Clyde men are idle.[15] Cheap labour of whatever colour or gender was a bone of contention during the war when dilution was considered an attempt to erode skilled men's wages and it is an acute issue now when full wartime employment is waning. However, there is more to Shinwell's divisive argument among seamen than a simple matter of one faction undercutting another's weekly wage.

Only a week ago, a riot occurred in James Watt Street between black and white sailors waiting at the mercantile marine office to sign on to a ship lying in the harbour. Shinwell had addressed a meeting that morning, stressing the need to exclude Chinese seamen and that 'action must be taken at once'.[16] When the violence began, only a handful of police constables were present and an additional fifty had been hastily mustered to deal with the ensuing riot. The spark that lit the flame was the perception that white workers had a greater right to employment than non-whites in a shrinking labour market. Outnumbered, the black sailors fled along Broomielaw to their lodging house, chased by a mob armed with knives, sticks and bricks fetched along the route, and the noise of revolver shots resounding behind them. Having reached their boarding house, the black sailors barricaded themselves inside and were reported to have fired down on the mass of white sailors below them, but the police had them cornered. Of thirty black sailors arrested, all were charged with riot and possession of weapons. None of the white rioters on the streets were arrested. Of the casualties requiring medical assistance, Duncan Cowan, a white sailor was shot in the neck and was taken by ambulance to the Western Infirmary. While Sierra Leonian Tom Johnson, described by a news reporter as a 'darkie' with little English, having been stabbed in the back, was remanded in the police office and, having been charged, he was then allowed to join his alleged victim, Cowan, at the hospital for treatment.[17] The entire business appears to have been based on the perception that black sailors were undercutting white seamen, combined with assumptions about racial superiority. However, black sailors hired in British ports were paid similar rates to white British sailors; it was only those hired overseas who might be contracted on lower wages.[18] But fears about job competition stoked by the likes of Shinwell promote divisions and hostility, which is especially easy where skin colour is concerned.

Among the seamen listening to Shinwell this morning are James Kennedy, a ship's fireman, and William Blamires, a delegate of the British Seafarers' Union. They hear Shinwell confirm the Forty-Hours strike has nothing to do with the sailors, they are not on strike, and he turns what happened last week upside down by declaring he has no issue with black seamen because they receive the same wages as Clyde men. It can only be an attempt to build camaraderie among the sailors to get their general support for the campaign. Shinwell tries again when he alludes to a dockside policeman they all know, Tom Russell, who one day may be on strike with them because, Shinwell claims, the police are dissatisfied too.[19] Elsewhere in Britain, that may be the case in the near future, but in Glasgow, no. Sergeant Steele and his men know where their priorities lie, and they too have their biases towards non-white labour. Why else were no riotous white sailors arrested last week, nor left-wing conspirators like Shinwell whom the police distrust?

By the end of the meeting Shinwell has elicited a promise from the sailors not to sign on to ships which may already be employing Chinese seafarers and offers his own promise to chase the Chinese 'for their lives' if the Government does not remove them from the boats. He gives the men gathered on the harbourside clear instructions to join their fellow workers in George Square tomorrow; he needs their moral support and presence to swell numbers.[20]

Further attempts to bring out recalcitrant workers occur across the city. Again, the Star Picture House in Orchard Street in Partick accommodates a strikers' meeting where speakers Allan Ireland, a member of the Amalgamated Society of Carpenters and Joiners, and Joseph Brennan encourage the men listening to them to attend the mass meeting planned for tomorrow in George Square. Detective Sergeant George Ross is in the crowd which he estimates to be somewhere between 2,000 and 3,000 men. He hears every word spoken, and later reports hearing the strike organizers inform the men that if the Square won't hold them tomorrow then, perhaps, they can hold an overflow meeting in the Municipal Buildings. At the trial, the defence will claim that such fighting talk is intended only to rally the men, make them laugh, keep them on-side; the prosecution will try to prove it is incitement to revolutionary occupation of the seat of city government. Ross accompanies a procession heading to Mechan's Yard, while a band of strikers unattended by police marches north to Anniesland to persuade the men at the optical firm of Barr and Stroud to come out and join them.[21]

Established by two university academics, Archibald Barr and William Stroud saw their company expand rapidly at the outbreak of the war, manufacturing rangefinders and other optical instruments for the navy. With the war over, they are now expanding into the production of binoculars and have hopes for supplying them to the navy as well as the British army.[22] Maintaining production with potential new orders on the books is vital if they are to continue to employ the men they have, but the strikers have other ideas. It is only two miles from the Star Picture House to Anniesland and nearly 2,000 men from the picture house form an orderly procession weaving their way through the streets. They arrive in time for Barr and Stroud's men coming out for their dinner, creating two cordons across the street to greet them. The workers are questioned and only allowed to return after their break on the promise they will hold a meeting to vote whether to join the strike. Outside, the pickets hear the factory's fire horn blow, followed by a man they call a 'scab' appearing at the gatehouse door wielding a revolver. He is an anomaly among the week's events so far and is quickly disarmed and arrested by police already in attendance. Inside Barr and Stroud's, the optical workers decide to fall in with the Forty-Hours movement.[23]

Other members of the picture-house meeting have arrived at Mechan's Ironworks in Scotstoun, further west along the Clyde, where Inspector Kenneth McLennan sees a large crowd approaching from the east along South Street. He observes the men marching in orderly fashion, yet it is anticipation of a change of mood that provokes him to enter Mechan's Yard to telephone the Partick Police Office for assistance. He is instructed to do his best with the twenty-three men he has with him, one of whom is Sergeant Robert Gordon in plain clothes.[24]

It is 2.45 pm when Gordon spies a large crowd approaching. Either Joseph Brennan repeats himself or Sergeants Ross and Gordon are confused, because again Brennan is heard telling the massed crowd that if George Square will not hold them then an overflow meeting can easily be arranged to spill into the Municipal Buildings. However, Sergeant Gordon hears him go further, because next Brennan informs the strikers that the trams will be off the rails by midday tomorrow because the power station workers will have joined them by then. There will be no gas or water workers at their works and Glasgow will be plunged into darkness except for the infirmaries for which he re-assures them provision will be made. Now that does sound like the workers taking control of the city's infrastructure and placing the lieges, its citizens, at risk. Brennan pays special attention to the apprentices still working at Mechan's Yard who he believes want to come out and he asks for volunteers to go inside to speak to the management. A flurry of hands goes up, but neither Sergeants Ross nor Gordon see who they are, and nor do they witness a deputation enter the yard.[25] However, Inspector McLennan, standing only twelve yards from Brennan, distinctly hears him tell the men that if the apprentices are not out within a quarter of an hour, they have licence to burst in the doors and take them out. McLennan feels this is highly likely because he considers Brennan has the men in the palm of his hand. To avert trouble, McLennan suggests to Brennan he should go to speak to the management on the men's behalf, which Brennan agrees might be better. He instructs the men to let the inspector through because, as workers together, they bear the police no ill-will, they have a difficult duty to perform.

Stationed at the works gate where he can always be found, 44-year-old timekeeper Michael McKeown confirms that 380 men are on the clock and his impression is they wish to recommence work after their dinner break.[26] Inspector McLennan goes inside seeking out Henry Mechan and informs him that he is under-resourced to protect the works. With pickets clambering on the windowsills, the threat of damage to his premises is real, so Mechan assembles the apprentices to ask if they want to leave; emphatically they reply 'no'. Next, he asks the engineers. They are less definite and wish to be allowed out safely rather than face a hostile crowd once their shift ends. With a split decision, Mechan takes a pragmatic approach. Walking at the head of both the engineers and the apprentices, Inspector McLennan emerges from Mechan's Yard and is met with loud cheers from the gathered strikers. Above the din, he explains the situation to Brennan: Mechan is closing the works of his own volition rather than countenance damage to his property. A man in the crowd interrupts. Apparently, some men remain inside. Henry Mechan is swift to step forward appealing to the pickets to allow a handful of men to remain until 5.30 pm to shut down the plant safely. Brennan reckons it can be done more quickly than that, but Mechan remonstrates with him, forcing Brennan to acquiesce in favour of a shutdown by 5.30 pm with the additional demand that no one will be allowed to return tomorrow morning. Mechan refuses. So, Brennan asks for the one man responsible for shutting down the works to step out to speak to him. He proves easier to persuade and it is quickly agreed he can have until 5.30 pm to close up if he promises not to return tomorrow. With Mechan's Ironworks at Scotstoun now only hours away from being completely out, although not necessarily all in support of the strike, Brennan and his crew advance on Albion Motor Works.[27]

While the mood in Glasgow continues at a roiling pitch, at Westminster the Lord Provost's telegram wired last night is under discussion. Three of the five members of the War Cabinet are present: Andrew Bonar Law, recently elected Member of Parliament for Central Glasgow, is in the chair; Austen Chamberlain, Chancellor of the Exchequer since early January and Sir Eric Geddes, who recently left office as First Lord of the Admiralty. They are joined by members of the wider cabinet, civil servants and army generals, among whom are: Robert Munro, Secretary for Scotland and Lord Advocate James Avon Clyde; also, Winston Churchill, Secretary of State for War and Air.[28] The Empire's most senior soldier, Chief of the Imperial General Staff Sir Henry Wilson, is also there. Meeting at 10 Downing Street, the War Cabinet addresses the week's events in Glasgow, which are not viewed as anything so debilitating as a national strike. Earlier in the week, Minister of Labour Sir Robert Horne stated clearly in the press he will only negotiate with the unions and their leaders, which relegates the ongoing situation in Glasgow to a regional labour dispute. Horne's intransigence on the matter has been a serious rebuff to the strike leaders, but it is the Lord Provost who now seems most to require the War Cabinet's advice. He is new to the role and has not benefited from the experience others around him in Glasgow's City Chambers gained in labour disputes during the war. It is the Lord Provost's responsibility, advised by the Sheriff of Lanarkshire and the chief constable, to maintain order in Glasgow and resolve the city's current problems. The War Cabinet's response will certainly make their position abundantly clear.

Bonar Law opens proceedings by reading the telegram to the War Cabinet and explains he has already discussed matters with Horne. Between them, they have drafted a response which the Prime Minister in Paris has approved by telephone. In essence, it rebuffs Wednesday's delegation's attempts to involve central government. It emphasizes the Government's policy of dealing only with the official, elected representatives of the trade unions. To become involved with local union and labour leaders would undermine current negotiations as well as the supposed wartime co-operation established between employers and employees. Everyone desires industrial peace, but the personal involvement of the Prime Minister could only diminish Horne's authority, which Lloyd George is reluctant to do. And while the trade unions have already agreed to a forty-seven-hour week, a breakaway movement striking for a forty-hour week contravenes the previous agreement. The Cabinet discusses the ramifications for the nation if the current strike spreads, which leads Munro to suggest deploying the

2,000 special constables available in Glasgow to operate the electricity and other municipal services; he would rely on them in preference to soldiers, but the trouble is, since the Armistice, the 'specials' have been partly stood down and may take time to muster.[29] Bonar Law broaches the issue of maintaining law and order, and the need to guard any men prepared to keep the city's services running. They estimate there are still 500 men from Glasgow's police force in the military. So, despite Munro's suggestion that Glaswegian police be identified and plucked from the vast numbers being demobilized and returned to duty, the police force will not be replenished any time soon. Churchill says it's impossible.

However, Munro is not prepared to sit quietly. He has been contacted by the Sheriff of Lanarkshire to enquire whether, if it were necessary, it would be possible to call on the assistance of the military if the civil authorities cannot cope with the current disturbances.[30] The sheriff has seventeen years' experience in his role and has managed serious labour disputes and protests on the Clyde before. As the man taking the city's temperature, MacKenzie has given the impression he is very worried. Consequently, Munro broaches the subject to the War Cabinet now.

Sir Thomas Munro from the Ministry of Labour is already on stand-by to head north to contribute his experience of labour conditions in Scotland to the situation, but Mr Chamberlain thinks that plan might inflame matters and comes dangerously close to implying that a Ministry of Labour man could assist in a matter of law and order. Having remained silent throughout the meeting so far, General Sir William Robertson, Commander-in-Chief of Home Forces, the commander of all troops in the United Kingdom, interjects to clarify that the civil authorities are responsible for law and order and in Scotland: the military can only step in if requested by the appropriate local authority; in Scotland that is the sheriff. Or if martial law is declared first, which is not the case. He can offer men from the nineteen infantry battalions stationed in Scotland, all but one of which are Scottish: one in Glasgow, another in Greenock just along the water, and twelve based fifty miles or so away around Edinburgh. They are reserve units consisting of all sorts of men and he explains further that their officers may not be the most efficient. However, it would be illegal for soldiers to operate the power stations or other municipal works. Someone recalls that during a rail strike before the war soldiers had been detailed as engine-drivers and guards. General Childs points out that that was when troops were well-disciplined and ignorant, unlike today's army which he considers to be educated and ill-disciplined. Is he suggesting he would not like to put the soldiers to the test in a labour dispute? There are, says Robertson, certain disadvantages to using Scottish troops, but on the whole it would be 'safer' to use them than to bring in English battalions.

Immediately, the Secretary of State for War shatters any enthusiasm for deploying troops to Glasgow. The time is not yet ripe for strong measures, the strikers are merely a disaffected minority and previous, more serious strikes have been weathered. However, some of the leaders could be seized under the Defence of the Realm Act which remains in force. DORA is a legal instrument with different policing guidelines from peacetime, allowing the authorities to seize potential malcontents if they so desire to prevent the commission of crime which might threaten national security.[31] Bonar Law agrees wholeheartedly with Churchill, but insists they need a man in the City Chambers to acquaint the Lord Provost with the Government's policy and to report back to London as matters develop. Sir Thomas Munro's ticket on this evening's night-train to Glasgow is handed instead to Assistant Under-Secretary of the Scottish Office, Mr John Lamb, a less prominent but equally trustworthy officer.[32]

He may have nothing to say directly to the strike's leaders, but Sir Robert Horne makes one last request as the War Cabinet meeting closes. Addressing the Secretary for Scotland, he asks that, if the possibility arises, the strike leaders should be seized. They are not elected trade unionists but well-known extremists. Churchill advises calm. Until the strikers are guilty of a serious breach of the law, the Cabinet should bide its time; the Government needs the people behind them, not among the ranks of the strikers. But haven't they crossed that line already? Churchill explains: the government should wait until some glaring excess is committed and the strikers exceed the limits of their wage dispute.[33] Munro believes they are planning to wreck the newspaper offices in Glasgow. He sounds frustrated at Churchill's imperturbability. Just before they leave, Sir Eric Geddes notes possible disruption of rail traffic over the weekend which might affect troop movements. Churchill assures him he will take all necessary measures to have troops ready to move and will consider arrangements to place troops in the vicinity of Glasgow.

Outside 10 Downing Street, London's street-lights add warmth to a dreary day in the capital. The War Cabinet departs, having approved the telegram response to be transmitted to Glasgow's Lord Provost. He is urged strongly to maintain the street lighting; he is assured the military will be held in readiness if requested by the civil authorities and he should maintain a firm yet not provocative stance to put down disorder and prevent intimidation. John Lamb grabs his hat and coat and other paraphernalia for his journey north. The Cabinet establishes a small committee to consult as the situation progresses: if difficult decisions need to be taken in the days ahead, it is preferable that the committee assuming responsibility understands the particularities of Scotland and can advise accordingly.[34] Three MPs for Scottish constituencies, the Scottish Secretary Munro, Lord Advocate Clyde and Horne, are joined by General Childs.[35] The meeting has taken a little over an hour. As the message's dots and dashes are transmitted from Downing Street, the flimsy, pale biscuit-coloured draft telegram sheet is time-stamped 4.20 pm.[36]

In Glasgow Chief Constable Stevenson prepares for possible trouble tomorrow. It seems unlikely a mass meeting of strikers and their supporters, waiting expectantly in the Square for their leaders to explain to them London's response, will behave calmly, especially if Westminster's answer is unfavourable. And so, Stevenson expands his directives already in place since Monday. He makes arrangements for meals to be provided to police who remain on duty beyond the end of their shift and overtime payments, with mounted police to be held in reserve at Henderson's Stables in West Nile Street, just to the west of George Square. He also instructs all police to work a twelve-hour shift which will increase the numbers on duty to around 570 across the whole of Glasgow, and he orders the number of men held in reserve in each division to be doubled. Constables on the beat will be allowed two meal breaks, each of thirty minutes. They are to focus on protection of public utilities and to protect those who remain at their work.[37] Apart from preparing for the worst, there is little more Stevenson can do, except perhaps pray the worst does not happen. His force of fewer than 600 men per shift is nowhere near up to strength to contain potentially tens of thousands of angry strikers. If so many turn out to demonstrate tomorrow, not only will they not fit into George Square, but he will be unable to police them wherever they care to march.

As it stands, today's meetings popping up erratically across the city are stretching Stevenson's resources and there appears to be no abatement in the numbers willing to attend as temperatures drop with the setting sun. At the Tradeston Gas Works Sergeant William Ferguson has certainly got the wind up. He has spotted a group of men proceeding along West Street without a leader, no one to calm their tempers if what they meet at the gas works is disagreeable. At present, they are marching quietly but Ferguson takes no risks. He gathers a further two sergeants, Sellars and Wishart, and a dozen constables and follows the procession. The crowd presses hard against the gas works' gate and refuses to budge when he asks; in fact, they shout and jeer at the police. There is nothing else to do except stand and be witness to events. At 5.30 pm the shift ends and out spill the municipal gas workers; they are met with a V-shaped crowd of pickets. The strikers encircle them, forcing them into the narrow end of their cordon and closing behind them. There is no retreat, the men coming off shift must stand and listen, and hopefully be persuaded, or coerced, into joining the strike. And to convince them to do so, they are introduced to this afternoon's speaker, Comrade Ebury.[38]

From the gate of the works, general foreman Thomas Moffat watches as George Ebury, an English socialist, jumps onto a bag of charcoal so that he is head and shoulders above the crowd. Sergeants Sellars and Wishart do not need any formal introductions; they recognize Ebury from socialist meetings going back to summer 1918.[39] Ebury is a member of the Gas Workers' Union and understands what the working conditions are like inside. He supports Gallacher's thirty-hour week, but this week is a strike for forty hours to accommodate demobilizing soldiers and to ease the increasing burden of unemployment. He knows the gas workers have plans for a meeting later tonight asking for a forty-four-hour week, but there is little point in a fragmented campaign that cannot decide what its single main thrust should be. He urges them to join the Forty-Hours movement tomorrow. But he oversteps the mark when he threatens to bring them out himself and damn the consequences. He goes even further, claiming that, by tomorrow night, there will be no tram cars running. Moffat is fearful his fiery words will incite the strikers.[40] Sergeant Ferguson agrees; he considers Ebury has certainly worded his speech to inflame the crowd to violence.[41]

There is no keeping up with the pace of pickets and closures for the police. At Mossend, to the far east of the city, Beardmore's Iron and Steel works have had to close because the electricians have come out, making some 1,300 men idle.[42] At the collieries at Hamilton yesterday, miners wishing to work described the pickets' actions as amounting to terrorism, with the red flag flying from Hamilton's Miners' Union office and official papers scattered like confetti from its balcony. Clearing up the street below will be delayed even though the carters have returned to work. There are already concerns for public health since rubbish is mounting across the city and at this time of year refuse collection is reportedly at its busiest. The authorities advise citizens to burn everything that is not insanitary to alleviate pressure on the municipal Cleansing Department.[43] There appears to be no end to the disruptions to everyday life caused by the strike.

However, the police force is in possession of some very helpful intelligence as they dash from meeting to meeting. The legacy of Clydeside's wartime fame is that photographs exist of all the main protagonists involved in this week's strike, so the police know who they are looking for and can readily identify key speakers. If it comes to it, they will be able to give credible evidence in court, naming names of who said what, where and when. Intended to promote the contribution of hardworking Clydesiders to a grateful nation, now those same publicity photographs that glamourized the shipyards are distributed among police offices so that even the most junior and newest policemen can recognize who drives the disturbances.[44] If it turns ugly tomorrow there will be no hesitation in arresting the culprits. They will know who they are and where they live because Glasgow's police force lives and has grown up among the community it serves. No longer heavily recruited from Highland villages, north-east Scotland or Ireland, constables born and bred in Glasgow now constitute a growing number among the force.[45]

Highland recruits have always been considered tougher, healthier and more robust than native Glaswegians and, more importantly, non-partisan in Glasgow's particular troubles and with a perceived loyalty to Crown and country.[46] These rural police recruits worked for low wages, often tens of shillings below the weekly pay of bricklayers and other semi-skilled trades, but they earned more than an agricultural worker back home.[47] But for some years, recruitment from lowland Scotland has been increasing, men who have lived in closer proximity to the main cities of Edinburgh and Glasgow.[48] Police wages are now comparable to the skilled and semi-skilled, and they live among their fellow workers. One thing that has changed little though is their chief constable's demand for courteous manners towards all members of the public and restraint in the use of force, which may be stretched somewhat before the week is out. At this morning's meetings, there has been evidence of an unruly element among the strikers, men unwilling to obey police instructions. If that disinclination continues, batons may have to be employed simply to maintain order. And when one considers known troublemakers, then there has always been licence for a spot of rough justice among the Glasgow force.[49]

Yet, so far today, there have been very few disturbances requiring forceful police intervention. Even this evening at a meeting at the public hall in Kinning Park south of the Clyde, Detective Sergeant James Mulherrin in plain-clothes stands among 500 people and has so far only witnessed them eject an unwanted news reporter. Mulherrin is joined by his colleague, acting Detective Constable William MacFarlane; they are experienced officers well into their second decades of service, but what they hear rattles them because later they will declare the speakers' words were a direct incitement to violence. Having finished his rousing speech at Tradeston Gas Works, George Ebury is now speaking at the hall in Kinning

Park and much of what he says is a polished repetition of his earlier robust and persuasive oratory. He attempts to win the crowd's empathy with tales of personal and painful experience of a policeman's baton; he is not afraid of the view down the muzzle of a revolver. He tells them the only thing wrong with the current Forty-Hours campaign is that it is too damned mild, but forty hours it is, and he wants them out. He hands over to John Thom.

Thom is just returned from Ireland. His enthusiasm for the successes in Belfast is palpable. Not only is the situation there excellent, but he was also a member of a delegation sent to speak to the lord mayor with demands to remove the tram cars from the streets. He recounts that a man accompanying them had tools to cut the cables there and then, but Belfast's lord mayor acquiesced and, within an hour, there were no trams running. The crowd gathered in front of him is surely aware of demands made yesterday by Glasgow's very own strike delegation during their visit to the Lord Provost. Thom is fired up and, while referring to possible solutions to difficulties discussed in Belfast, he places his hand in his hip pocket and taps on what is supposedly inside, which Mulherrin understands refers to a revolver. The police will not stand in Thom's way, he wants the men at the gas works out and threatens there will be no trams by the weekend. Interestingly, he suggests that the soldiers are with them, which the next speaker will also claim, without any basis.[50] This evening's key speaker is James Dunlop MacDougall, a serious political activist.

In the December 1918 election MacDougall stood as the British Socialist Party candidate for Tradeston in Glasgow and lost. Despite being only 28 years old, he has had a long career agitating for better housing for Glaswegians, supporting John Maclean at socialist meetings and doing a spell in gaol for it, as well as organizing miners across Scotland and South Wales to unionize. He is militant and has been described as dangerous.[51] He is introduced to the meeting as the man most likely to be the first president of the 'British Republic'. Neither Mulherrin nor his uniformed colleague Constable Archibald McGlachan mention any hint of irony at this statement in their later reports. It is 9.00 pm and McGlachan stays only ten minutes, but it is long enough to hear young MacDougall declare bloodshed will be inevitable and the men must be prepared because the authorities are laying traps for them. Somehow, he has magicked up 600 police from an overstretched and undermanned force – virtually the entire available Glasgow force – already waiting for them at the gas works. He too involves the soldiers in their strike because he tells them that, only yesterday, he was at Hamilton speaking to the miners and when asked to preserve order on the streets the men in Hamilton Barracks told their officers to go to hell.[52] A soldier listening in the crowd tonight takes exception to this and an argument ensues. Constable McGlachan does not hear the outcome, only the voice of Ebury shouting above the tumult, asking for quiet and explaining that it does not matter if the police are taking notes, they will take them whether the men shout or not. McGlachan is clear that Ebury takes control of the uproar because he has seen him before and recognizes him. Perhaps too concerned for his safety to do so during the meeting, once outside McGlachan scribbles hurried notes on what he has just witnessed.[53]

However, Mulherrin and MacFarlane remain and receive the full blast of MacDougall's desire for revolution and a British republic. He describes mutiny in the navy and on board the fleet's largest battleship moored in the Firth of Forth where twenty men have recently been killed in a skirmish. The faces of the crowd must look horrified because MacDougall hastens to add that that kind of news is never reported; this is probably because it is untrue. He regales them with details of a visit around New Year from a naval man asking how to raise a revolution in the navy and MacDougall's answer, as Detective Sergeants Mulherrin and MacFarlane hear it, is disquieting as well as fanciful. To foment a revolution in the navy, one must wait until the appointed time, then sail to the middle of the English Channel, raise the red flag while simultaneously sending out a wireless message declaring the revolutionaries' standard has been raised and, even if revolution fails in Britain, capitalism will be crushed. They have not enjoyed the revolutionary successes of Russia and Germany, but this strike here this week could be the start of something momentous. MacDougall wouldn't be surprised. If Mulherrin has heard him correctly, his evaluation of MacDougall's words is alarming: the Forty-Hours movement and industrial matters are secondary to MacDougall's campaign for absolute revolution.[54]

At a municipal workers' meeting this evening at St Mungo's Hall, pickets stand outside brandishing placards telling those inside to 'Strike now, not next week'. Many in tramways' uniform, there are nearly 2,000 Corporation employees here with a decision to make: decide on a show of hands at the meeting or organize a full ballot of members to vote for or against the strike. They opt for a ballot which will delay them joining the stoppage in time for tomorrow.[55] In Govan, Shinwell rallies support at a 'Victory at Home' meeting where recent Labour party successes are being celebrated. District Nurse Allison Moir is there, so is Neil Maclean. They both hear him give clear instructions that tomorrow's demonstration must be peaceably conducted and Moir claims he also tells the meeting that he has it on good authority: the military are already arrived in Glasgow.[56] How could he possibly believe that? No one has requested their presence, nor given the order for them to move.

South-east of the city, in the mines of Lanarkshire, tonight and continuing into the early hours of Friday there is a disturbance already underway. What appears to have started as picketing by a group of eighty men has turned very ugly. They have gained numbers visiting the Independent Labour Hall en route and, reaching Craighead Colliery, they have broken in and stolen lamps. Moving on to Hamilton Palace Colliery, where the men have voted not to strike, they have smashed windows, ransacked an office and attempted to break a safe containing £5,000 in wages. Calls between the Glasgow and Lanarkshire forces have alerted Constable Cameron and others to what is underway. For a while, Cameron is alone in the colliery office and has drawn his baton to confront fifteen men. He is coshed by one of the leaders, but fights on bravely. Then, as seven colliery firemen arrive for duty, they meet the 200-strong angry and abusive crowd. Threatened with being stranded underground if they start work, they escape over the spoil tips. Discussing the strike with a picket line is one thing, but what they believe they are facing is a gang of hooligans and 'Bolshevists' prepared for mischief; the violence and intimidation is too much. Of the 200 men who left the meeting hall, it is estimated twenty are the main culprits for the violence which continues into the early hours. The men who are caught will be prosecuted for mobbing and rioting and the eight men convicted will receive sentences between ten days and six months.[57] It is a worrying signal of how high tempers are running and the element of violent disorder among legitimate strikers.

In the city centre at 105 West George Street news of the Hamilton colliery disturbance has yet to reach the eleven representatives of the North-West Engineers' Association and twelve members of the Clyde Shipbuilders' Association who are in a meeting with Mr Thomas Biggart; he joins them in an advisory capacity. The joint meeting of both Associations' executive committees discusses the ongoing irregular strike and agrees to send a deputation to interview the Lord Provost. The four men chosen intend to raise the matter of the electricity supply having been cut off by the Corporation Electricity Department and mean to protest strongly against such action without first consulting the employers. They will place before the Lord Provost a full statement of their position and they will convene a meeting for tomorrow, Friday 31 January, of all their members to discuss the entire strike business and the city's response to the disruption so far. They also intend to have words with the press authorities to discourage them from reporting on the strike and naming its leaders. It is felt such measures would assist in the collapse of the strike.[58] Misguided or insufficiently informed about the seriousness of the situation, their plans may prove insubstantial in the face of what is happening in Hamilton's collieries and beyond. But news from the city's streets is available to those prepared to spend a penny on the strikers' own newspaper.

A deputation of four men to visit the Lord Provost tomorrow sounds tame compared with what is splashed across the back page of the *Strike Bulletin* exhorting all strikers to join the great demonstration in George Square at 12.30 pm tomorrow, come along to hear the Prime Minister's reply to Wednesday's telegram, all districts to attend, come with bands and banners, but above all, be sure to 'Be in Time and Be There'.[59]

Chapter 6

Friday, 31 January 1919

Afternoon

They came to hear the Government's response to Wednesday's telegram from their leaders, but instead they have heard the opening words of the Riot Act, the sound of bottles smashing against walls, tram windows shattering under the impact of bricks and bolts, and the entreaties of their strike leaders to depart George Square and head instead to Glasgow Green. For those gathered at the rear of the Square, William Gallacher's and David Kirkwood's pleas to leave, to bide their time, are a hoarse whisper conveyed throat by throat from the City Chambers' balcony where they stand waving to the crowds below.

Since midday, 20,000 perhaps as many as 30,000 strikers and their supporters have gathered in the city centre; some will later claim as many as 100,000 are squeezed quite impossibly into George Square. Inside the Municipal Buildings, the Lord Provost has been in conference with the Town Clerk, Sir John Lindsay, and the Sheriff of Lanarkshire, Alastair MacKenzie, and he has attended a magistrates' meeting. Kirkwood and Gallacher have been dragged from the quadrangle where they have nursed their wounds and have made a plea bellowed from the balcony for the crowd to move peacefully to Glasgow Green. Timings on what started first are confused: the riot or the police baton charge? Is everyone in the Square really here to receive the Government's answer to the strike leaders' demand for intervention? Or have some been intent on violence from the moment they got out of bed? Some will argue that is an unthinkable accusation, yet for others it is a possibility. How far is Shinwell prepared to rouse the crowd?[1] The men gathered at the junction of the Square with North Frederick Street, where a perfect hail of bottles is being hurled from a stricken lorry, are a case in point.[2]

At 12.15 pm, as the violence begins at the south-east corner of the Square around the trams, at the north-east corner a little way up North Frederick Street, a lorry pulls up at No. 46, the licensed premises of Mrs Agnes Graham, managed by 22-year-old Owen Quade and his older brother John.

Owen has been employed here since October 1917 when he was medically discharged from the army; he is a Gallipoli veteran. This is their Friday order arriving: fourteen dozen bottles of beer in return for sixteen dozen empties. North Frederick Street is a straight road with no obstructions except the parked lorry, so Owen and the driver George Binnie have a clear view of events unfolding at the bottom of the steeply sloping street where it joins George Square. The driver is very young, just 17 years old, and unsure how to proceed; he has other deliveries to make but does not like the look of the crowd nor does he wish to take responsibility for whatever might happen next. He asks to use Owen's telephone and calls his depot for instructions. Owen does not hear the exchange but plainly the driver is told to continue with his next stop at No. 41, Mr Slater's down the street. But it's a mistake. As he leaves No. 46, Binnie's lorry is surrounded, rioters crawling over it pulling bottles as quickly as they can and throwing them at the approaching police. Binnie jumps down from his lorry while the rioters hold the horse's bridle. At last count, before he is dragged away from his horse and lorry, Binnie reckons there are forty-eight dozen bottles of beer and seventy dozen empties on the dray.[3]

From the foot of North Frederick Street, Constable Gargan is among those detailed to stop the violence occurring halfway up the road around the lorry. The police are too experienced not to realize what might happen if the crowd takes possession of the beer crates. But, for anyone rushing towards the fracas from the Square, this is going to become a decidedly uphill battle. As Gargan and his colleagues approach, the mob, now barricaded behind crates pulled from Binnie's lorry, throw their former contents at the police. Only just arrived in the Square in time to catch the sheriff's attempt to read the Riot Act, Alexander McKendrick, a juvenile delinquency board officer, quickly surveys the scene. In his opinion, the barricade has been erected to prevent mounted police advancing up North Frederick Street. Further, he reckons it is a wonder no one has been killed since the violence is so terrible.[4] Full and empty bottles whizz through the air; most find their mark hitting the oncoming police or exploding at their feet, but others smash through the windows of Owen's shop or fly further down the street to the sheriff's party on the corner of the City Chambers. As he hurries to take cover inside, a bottle strikes him on the shoulder and he has the presence of mind to catch another two before they hit him in the face. Gargan remains in the street and does not witness a man jump up onto the window of Owen's shop, threatening the young man with a revolver. Having survived being buried in a trench during the Dardanelles campaign in Turkey in 1915 and returned home to Clydeside with shellshock, Owen does not fancy defending the premises. He yells to the man to wait until he has his coat and then he takes his brother outside with him, locks the door and informs the crowd that, if they want any of the full bottles inside, go get them – through the broken window. No one enters.[5]

Among the malcontents Constable Gargan spies a marked man, the former night warden at a lodging house in the Trongate, who is inciting the crowd to attack the police and whom Gargan has every intention of arresting as soon as he next sees him.[6] Somehow, the police struggling at the bottom of North Frederick Street must find their way beyond the barricade to assist their fellows at the top of the street involved in a running battle along Cathedral Street. It is only 200 yards but from here Sergeant Blackhall can see the police being seriously mauled.[7] One of the mob yells out 'Police, police' and the rioters disperse northwards, diving into alleys, which is Binnie's cue to take back the reins and lead his horse and lorry into the relative safety of North Hanover Street.

Only one block away city life continues relatively undisturbed. The tall stone buildings block out the uproar coming from the Square and only a lack of trams trundling by might raise suspicions something is amiss. Binnie takes a moment to rest but, worried for his stock, he returns to North Frederick Street intending to retrieve as many crates as he can, but the ominous threat of a good kicking from a rioter deters him. Later this afternoon Binnie will manage to report the incident at the Northern Police Office before returning to his employer's depot.[8]

From his position in the Square, Lieutenant Lawrence Gray is fearful the rioters in North Frederick Street are intent on changing direction and rushing the Municipal Buildings. Stones, sticks and dirt are thrown at him as he recalls his men to the City Chambers, but it is a bottle from the overturned lorry that lands a direct hit on his right jaw, knocking him down.[9] As he turns back to the Buildings, Gray hears Sheriff MacKenzie struggling through the opening sentence of the Riot Act and watches Gargan and twenty constables dashing through the same hail of bottles. As the detachment of police reach the rioters, they flee north joining those already embroiled in fighting the police on Cathedral Street, systematically smashing windows on both sides of the street as they run.[10]

Both officers of the Central District, Chief Detective Inspector Duncan Weir and his colleague Detective Inspector Louis Noble had a quieter day yesterday after their efforts attending Wednesday's picketing events, but since mid-morning they have been in the thick of things in front of the Buildings and now a further baton charge is ordered. Noble is perplexed because he recalls hearing Shinwell state, as he entered the City Chambers, that the Government's reply to the workers was already well-known through the press which, if reading the right morning papers, published Westminster's telegram in full at breakfast. *The Scotsman* has also published the time and date stamp for Bonar Law's telegram to the Lord Provost, which reveals that James Stewart knew of the Government's answer late yesterday afternoon.[11] Might it explain his elusiveness so far today?

Neither Weir nor Noble is directly involved in the mêlée; they are too senior, but they observe the crowd still milling in the Square who are now again induced to leave, because at 1.00 pm it appears the demonstration in the Square is finally moving on.[12] No longer a mass meeting to hear the resolution to their demands for a forty-hour working week, what has developed into a protest riot for the past half hour has been transformed once more, this time into a looting spree. Watching the violence unfolding at the top of North Frederick Street, Detective Sergeant James Wilson takes decisive action. He darts inside the Municipal Buildings to use the telephone and calls St Rollox Police Office to request reinforcements to be deployed to Cathedral Street where the worst of the fighting is now taking place. The St Rollox office is not far away and police hurrying on foot could be there within fifteen minutes. As he heads north to join the charge, Wilson witnesses Constable Smith being knocked over and kicked on the face as he drops to the ground and the mob wielding road metal to attack the brave cohort of ten constables led by Lieutenant Walter McGowan who have come direct from St Rollox as requested.[13] It is a vain attempt to hold back a mob that far outnumbers them. Yet somehow the small contingent chases the men as far as Canning Place only to be chased back again. Lieutenant McGowan orders a baton charge and the crowd scatters down a side street and towards the Square where they disperse into the raging sea of dark jackets and coats and flat caps.[14]

However, one man cannot evade recognition so easily. Already this morning, James Murray, an ex-policeman once employed by the Central Police Office, has been observed by his former superior officer, Inspector Sutherland, who believes his actions amount to incitement to violence, rallying protestors in the middle of the Square to rush the police. Now, temporary Constable Frederick Cameron, who had a word with him yesterday during the mass picketing outside Mechan's Ironworks, can see him leading the rioters in Cathedral Street. Yesterday, Murray threatened that there would be a brick for the police's heads today, especially those from the Central Office: only at the moment Cameron spies him, it is not a brick he is holding. As the mob and police to and fro along the road, Cameron believes Murray is the last to run, standing his ground grasping

97

an iron bar ready to throw at the police. He retrieves it after it hits the pavement and places it for safe-keeping, and later to be used as evidence, at 280 Cathedral Street.[15]

Sergeant Blackhall watches a steady trickle of his colleagues heading back to the first aid post at the Municipal Buildings with severe cuts and wounds. Constable Smith has been surrounded by a mob he estimates was fifty strong, kicked to the ground, rendered unconscious, but luckily colleagues carried him to Cathedral Street where he comes round. He has a deep cut on his face and will be off duty for ten days. Constable Gallagher takes a hit to the back of his head from a half brick which fells him. The resulting scalp wound will take a week to heal. At some point in Cathedral Street, Constable Cochran receives a violent blow to the head. He drops to the pavement, manages to stand up again, only to be hit by a man armed with a length of iron; Constable Cameron makes the connection between it and Murray who he saw just a moment ago with an iron bar.

Shortly after noon in St James Street, two blocks to the north-east of the Square, 60-year-old Inspector Alexander MacDonald is on duty with Sergeant Caskie. Realizing there is serious trouble in the vicinity, they proceed to Cathedral Street where they are spotted by a large crowd which pins them against a wall deluging them with bricks and stones for ten minutes. MacDonald manages to collect a piece of iron which will later become evidence and is confounded why 500 protestors would assault just two policemen who gave them no provocation. His injuries will heal, but he is not a young man and the shock to his system is so severe that by mid-April he will not have returned to work; in fact, he never does. Neither can he give evidence at the trial. Constables Smart and Beaton, on reserve duty at St Rollox Police Office, are called at 1.00 pm to assist in Cathedral Street where Smart is stunned by a knock to the head. Thomas Graham, a clerk working at Messrs Graham and Co. at 400 Cathedral Street, decides to take his lunch break at this moment and walks out into the maelstrom but swiftly returns, accompanied by an injured constable and his colleagues. It is probably Constable Beaton who helps Smart, now close to collapse, into Graham's premises to take refuge. Detective Inspector Noble has walked up to Cathedral Street where he has a panoramic view of the Square and the Buildings below and where he observes Sergeant McKenzie attempting to apprehend a man. From among the crowd, another man dashes forward with what appears to be a broken bottle in his hand. He thwacks McKenzie on the back of the head and, as the policeman turns to see who is assaulting him, the bottle slashes his face too. He makes it to the City Chambers, but not back to work for three weeks. By 1.30 pm the riot has calmed down sufficiently for Smart and Beaton to leave the premises where they took shelter. Later Smart will describe the Cathedral Street riot as worse than anything he experienced in France.[16]

The *Glasgow Herald*'s reporter manages to maintain a degree of impartiality. He has watched as strikers fell like ninepins under the sweep of police batons with half a dozen mounted police entering the last of the fray. Now he counts the numbers of injured police, demonstrators and innocent bystanders streaming towards the casualty station within the Municipal Buildings. Whether the young girls he sees are horror-stricken at the violence, or personally injured, he cannot quite tell.[17] However, when the official lists of the injured are compiled, if there are any female casualties, they go unmentioned. Casualty reports are confused. The *Evening News* journalist names thirty-six civilian men injured and eighteen policemen, while the *Glasgow Herald*'s man calculates fifty-three casualties, most of whom are treated at the Royal Infirmary; the police's physician, Dr Halliday, tallies forty-one police casualties in George Square alone; no strikers are tended by him.[18]

Since it is apparent the strikers will not receive their answer in George Square, some drift away while others, following their leaders' instructions, begin to move southwards to find somewhere they might be able to re-congregate and decide how to proceed. From his vantage point on the second-floor balcony of the Municipal Buildings, Rosslyn Mitchell cannot see very far up North Frederick Street, although his attention is held by Herbert Highton in the Square immediately in front of him. Somehow, he can hear Highton's voice ringing out above the general din; he is instructing the crowds to form up and head to Glasgow Green.[19] To help them organize themselves, the ex-servicemen who have attended the demonstration line up and lead the protestors on the mile-long walk south to the open park on the north bank of the River Clyde.[20] There is sufficient space at Glasgow Green for any number of protestors to gather but getting the crowds there in an orderly fashion is a problem.

At 1.25 pm, 28-year-old Mary Beattie arrives at Saltmarket, opposite the High Court of Justiciary buildings in Jail Square. Employed by the Corporation Tramways Department, Mary drives the Polmadie to Garngadhill route. Where she halts is to the immediate west of Glasgow Green. What she experiences is a repeat of Margaret Buchanan's tussle only an hour or so earlier. The crowd of several thousand holds up their hands to stop her and, as she slows, they clamber onto the tram platform where someone seizes her reversing handle. There is no hope of backing up anyway and thankfully they do not grab the driving handle, although Mary will not be going forwards either. The trolley rope is cut, the windows are in the process of being smashed and then she is threatened. Too scared to stand her ground, particularly since some strikers have already knocked the ticket box from her young conductor's hands, Mary flees home, skirting the police who she notices chasing strikers towards the Green. As she runs, she also sees several other stricken trams experiencing the same abuse and a policeman wounded by a piece of flying glass.[21]

A little to the north in the Trongate a tram-driver on the Ibrox to Uddingston line, John McNair's vehicle is brought to a standstill at approximately the same time. Having checked what has caused the stoppage and realizing there is nothing he can do to replace the trolley onto the wire, he returns to the front of his car where he raises his whistle to his lips to blow for assistance. However, before he can make any noise, a striker attempts to relieve him of the whistle. Quickly, a plucky lady passenger intervenes, snatches the whistle and rushes upstairs where she blows it from the top of the tram. McNair manages to keep his tram moving at a snail's pace but, at the junction of London Street with Gallowgate, he needs to alight to shift the points; he holds the iron rod he uses to change the points in his hand. He swings it round his head to keep the small group of angry strikers surrounding him at bay, then it is snatched from him. A policeman assists him back to the tram, but his passengers have deserted the car to avoid flying glass as the windows are destroyed. Amid shouts of 'blackleg', McNair is injured by a bottle or stone; he does not stick around long enough to discover which. He has the fortitude to take a moment to remove the handles from the driving mechanism, lock the controls and retreat inside the car, where he lies down, clearly feeling faint. A policeman, probably Constable Joseph Orr, lies face down and senseless on the floor having presumably taken cover away from the mayhem on the streets. Orr has escorted six passengers from the tram but, after being struck on the head with a brick, he will remember nothing more until he regains consciousness in the Royal Infirmary and afterwards requires three weeks' sick leave. Confronted with a pole-axed policeman, McNair is unable to help because he is stunned himself and in need of assistance when two ladies take hold of him and usher him into Tron House, a massive edifice on the corner with Albion Street. Bleeding and shocked, he remains there for the next two and a half hours before bravely returning to duty at Whitevale Depot.[22]

Clearly, the protest has turned very ugly, with no respect for or quarter given to uniformed police or tram workers doing their job now the strikers have moved towards Glasgow Green. Constable Christopher Player is in the vicinity of Tron House when McNair's tram is stopped.

He is unable to help his colleague Orr because he is struck across the nose with a metal rod. While he takes a moment to recover, the crowd demands his baton or else they will hit him across the head with an axe they have with them. He is a proud policeman and he will later describe how he told the crowd that his baton is worth more than his life. Seeing his predicament, the ladies who helped McNair take hold of him and guide him into the Tron warehouse, but he stays only long enough to catch his breath before leaving by a side door.[23]

Standing a short distance from the violence, Tram Inspector James Erskine receives word from a passing gentleman that one of his drivers is in trouble in the Trongate. He attempts to reach him before matters become too serious, but is delayed by the crowd swarming across the street. Thwarted, Erskine diverts to the Central Police Office to report untold damage to the Corporation's cars. By the time he returns to the disabled tram, John McNair has been rescued and has retreated to Tron House, so Erskine gets the abandoned vehicle moving and delivers it full of shattered glass, bottles and stones to the Whitevale Depot. He does not witness the crowd actually damaging the cars, but the evidence of vandalism is all around him as he focuses his attention on clearing the backed-up traffic and getting the tram network moving again.[24]

Mrs Margaret Quail is nothing to do with the strike or the current wave of violence. At 1.40 pm she is going about her own business with a friend in the Trongate when she does a remarkable thing. At 48 years old, Margaret is apparently unfazed by Glasgow's endemic violence and she does not react to today's events as anything particularly noteworthy. Seeing a constable assaulted from behind, she takes matters literally into her own hands, disarming the rioter who is about to strike the constable again with a broken tram handrail. Perhaps realizing just how brave she has been, she does not hang around for matters to escalate but, being a decent citizen, she hands in the rail at the Southern Police Office. She says she would recognize the 25-, perhaps 30-year-old clean-shaven respectable-looking assailant, who, like everyone else, is wearing dark clothes, that is, if she saw him again.[25]

The situation is evidently out of control. Many strikers are heading to Glasgow Green as instructed, but there are small pockets of rabble-rousers intent on damage and violence – are these only 'hooligans' and 'corner boys', who, the defence will argue in court, are causing all the trouble? It may have been their intention when they arrived in George Square before midday, or it may be that the mood of the crowd has changed in the intervening hour and a half. Seeing police baton-charge their fellow strikers, a misinterpretation of events may have spawned anger and aggression. When it is impossible to see above the swarming heads of the crowd, rumours and fear can spread rapidly. Reports of the violence are communicated to the Southern Police Office just south of the River Clyde, where Inspector Innes responds. He is on duty with another inspector, four sergeants and thirty constables. He has only the information conveyed to him by telephone from headquarters and does not know exactly what his men might face until they reach the Trongate, where, at 1.45 pm, they encounter a huge and hostile crowd advancing towards the Green. Innes's men have been joined by other constables and now number nearly forty police, so he gives orders to draw batons. Despite the shower of bottles and stones hitting their marks, his men manage to break up this section of the crowd. They move on to Jail Square where Innes repeats his order with the same success. The strains of a pipe band approaching from behind catch his attention and he turns to see another crowd leaving Glasgow Green led by their band flying a red flag with white lettering – it is the Discharged Servicemen's Association flag. Seemingly peaceful until they see the police, they, too, turn nasty and begin to hurl missiles. Innes is not especially alarmed until he turns again and spots another crowd advancing northwards towards him over Albert Bridge. His men raise their batons again and break through them. Apart from occasional stragglers who take a swipe at the police, the crowd passes peacefully on to East Clyde Street. Except for those absolutely out for trouble, it appears the majority of marchers are here to protest and their violence against the police is opportunistic when their paths cross, conducted by small groups, because Innes and his men are permitted to follow the crowd which he estimates to be up to 3,000 strong.[26] If they intended to put his contingent out of action, they would be able to do so without much effort.

It is 2.15 pm when Constable Player emerges from Tron House onto Candleriggs and heads to the Saltmarket to seek help. He finds another constable trying to clear missiles from the street to prevent the crowd from re-using them but, in East Clyde Street, Player is struck again, this time by a bottle which cuts through his helmet and injures him badly on the forehead, putting him out of action for a week.[27] Close by, in Great Clyde Street, Inspector Innes's men encounter a lorry loaded with barrels and bottles of stout. Again, half the crowd ignores its presence while the other half surrounds it, jumping on top and throwing the boxes down. This time, the men are not only using the bottles as missiles, they are seen stealing many, but Innes is not in a position to arrest anyone. Instead, he decides to keep the main culprits in line of sight, one of whom he watches tuck a bottle into his right jacket pocket. The man may have plans for enjoying his free bottle of stout later because, when he throws a bottle at the police, it is not drawn from his pocket and is an empty. Innes follows him further biding his time until, with Sergeant Sellers, they pounce on their man, seize him and swiftly head for the police office where he is detained. It was a close shave in many ways. Not only does the crowd take umbrage at the arrest by throwing yet more bottles but, when they search their man, they find a butcher's sticking knife concealed in his coat.[28]

Despite some defence witnesses who will later claim they did not observe the crowds smashing windows or disrupting the tram network, the *Glasgow Herald*'s reporter witnesses both occurring as a procession crosses the Albert Bridge. The battle on the bridge lasts an hour, during which the reporter is horrified to note the crowd jostling a van full of disabled schoolchildren. Their mood is too heated to realize there are small children in the van; he watches as the crowd smashes the windows, although thankfully none of the children are physically hurt. It is apparent that the curiosity of some people leaving their workplace to see what is going on in the streets has placed them at the storm's centre; until the mob moved south of the Square, they were unaware of such a huge disturbance just streets away. Although the journalist believes the police might be mastering the situation, the mayhem continues and police casualties mount. No one else remarks on it, since everyone else is concentrating on the fight rather than searching the skies for inspiration to pepper their copy in the morning's papers, because the reporter is the sole person to comment on an aeroplane flying above Glasgow Green, supposedly performing aerobatics.[29]

Trouble in the Trongate commenced shortly before 1.30 pm, which coincided with the ongoing riots in North Frederick Street and Cathedral Street and occurred shortly after the demonstrators were asked to leave George Square. Throughout these disturbances, the sheriff receives reports from across the city. He is rapidly building a picture of escalating and widespread and, according to many, violent disorder. His colleague, the chief constable, has around 140 men in the Square and now another forty from stations on the north and south sides of the Clyde have become involved. He has only 180 policemen to attempt to contain the outrage: there are fewer than 600 on duty across the whole city. Alarm is growing in the City Chambers where he has conferred with the Lord Provost and Chief Constable Stevenson.[30] It is not a decision he takes lightly but reading the Riot Act has had no effect except to create embarrassment for him and Stevenson. This riot must be contained, and he believes there is only one option remaining to him, an idea he floated on Wednesday.

At approximately 1.30 pm the Sheriff of Lanarkshire reaches for his pen and writes a formal request, as required by the *King's Regulations for the*

Army, to the local army district command in Glasgow. The seriousness of his request requires it to be conveyed in writing; a telephone call will not suffice. He requests the army's assistance. In turn, the regulations require the district commander to inform the War Office that such a request has been received.[31] Whether the district commander's communication reaches London first, or the Scottish Office's man on the spot, John Lamb, telephones Robert Munro, by the time the War Cabinet convenes for its routine mid-afternoon meeting, they are aware of the situation in Glasgow.[32]

At 3.00 pm at 10 Downing Street two War Cabinet members are present: the Right Honourables Andrew Bonar Law MP, who is in the chair again, and Sir Eric Geddes MP. They are joined by twenty-one others, among whom are familiar faces from Wednesday's meeting: the Right Honourable Winston Churchill MP and Secretary of State for War and Air; the Right Honourable Robert Munro KC MP, Secretary for Scotland, and the Lord Advocate J.A. Clyde KC MP. Also attending is Major General Romer who saw action on the Western Front during 1917 and 1918 and now has an undefined role in internal security. His superior is the Chief of the Imperial General Staff, a fervent anti-Bolshevik, but his more moderate deputy, Major General Sir Charles Harington KCB attends today. The situation in Glasgow is top of the agenda. The most recent news has overtaken talk of Belfast to become the most pressing matter of the day.

Sir Robert Horne, the Minister for Labour, explains they have limited details at present and can only inform the assembled War Cabinet there has been a riot, in response to which foot and mounted police have charged the crowd; this has resulted in casualties. Robert Munro informs them that intelligence from the Commissioner of Police indicates the strike will break up at an early date because there is strong feeling against its leaders. However, what catches everyone's immediate attention is Munro's claim that the situation in Glasgow can no longer be viewed as a strike: it is a 'Bolshevist rising'.[33] That's a strong and panicky claim to make on such limited evidence; indeed, it's absurd and has come out of the blue. Nothing of the sort has been mentioned this week in the War Cabinet.

Since mid-November, when the Armistice was declared, the Scottish press has bandied fears of the disease of Bolshevism spreading to become an epidemic of squalid terrorism; they have also suggested revolution is doomed to fail on British soil because political conditions are unfavourable and the people are 'hostile to anarchism'.[34] So, how red are the workers? There have been occasional red flags flying throughout the week's meetings and on picket lines. It is a symbol of the working class's increasingly vociferous confidence learned during wartime labour negotiations, but is it recognition of their comradeship with recent events in Russia and post-war disturbances now spreading across Europe?

For several years men such as James Maxton and John Maclean have lectured and educated many workers, gaining support for socialism, but the extent of Clydeside's red politics is unquantifiable. No one knows how many men and women attended Maclean's evening classes nor how many have become committed socialists. The results of December's general election do not point decisively to burgeoning radical left-wing tendencies.[35] Government has remained in control throughout discussions on dilution and pay, cajoling Clydeside's labour leaders into working relationships with their employers. Largely, the policy has been successful even if, in the opinion of the employers, men such as Kirkwood and Gallacher have become too powerful. And the Clyde Workers' Committee's first direct communication with Westminster on Monday only stated its aim of a reduced working-week; there was no intimation of 'or else we shall rise up in revolt'. Some of the language used this week could be construed as threatening, but hardly revolutionary. Removing whisky from the Municipal Buildings for the benefit of all or dining at the British Hotel where the meals are reputedly lavish is rabble-rousing banter; it is not revolutionary incitement. And what does 'unconstitutional methods' really mean? Shinwell threatened it on Wednesday in the Lord Provost's office and today some of the trams have been decidedly halted, but the network continues to run and electricity is still being generated. If this were the moment for a red revolution, then any political education of the workers attained during the war has been overwhelmed by the over-exuberant element among them now intent on wilful damage of property across Glasgow. For today to have become a successful red revolution would have required greater, longer-term and more widespread organization of the entire nation's workers. What will be written in the coming months and years is reminiscent wishful thinking for a missed opportunity that did not exist.

So far this week the War Cabinet's tone has been one of restraint and calm, concerned to keep the streetlights on, with no fears expressed of revolutionary intent. Yet, given today's report from Glasgow, they need to be prepared for any eventuality. How red Glasgow might be at this very moment on Friday afternoon 31 January 1919 is subjective. Special Branch's reports are alarmist but how they are interpreted depends on the individual's fears, on their choice of newspaper and their class, on what they think they have to lose. The Secretary for Scotland has the War Cabinet's focused attention. Munro has used the trigger words 'Bolshevist rising'. The sheriff has requested military aid.

At some point between 1.30 pm and 3.00 pm the military is on the move. Major General Romer informs the Cabinet that up to 12,000 troops can be put into Glasgow at short notice. He confirms that an officer sent north last night has explained the situation to the General Officer Commanding for Scotland and troops are already on the move. The Deputy Chief of the Imperial General Staff reports that six tanks and 100 lorries are ready to be transported by rail tonight. When the army provides 'military aid to the civil power', the army decides what force is to be deployed, not the sheriff who seeks the aid, nor the Government. The army is deploying 10,000 soldiers – the largest domestic deployment in the history of mainland Britain: is a repeat of the Easter Rising in Dublin in 1916 expected?[36]

The Lord Advocate says various possibilities are open to them for arresting the strike leaders under Defence of the Realm legislation which Churchill confirms he can authorize in minutes. The Naval Intelligence Department understands from its men on the ground in Glasgow that many of the men desire to return to work and the agitation has been poorly organized. They have done all they can for now; Glasgow will have troops and matériel later tonight and certainly by the morning. The conversation moves on to matters in Calais where three men will be court-martialled tomorrow for leading a disturbance among the railwaymen and Royal Army Ordnance Corps.[37]

In Glasgow the rioters have re-focused their attentions too. Part of the mob has moved south of the river and west along Paisley Road. Now they are throwing lumps of coal at a jeweller's windows. Lawrence Hunter, the 54-year-old owner, watches as hands reach through the smashed windows lifting out trays of rings. He cannot stand idly by while they steal his merchandise, but a hit to the head stuns him. Leaning out of her upstairs window, Mrs Agnes MacFarlane can only see fleeting glimpses of the action. Hunter has a large advertisement hanging outside his shop, which obscures her view, but she can definitely see the men assembled outside looting the shop and she sees Lawrence put his hands up to protect his head as he is struck from behind. With blood pouring from his wound, Lawrence manages to return to the shop where his assistant Margaret is just returning from a late lunch break. She has had a terrible time getting inside. She helps Lawrence to retrieve what is left in the window, pulling the trays further back into the shop beyond prying fingers, by which time her coat is spattered with Lawrence's blood. He reckons he has lost £600-worth of rings and at least forty-five watches from a case to the side of the window. A passing constable reaches the shop but by now only a handful of men remain outside. Constable Stewart watches one man pocketing jewellery, so he follows him as he slinks

106

off into the crowd. His opportunity to arrest him comes when he approaches two colleagues but, as they take hold of him, the crowd pelts them with bottles and stones. Undeterred, they reach Plantation Police Station where the man's pilfering is confirmed.[38] He is not a striker, but an opportunist.

A demonstration that started with pipe bands and expectation has taken just three hours to descend into violence, vandalism and looting. Whether the strikers turned sour after events in George Square or a contingent of troublemakers was always among them planning such terrible disruption is still unclear. By the time he goes off duty at 3.00 pm, Sergeant Blackhall reports that events in North Frederick Street have returned to comparative quiet. Similarly, to the north-east of George Square the scene has calmed down.[39] By 3.30 pm Tram Inspector Erskine feels it sufficiently safe to return to the Saltmarket where he finds the fragments of tram windows scattered across the streets. He identifies Mary Beattie's abandoned tram and gets it going, thus freeing up trams backed up behind it. He notices most of the crowd has moved into Glasgow Green.[40] However, the sharp cold descending as the sun sets does not deter either Detective Inspector Louis Noble or a mob of 200 men from conducting a last sweep of North Frederick Street. At 5.15 pm, half an hour after sunset, Noble telephones to the Western Police Office for assistance; the crowd has stopped under a railway bridge where they are smashing plate-glass windows. In the darkness, they get away from him.[41]

By 6.00 pm, Tram Inspector Imrie is still on duty and returns to the Square five hours after his last ordeal trapped on the tram as the police made their first baton charge. He surveys the damage and hangs around until 10.30 pm. He will give a statement in seventeen days by which time he will have decided the police were justified in their response to the unruly crowd.[42] Chief Detective Inspector Duncan Weir has been on duty all day. It is 7.00 pm when he retires for the night, taking with him two pails brimming with broken glass, stones, mud, pieces of iron and other missiles. He places the evidence in the Municipal Buildings for safe keeping, but they will later be disposed of by the soldiers who are imminently to be stationed there.[43]

After today's events, the city is exhausted and now dark, but there are further movements underway at Queen Street Station, north of George Square. Around 10.00 pm, soldiers from the closest camps begin to arrive by train. They are men of the King's Own Scottish Borderers, Royal Scots, Argyll and Sutherland, and Gordon Highlanders, along with soldiers from the East Surreys based near Stirling. They were requested by the Sheriff of Lanarkshire and, just over eight hours later, they have arrived, but before they can be dispersed to their posts they need to be fed. The Highland troops march half a mile to Central Station accompanied by their pipe bands where food and hot drinks await them, while the East Surreys are directed to St Enoch Station to take up positions between platforms 5 and 6. Great mounds of blankets, baggage and other essentials pile up as they stand huddled in their greatcoats, smoking and teasing the station hands. The atmosphere appears relaxed; they are buying more cigarettes and writing postcards surrounded by stacks of rifles and a few Lewis guns.

Young and old soldiers rub shoulders with an occasional glimpse of a medal ribbon on familiar uniforms for anyone watching. With their arms swinging back and forth as they march between stations, a gold stripe on the left sleeve of some can be seen; it signifies a man who has earned a wound in the field of battle, who has returned home but not yet demobilized.[44] These are not inexperienced recruits despatched to a volatile city to keep the peace, which will be claimed in later years. They are largely steady men who can be relied upon however uncomfortable the task. The army has not deployed Royal Scots Fusiliers from the local Maryhill Barracks nor the local regiment, the Highland Light Infantry based east of Edinburgh, because army policy is always to use men from a distant locality.[45] Still on duty at the Municipal Buildings, Inspector Gillies notes the first soldiers marching up. They are abused by the remnants of the mob lingering amidst the day's debris.[46]

All is still not quiet in the city. In Argyle Street, the windows of the Polytechnic Warehouse are smashed as well as the nearby windows of the Cable Shoe Company. A tobacconist's and a jeweller's receive the same treatment and the police are quick to respond.[47] A partial interruption to the electricity causes alarm in some sectors as houses and restaurants fall dark, resorting to candles until the power can be restored. Rumours of strikers sabotaging Port Dundas are quickly denied, although plans for such extreme action have been destroyed this afternoon at the strike committee's office.[48] The restoration of the city's lighting allows a performance at St Andrew's Hall to go ahead. It is the second entertainment for returning prisoners of war staged by the City of Glasgow Corporation. And the Lord Provost, James Stewart, is presiding. His city is literally shattered, and soldiers are being deployed to the Municipal Buildings, the Post Office and railway stations. Trained men shouldering rifles walk Glasgow's central areas. Mr Stewart takes the stage, expressing regret that the bravest of the brave who have endured the privations of a cruel enemy are confronted by the aftermath of war at home. Please have patience, do not despair, because the Lord Provost and his colleagues will not shirk their duty to restore order to this most grateful of cities.[49]

Chapter 7

1 February to 6 April 1919

Aftermath

The clear up begins. Manny Shinwell is arrested just after midnight on 1 February. He spends the evening at home with his wife at 10 George Drive in Govan, close to the water on the south side of the Clyde. This is where Chief Detective Inspector John Storrar and his colleague Detective Inspector Coulter find him at 12.10 am. If the knock at the door is a complete surprise, being roused from slumber confuses Shinwell because later he will recall it is 1.30 am. The chief constable has selected two very steady officers to arrest Shinwell. Storrar has been with the force for twenty-seven years and Coulter only two years less. As experienced policemen, they are unlikely to be flustered if Shinwell, councillor and Trades Council chairman, becomes difficult; and if he is where he should be – tucked up at home at this time of night – then two senior officers coming to arrest a leader of the community shows a degree of respect. As he emerges from behind the door, Storrar gets straight to business and informs Shinwell he is charged with inciting the mob to riot yesterday in George Square and on several days prior to that in other places around Glasgow. The charge is sufficiently detailed but also vague enough for there not to be an argument on the doorstep about the minutiae. Storrar continues with the familiar injunction: Shinwell is not required to say anything but anything he does say may be used as evidence against him. Shinwell heads upstairs to get dressed followed by Storrar and Coulter.

In their bedroom Manny soothes his wife and says goodbye to the children who have been woken by the disturbance. Storrar and Coulter remain in the shadows; if he attempts to bolt, he will not get far – there are constables gathered outside in the street – unlike yesterday afternoon when magically Manny disappeared completely.[1]

Because he vanished without anyone noticing quite how he managed to leave the Municipal Buildings, the rumours about Shinwell's lack of involvement among the crowds in the Square and afterwards at Glasgow Green began almost immediately. Within hours of the crowds dispersing, the *Evening Times* queried Shinwell's whereabouts after supposedly last being seen on the far side of the Square.[2] Some believe he rushed out with David Kirkwood and, when Kirkwood was knocked to the ground, the strikers secreted Shinwell away from the violence.[3] Shinwell himself will claim he stood up on a seat to speak to the crowd urging them to leave the Square after which he headed to the Trades Council offices; later he will tell his biographer he left the Buildings by a back entrance and went straight to the strike committee's office. One thing is true: when he reached his destination, papers detailing plans for sabotage which had been discussed by the committee were burned.[4] Either Shinwell did the burning or, as he later claims, the organization's secretary destroyed the incriminating papers. Others recall that as chairman of the strike committee he was involved in meetings all afternoon strategizing the continuation of the strike. Even later, a fanciful notion will emerge of Shinwell pulling off a second disappearing act disguised with a broom for a beard and heading for home.[5] Clearly, there is confusion concerning yesterday's events but not about where to find the other ringleaders.

Gallacher and Kirkwood have been in jail overnight in the centre of the city. Constable Turner was present yesterday evening when Gallacher was charged and he heard him say he did not have a stick in his hand during his altercation with the chief constable, which concurs with Turner's own recollections because he was not sure he had seen a stick at the time.[6] And then, in the early hours, Shinwell arrives at Albert Police Station in Govan. Detective Inspector Storrar searches him and finds £2 15s 10d in his pocket and a notebook which could be very useful if his case goes to prosecution. The notebook states quite clearly the intention to create a 'socialistic republic', that the people cannot wait a few years for the Labour Party to win a majority in Parliament, instead they must smash the capitalists to dismantle government because ultimately their rulers fear industrial strife and revolution.[7] Not destroying this notebook like so many other papers yesterday is an incriminating oversight which may pose difficulties for Shinwell's defence team: how to persuade a jury that it is nothing more than naïve politicking?

Not far away in Partick, of all the men who were seen smashing tram windows, quiet tempered 34-year-old David McKenzie is arrested at home. He is a dock labourer and, although not part of the strike, he has not been at work while he attended strike meetings. Perhaps the reason why Detective Constable James Mair and his colleague Constable McIntyre are sent to arrest him so soon at 2.20 am is his profile as a member of the Independent Labour Party and a seller of socialist literature, something Mair has

1. Postcard showing George Square, looking from the south-east corner towards the Merchants' House. First decades of the twentieth century.

MUNICIPAL BUILDINGS AND GEORGE SQUARE, GLASGOW.

2. Postcard showing George Square, looking from the west side towards the City Chambers, showing the south-east corner (right). First decades of the twentieth century.

3. The procession from St Andrew's Halls to George Square, Monday 27 January 1919. (*Bulletin* 28 January 1919)

4. Crowds in George Square, Monday 27 January 1919. (*Bulletin* 28 January 1919)

5. Emanuel Shinwell and Harry Hopkins speaking to the crowd from the plinth of the City Chambers, Monday 27 January 1919. (*Bulletin* 28 January 1919)

6. The red flag flying from the corporation flag pole, George Square, Monday 27 January 1919. (*Bulletin* 28 January 1919)

7. The most frequently used image to represent the events of 31 January. In reality, the red flag in George Square five days earlier, on Monday 27 January 1919. (*Daily Record*)

8. A strikers' procession, Tuesday 28 January 1919. (*Bulletin*, 29 January 1919)

9. A placard in a procession on Tuesday 28 January 1919, showing a blackleg being hanged. (*Bulletin* 29 January 1919)

10. A strike picket at Weir's of Cathcart's works, Thursday 30 January 1919. (*Illustrated London News* 8 February 1919)

11. Kirkwood being brought round in the City Chambers quadrangle. (*Graphic* 8 February 1919)

12. Gallacher, bandaged, in the City Chambers quadrangle. Kirkwood, is just visible, still prone, at the bottom right. (*Illustrated London News* 8 February 1919)

13. A police casualty being put in an ambulance. (*Illustrated London News* 8 February 1919)

14. Kirkwood being batoned by Sergeant Steele between the door of the City Chambers and the Gladstone statue. Note that there is no crowd for Kirkwood to incite, as was claimed by Steele and others. The figure immediately to the right of Kirkwood is probably Neil Maclean MP. Reproduced by kind permission; Crown copyright. National Records of Scotland, AD15/19/11/7

15. Sheriff McKenzie (marked with a cross) shortly before reading the proclamation of the Riot Act. Assistant Chief Constable Mennie is on the right; Chief Constable Stevenson is third from right. Friday 31 January 1919. (*Bulletin* 1 February 1919)

16. The police withdraw after a baton charge in North Frederick Street. The barricade of boxes taken from George Binnie's lorry is visible. (*Illustrated London News* 8 February 1919)

Left: 17. George Square in the immediate aftermath of the riot. (*Graphic*, 8 February 1919)

ST. GEORGE'S SQUARE, THE SCENE OF THE BATON CHARGE

Below: 18. The immediate aftermath of the Battle; the broken flag pole outside the City Chambers, and Gladstone's statue, from which the strike leaders addressed the crowd. (*Bulletin* 1 February 1919)

19. Soldiers guarding a railway bridge, 1 or 2 February 1919. (*Illustrated London News* 8 February 1919)

20. Mortars set up for the cameras in the quadrangle of the City Chambers, 1 or 2 February 1919. (*New York Times* 2 March 1919)

21. Soldiers guarding a railway bridge over the Clyde, 1 or 2 February 1919. (*Illustrated London News*, 8 February 1919)

22. Soldiers with fixed bayonets, some wearing steel helmets, escort a supplies cart, 1 or 2 February 1919. (*Illustrated London News*, 8 February 1919)

23. Troops marching in George Square 1 or 2 February 1919. Note the variety of headgear: flat forage caps; Tam o'Shanter bonnets; fore-and-aft caps; even a bush hat, such is the variety of units represented. (*Illustrated London News* 8 February 1919)

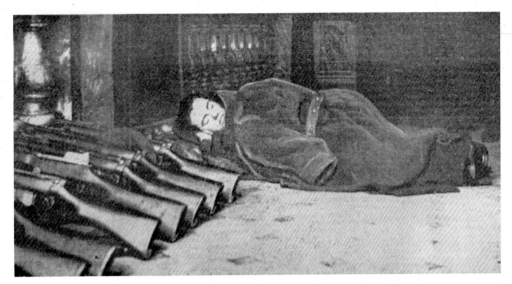

24. A soldier sleeping in the City Chambers, 3 February 1919. (*Bulletin*, 4 February 1919)

25. A soldier inspects a damaged tram. (*Graphic*, 8 February 1919)

WINDOWS WERE SMASHED
for showing lights.

Above left: 26. One of the smashed and looted windows of the Cable Shoe Shop, as joiners prepare to board it up, 31 January 1919. (*Graphic*, 8 February 1919)

Above right: 27. Two Royal Scots signallers on a roof, probably that of the City Chambers, 1 or 2 February 1919. (*Graphic*, 8 February 1919)

28. The most frequently used image of the tanks in the Cattle Market, 3 February 1919. Three Medium C tanks are in the front rank; parts of the Mark V* tanks in the second rank can be glimpsed. (*Daily Mirror*, 5 February 1919)

Right: 29. Soldiers pose
on one of the three Mark
V* tanks stationed in the
Cattle Market. (*Bulletin*,
3 February 1919)

Below: 30. Some of
the accused in court,
April 1919. According
to Shinwell's caption in
Conflict without Malice:
L to R Shinwell; Gallacher;
Ebury; Brennan;
Kirkwood; Hopkins;
Murray. Out of copyright.

31. 'Julian's
Baby' in a fund-
raising parade
in January 1919,
almost two
weeks before
the Battle. The
image has been
passed off as a
tank in Glasgow
after the Battle.
Out of copyright
image.

32. Tank 'Julian' parading along Trongate on 17 January 1918, during the 'Tank Week' War Bond sales drive. This image has frequently been misrepresented as a tank in Glasgow after the Battle of George Square. (*Bulletin* 18 January 1918)

33. Soldiers and police on guard at the docks. Out of copyright image used in Webb, 2016

WILLIAM GALLACHER (37) of 43 Well Street, Paisley, was born in Paisley, where he learned the trade of a Brass Finisher. He is a life long abstainer and in his youth was a very active worker in the temperance movement. For the past 16 years he has been a recognised Socialist leader and a prominent speaker at their meetings. He was born of respectable parents both of whom are dead. He has a brother in Chicago a minister, and another brother as art painter, and a member of that Society.

About seven years ago he stood as an independent candidate for the Town Council of Paisley, but was unsuccessful.

On 13th April 1916, Gallacher was convicted before the High Court in Edinburgh, for a contravention of the Defence of the Realm Regulations - printing and publishing a seditious article in a newspaper - and was sentenced to 12 months imprisonment.

Apart from his Socialist ideas nothing can be said against his character.

Gallacher conducted the election campaign on behalf of John McLean who stood as Bolshevik candidate in the Parliamentary election in the Gorbals Division Glasgow.

34. Biographical details on William Gallacher from police perspective gathered as evidence prior to trial; Reproduced by kind permission; Crown copyright. National Records of Scotland, AD15/19/11

DAVID KIRKWOOD (47) of 3 Saint Marks Street,
Shettleston, was born and bred in the Shettleston
District of Glasgow.   He is an Engineer to trade
and was the Convenor of Shop Stewards in Messrs
Beardmore's & Co. Ltd., Parkhead, prior to the
strike in February 1916, in connection with the
Governments dilution of labour scheme.   As Kirkwood
had taken an active part in causing same he was arrest
ed on 25th March 1916, and deported to Edinburgh on
same date, under Regulation 14 of the Defence of the
Realm Regulations 1914.   He subsequently refused
to sign any obligation and remained in Edinburgh up
till 24th January 1917, when he got permission from
the Competent Military Authorities to go to Manchester
to attend the Labour Conference, where he made a
violent speech against the authorities and said he
would return to Glasgow in defiance of the Order
served on him.

    He returned to Glasgow as he threatened and
then went to the Crieff Hydropathic where he was
arrested on 31st January 1917, and lodged in
Edinburgh Castle from which he was released on 2nd
February 1917, on promising to obey the Order of 25th
March 1916.

    Remaining in Edinburgh until the restrictions
were withdrawn in June 1917, he returned to Glasgow,
and was for some time idle.

    Kirkwood was afterwards employed in the
National Projectile Factory in David Street, Bridgeton
up till the 12th December 1918 when his services were
no longer required.

    He is a member of the I.L.P. and a prominent
Socialist speaker for a number of years.

    In November last he unsuccessfully contested
the/

68

35. Biographical
details on David
Kirkwood from
police perspective
gathered as evidence
prior to trial;
Reproduced by kind
permission; Crown
copyright. National
Records of Scotland,
AD15/19/11

EMMANUEL SHINWELL, 10 George Drive, Govan, Glasgow; WILLIAM GALLAGHER, 43 Well Street, Paisley; DAVID KIRKWOOD, 3 St Mark Street, Shettleston, Glasgow; JOSEPH BRENNAN, 1 Hayburn Street, Partick, Glasgow; GEORGE EBURY, 284 Scotland Street, Glasgow; HARRY HOPKINS, 18 Carlton Place, Glasgow; DAVID M'KENZIE, 66 Bridge Street, Partick, Glasgow; ROBERT LOUDON, 47 Mordaunt Street, Bridgeton, Glasgow; NEIL ALEXANDER, 110 Green Street, Calton, Glasgow; JAMES MURRAY, 2 St Andrew's Square, Glasgow; DANIEL STEWART OLIVER, 181 Snowden Street, Southside, Glasgow; and WILLIAM M'CARTNEY, 1076 Argyle Street, Glasgow; you are Indicted at the instance of the Right Honourable JAMES AVON CLYDE, His Majesty's Advocate, and the charge against you is that you, Emmanuel Shinwell, William Gallagher, David Kirkwood, Joseph Brennan, George Ebury, and Harry Hopkins did (1) on 27th and 29th January 1919, in George Square, Glasgow; (2) on 30th January 1919, in James Watt Lane, Broomielaw, Glasgow; (3) on 30th January 1919, in West Street, Glasgow; (4) on 30th January 1919, in the Star Palace Picture House, Dumbarton Road, Partick, Glasgow; (5) on 30th January 1919, at Messrs Mechans, Limited's Engineering Works in South Street, Scotstoun, Renfrewshire, ~~and elsewhere in Glasgow~~, instigate and incite large crowds of persons assembled at said respective places to form part of a riotous mob to be assembled in George Square, Glasgow, on 31st January 1919, for the purpose of holding up the traffic FRIDAY in said Square and adjoining streets, and of overawing and intimidating the police officers on duty there, and of forcibly taking possession of the Municipal Buildings and North British Station Hotel both situated in said Square, and a riotous mob of 20,000 or thereby evil-disposed persons, of which you Emmanuel Shinwell, William Gallagher, David Kirkwood, Joseph Brennan, George Ebury, Harry Hopkins, David M'Kenzie, Robert Loudon, Neil Alexander, and James Murray formed part, did assemble in George Square aforesaid, and acting of common purpose, did conduct itself in a violent, riotous and tumultuous manner to the great terror and alarm of the lieges, and in breach of the public peace, and did

on 31ˢᵗ Jany 1919

Wt. 1/326—80—2/19. Gp. X., Sc. C.

134

Above and overleaf: 36. Amended indictment sheet prior to trial. Reproduced by kind permission; Crown copyright. National Records of Scotland, AD15/19/11

forcibly stop various tramway cars, the property of the Corporation of Glasgow, and smash windows of said tramway cars and
of shops and other premises situated in George Square aforesaid
and in North Frederick Street and in Cathedral Street, all in
Glasgow, and did assault Owen M'Quade, 165 Dunn Street,
Bridgeton, Glasgow, who was then in charge of a shop at
46 North Frederick Street aforesaid, and attempt to rob him of
the stock and goods then in said shop, and did rob George
Binnie, 27 Abbotsford Street, Glasgow, who was then in charge
of a vehicle in North Frederick Street aforesaid, of the bottles
and boxes then under his charge on said vehicle, and did throw
bottles and other missiles and perform other acts of violence to
the danger of the lieges, and in or near George Square aforesaid did assault Alastair Oswald Morison Mackenzie, K.C.,
Sheriff of Lanarkshire, and strike him with a bottle or other
missile, and snatch from his hand a copy of the Riot Act from
which he was then making proclamation to the lieges, and in or
near George Square aforesaid did also assault the following and
other officers of Glasgow Police then on duty, viz.:—(1) James
Verdier Stevenson, chief constable, and beat him; (2) Alexander
Ferguson Mennie, assistant chief constable, and strike him with
a bottle or other missile and stab him to the effusion of blood;
(3) Lawrence Gray, lieutenant, and beat him; (4) Archibald
Swan, inspector, and strike him with a bottle or other missile,
and beat him; (5) Alexander Sutherland, inspector, and strike
him with a bottle or other missile; (6) Simon Fraser, inspector,
and beat him; (7) Alexander M'Lennan, detective inspector,
and strike him with a bottle; (8) Duncan M'Donald, sergeant,
and beat him; (9) David Murdoch, sergeant, and beat him with
an instrument; (10) Neil Martin, constable, and beat him and
stab him; (11) Thomas Gargan, constable, and strike him with
a stone or other missile; (12) Alexander Johnston, constable,
and beat him; (13) John Lally, constable, and beat and
kick him to his severe injury; (14) Andrew Gallacher, constable, and strike him with a piece of glass or other missile;
(15) Andrew M'Donald, temporary constable, and beat him;
(16) Charles Smith, constable, and kick him and beat him to his
severe injury; (17) Thomas Burke, constable, and stab or cut
and beat him; (18) George M'Kenzie, sergeant, and stab or
cut and beat him; (19) Neil Gillies, inspector, and kick and
beat him; (20) Alexander Calder, constable, and strike him

135

A no one would be so silly as to give such instructions. The other had some grievance which I did not understand.

But they seemed to have a grievance that the cars had been driven through the procession? - Yes, and another had a grievance that women were employed on cars

B at all, and Mr Shinwell pulled him up and said. "We did not "come here to discuss questions of that sort", and another dixheraged discharged soldier seemed to have a grievance that not sufficient was being done for them.

So that there was a general conversation or

C discussion going on the whole time? - Yes.

It was a perfectly pleasant interview? - Yes. I got a fraternal grip of the hand by some member, and he said he was very pleased to meet me.

After further discussion you shook hands with

D the deputation as it was going out, and then you went and saw Sheriff Mackenzie and the Chief Constable to make preparations for the deputation coming back again? - I did not know whether they were going to return or not.

Do you mean to say when the deputation left

E you on Wednesday you did not know they were coming back on Friday? - I did not know.

Did you have a talk with Sir John Lindsay when they had gone? - I had many meetings with Sir John Lindsay that week, also with the Chief Constable and the Sheriff of

F Lanarkshire, and others associated with me in preserving order in the city.

But/

37. Lord Provost James Stewart denies knowledge of Friday's deputation having arranged to meet him; Reproduced by kind permission; Crown copyright. National Records of Scotland, JC36/31/03

What was he doing? Was he walking or running?- I did not see him run; he was on the steps.

Did he get on to the street? - My attention was taken from him to other incidents that were happening near by, and the next I saw of him was just when he was face to face with me.

And was he shouting? - Yes.

And had he still his hands up? - Yes.

What was he shouting? - He said, "Come on, men; "rally round; rush the Buildings; rush them".

Did he repeat these words over and over again?- These are the words I heard him say, and in the middle of that I told him to clear out, and he said, "To hell with you", and pushed me to the side. He then repeated these words, "Rush the Buildings", and I struck him with the baton.

Did he fall? - Yes.

And as soon as he fell, did you apprehend him? - Yes.

And did you take him right back to the Municipal Buildings? - Yes.

I think you charged him at the Central Police Office with mobbing and rioting? - Yes.

He made no reply? - No.

On the 30th of January, were you at James Watt Lane? - I was.

James Watt Lane is off the Bromielaw? - It is off James Watt Street, and James Watt Street runs from Argyle Street to the Bromielaw.

Was/

38. Sergeant Steele at the trial describes his assault on Kirkwood; Reproduced by kind permission; Crown copyright. National Records of Scotland, JC36/31/03

announced that the deputation had arrived and were
then in the adjoining room.   The Lord Provost asked
those in the room with him to excuse him and went
into the adjoining room and met the deputation which
consisted of eleven persons including the accused,
(Shinwell, Kirkwood and Hopkins).

At his request I accompanied the Lord Provost
to the meeting with the deputation.   The majority
of the deputation took part in the conversation but
certainly the prominent speakers at it were these
accused Shinwell and Kirkwood and I think Hopkins
and Mr. McLean M.P.   They submitted to the Lord Provost the request that he should next morning remove
or cause to be removed the tramway cars from the
streets all over the city.   He explained that that
was impossible, that he was only one of one hundred
and thirteen members of the Corporation.   They
immediately told him that he could call a special
meeting of the Tramways Committee, who, if influenced
by him could remove the tramway cars.   He replied
that that also was impossible.

He enquired why the tramway cars should be
removed from the streets and was told that it was
with a view to compelling the Government to intervene in the dispute so as to secure a forty hours
week without reduction of wages and to enable the
demobilised sailors and soldiers to get employment.
They added that if the Government did not comply
with that request they would themselves enforce it
and not by constitutional methods such as they had
been pursuing up till that time, but by any methods
that would help them to realise the object they
had in view.   They explained that the effect of
these/

39. Town Clerk Sir John Lindsay's precognition describing the start of
Wednesday's delegation conversation; Reproduced by kind permission;
Crown copyright. National Records of Scotland, AD15/19/11

31/Jany

Friday 31st ultimo, somewhat to my surprise I read
in the Glasgow Herald, full copies of the telegrams
sent by the Lord Provost and of the reply received
thereto.

On Friday 31st January 1919 shortly after 11
o'clock the strikers began to assemble in George
Square. I was with the Lord Provost in his room at
the time. There were also in the room the Sheriff
of Lanarkshire and Mr. Lamb of the Scottish Office.

Before the great mass of strikers arrived small
knots of them gathered but the Sheriff directed my
special attention to the fact that on the South side
of the Square, on the pavement at the General Post
Office, men were assembling and taking up positions.
He remarked that he had not seen on any previous day
such a position taken up there and he wondered what
it meant. Shortly thereafter, about 12 noon the
procession arrived in George Square and probably
numbered from 15,000 to 20,000. The greater part of
the procession came by way of the south side of the
Square from the west and turned into the space in
front of the City Chambers. On the roadway between
the tramway rails and the pavement at the south east
corner of the Square immediately opposite the Lord
Provost's window a company of the strikers, numbering
I should say about 100 or so, stopped in the march
and remained there. Then a few minutes afterwards
another similar company stopped almost immediately
behind the first. These two companies arrived and
took up their positions before the great mass arrived.
A few minutes after I should say about 5 or 10, the
mass arrived and passed into the space in front of the
Chambers. The two companies remained in their places.
The point at which they stopped is a tramway stopping
station/

40. Town Clerk Sir John Lindsay's precognition describing his view from
the City Chambers' window onto the south-east corner of George Square;
Reproduced by kind permission; Crown copyright. National Records of
Scotland, AD15/19/11

station and the Sheriff and I discussed the stopping
of these two companies. It appeared to explain
to us why the other crowd was on the south side of
the street, on the pavement in front of the Post Offic
and that the intention was to interfere with the tram
way cars at that stopping place.

The procession having fully arrived there was a
large concourse of people and our suspicions as to
the interference with the tramway cars were at once
realised. A car had come along and was necessarily
stopped by the traffic. One or two other cars followed. The first car being ready to start, the
police, who were at that point, endeavoured to clear
the way for it and after some trouble did so, but
when they attempted to keep the way clear for the
second car the companies of men, already referred to
swept in and entirely impeded the way. The others
from the Post Office side closed in on the off side
of the car. They interfered with the woman driver
and practically took possession of the tramway car.
A soldier in uniform got on the platform of the car
with the obvious intention of assisting the woman
driver but was shoved about by the strikers. The
Police did all they could to clear the way and at
this point managed to make some clearance.

A few more policemen arrived at the moment and
tried to maintain the clearance but the crowd at this
point where the two companies were made a deliberate
and united attempt to sweep the police aside and
prevent the car moving. I should say that at that
time there would be about 15 or 20 policemen at that
point and they were under the charge of Inspector
Sutherland of the Central Division. They were
actually being swept aside and overpowered by this c
crowd/

41. Town Clerk Sir John Lindsay's precognition describing his observations
of the tram stoppage and the soldier assisting Margaret Buchanan, tram
driver; Reproduced by kind permission; Crown copyright. National
Records of Scotland, AD15/19/11

42. Glasgow women tram driver and conductress around the end of the First World War. The photograph shows how unprotected the driver was from anyone in the street; © Imperial War Museum Q28389.

witnessed for himself. McKenzie offers an immediate explanation: he was certainly by the Municipal Buildings, but he had his hands in his pockets and could not pull them out to throw missiles because he was being crushed by the crowd.[8]

As the city wakes up there are thousands of shards of smashed glass to clear away, and a stunned silence hangs over Glasgow's wide central streets. Several of the High Court of Justiciary's windows are smashed as well as windows at the police barracks in East Clyde Street. Along with Mr Hunter's destroyed jeweller's shop-front, this is the result of the riot near Glasgow Green which spread south of the river. In Queen Street south of the Square, the remnants of looting are strewn across the road and the process of boarding up windows begins. The mob has randomly stolen bed linen, shoes and smoking paraphernalia from a range of shops. Several jewellers have been burgled and, when caught, the perpetrators will be charged with assaulting police officers, stealing and mobbing. Five men are apprehended, two of whom are strikers, and will be found guilty and sentenced to three months' imprisonment.[9] A few blocks to the north, George Square is littered with stones, pieces of metal, broken sticks and uprooted flower bulbs and grass.[10] And in North Frederick Street and Cathedral Street, the situation is much the same: glass everywhere as evidence of the storm of bottles that rained down. Owen McQuade and his brother fill three large buckets with the remains of bottles and glass from the windows and shop lights at the licensed premises they run. They are amazed by the quantity of glass, but more so by the fact their stock remains untouched.[11]

However, the most striking feature of the streets this morning is the presence of troops. Sentries with bayonets fixed are stationed at what the army calls the city's 'vulnerable points': the City Chambers, post office, railway stations, bridges and, probably most importantly given the threats delivered during the week, the power stations. The Chambers' quadrangle which yesterday briefly housed Gallacher and Kirkwood is today filled with men and military materiél.[12] Thousands of troops have arrived to protect the city and its citizens from further excesses like yesterday's, but the claim they are here to crush the strike or any revolutionary spirit supposedly expressed by the strikers is journalistic licence because the strike continues.[13] Although in Paris, Chief of the Imperial General Staff Sir Henry Wilson, the 'political general', is alive to the potential for revolutionary upheaval anywhere in the country; his private crusade against Bolshevism and personal perspective on the political hue of Britain's working classes has probably driven the need for so many men and so much equipment to be sent to Glasgow.[14]

Press photographs show soldiers in the Chambers' quadrangle erecting trench mortars and posing with Lewis guns. Positioned inside the quadrangle, the public cannot see the extent of the army's hurried arrival or the soldiers' preparations.[15] There is an array of Scottish bonnets and regimental badges alongside the steel helmets and khaki greatcoats, and a mixture of Scottish and English accents among the troops. The soldiers' faces tell a story of hurried deployment; some are tanned which is most unusual in Scotland in winter. There are younger men posing for the photographer alongside older soldiers, and the *Guardian's* reporter believes the speed of their deployment indicates they are recently returned from France and have been rushed to Glasgow from demobilization camps.[16] Wherever they have come from, this Saturday morning, the soldiers are a day late if the intention was for them to suppress yesterday's violence. And they await the arrival of a hundred promised lorries; wherever they are ordered to deploy around Glasgow, for the moment they tramp there on foot. For Glaswegians out and about in the city's business and shopping streets this morning, the evidence may suggest martial law has been declared, but no such thing has happened.[17]

With the military on hand to support the police, the Lord Provost is keen to inform Glaswegians he will not shirk his duty to help the city through the crisis. His words frame the situation as an ongoing, not diffused, crisis.[18] Yet the unparalleled scenes of disorder and skirmishes with the police are unlikely to spread beyond Glasgow. This is the first day after 'Bloody Friday' and already the engineers on strike at Rosyth naval base near Edinburgh have reached a settlement. In Dundee men in the shipyards and foundries started their return to work yesterday and in Edinburgh the strikers are requesting financial assistance from the city's corporation. It amounts to a farthing a week per man which shows how close to the edge their families are after only a week on strike. This is not what a full-scale national stoppage looks like. South of the border, the miners' federation has persuaded Sir Robert Horne to put the matter of a wage increase and the priority demobilization of miners from the military before the Cabinet, which the Minister of Labour is happy to do because the request comes from the miners' national body, its official representation.[19] The miners have traditionally been the backbone of industrial strife, a body of men joined together by a single industry across the country, but even their solidarity with other unions is collapsing.

Already this morning, Gallacher's front-page article in *The Worker* placing the ferment on the Clyde as part of a worldwide struggle feels like yesterday's news. Indeed, the strike leaders chose 31 January as the day but, on 1 February, Gallacher's rallying cry to fight against the evil bosses driven by profit and to support a shorter working week is muffled by the exhaustion of strikers who had not expected yesterday's events to turn so sour.[20] Gallacher did not anticipate the demonstration in George Square turning ugly, otherwise his exuberant piece written some days beforehand might have been more considered. The mouthpiece of the Forty-Hours movement, the *Strike Bulletin* has coined a phrase to describe yesterday's uproar. They are calling it 'Bloody Friday', making accusations of pre-planned and unprovoked attacks on defenceless strikers, of the city elders using the police against them to club them into submission and even describing how mounted police used 'trick' riding to bring their horses down on the demonstrators. They are attempting to convince their readership that the 'desperadoes in blue' acted like madmen.[21]

To challenge the strike leaders' version of events, the Clyde employers have put out their own statement blaming the malcontents among the strikers for the violence, the revolutionary element among the trade unionists who have used unemployment as the catalyst for their ulterior political motives. They state the Forty-Hours campaign is not simply an industrial movement, but one aimed at unravelling society as they understand it.[22] The causes of the strike are not black and white; there are decades of industrial agitation and social deprivation behind yesterday's outburst, but now the race is on: the winner will decide how best to represent Friday's outrages. The soubriquet will stick and yesterday will become known as 'Bloody Friday', but today is definitely 'Spin Saturday'.

As the only leaders currently in custody, Shinwell, Kirkwood and Gallacher appear in court this morning before the stipendiary magistrate. They are charged with incitement to riot; bail is refused. They are remanded in jail until at least Thursday.[23] With the leaders incarcerated, the search for evidence of their real intentions begins. At the Glasgow Trades and Labour Council offices in Bath Street, the police are accused of entering without a warrant; they request all papers concerning the organization of the strike. The secretaries place what is left in front of them.[24] Is either side yet aware of yesterday's destruction of papers at this stage? Detective Inspectors Storrar and Coulter return to Shinwell's home during the day, searching for further evidence. They discover a pamphlet calling the workers to arms and, beside it, a letter from the Independent Labour Party acknowledging Shinwell's recent unsuccessful election campaign in Linlithgowshire.[25] One item may well add grist to the prosecution's case, while the other is a personal reminder of a more constitutional approach to leading from the left.

From Shinwell's home, Storrar and Coulter proceed to survey the damage between 467 Paisley Road and 75 Paisley Road West. They find eighteen plate-glass windows smashed belonging to the properties of four spirit merchants, a tobacconist, two banks and two jewellers. They estimate the cost to repair the windows will be in the region of £200. From the type of trade at the premises attacked by the looters, obviously they were intent on a good time with a little cash to spend afterwards, but of the jewellers only one reports valuables stolen, snatched through the broken window by greedy fists. The detectives' last visit at 75 Paisley Road West is the jewellery shop belonging to Lawrence Hunter who was so badly shaken by the assault yesterday that one of his lads accompanied him home where his wounds were dressed. He is now confined to his house which is where Storrar and Coulter ask him to identify a number of items, which they have found on the thief now in custody. Immediately he recognizes a watch, four badges, a gold locket, three gemstone rings, a signet ring and a delicate shell tray as his goods. They ask him to estimate the value of the items still to be recovered and he suggests it is around £1,000.[26] Hunter has not yet had time to request estimates for the repair of his windows, but the looting spree along Paisley Road seems to have been most lucrative for the vandals as well as the local glazier. From south to north of the river, the city would sparkle like winter frost if only the sun would come out.[27] At Messrs Graham and Co. in Cathedral Street, north of the Square, ninety-one panes are smashed which will also be expensive to replace.[28]

After such unprecedented events, Sunday 2 February is neither a day of rest for the police nor the suspects they seek. Detective Inspector John Lobban is instructed to arrest George Ebury. He lives in Scotland Street on the south side of the Clyde and, after being charged with inciting a crowd to violence on Thursday, he makes no answer. As he walks along Paisley Road with Lobban on one side and fellow officer Livingstone on the other, his response to a passer-by asking what is wrong is also sparing: he doesn't know. 'What, do we live in Germany?' Ebury expresses his preference for Germany where the Spartacist Uprising has ended in violent reprisals. It is glib banter, but he won't mind repeating it for his audience when he appears at the Central Police Court tomorrow. When searched, Ebury's pockets are full of documents, diaries, notebooks and money, and still he says nothing when cautioned, except to ask for bail. Detective Inspector Lobban pushes the boundaries of credibility when he suggests Ebury's bloodstained white handkerchief and a scrap of red cloth attached were apparently intended to excite the crowds.[29]

North of the Clyde, Temporary Constable Frederick Cameron, who recognized ex-policeman Murray in the crowd on Thursday and again in

Cathedral Street on Friday, arrives to speak to him this morning. It is 7.00 am when they rouse James Murray and his family from bed at 2 St Andrews Street, a ten-minute walk from George Square. With Cameron are another uniformed colleague, Constable Smillie, who was on the receiving end of Murray's iron bar yesterday, and two plain-clothes officers. They charge Murray with mobbing and rioting, assaulting a constable and convey him to the police office where he has the audacity to ask the desk officer where Cathedral Street actually is. His recollection is immediate when Smillie points out it's where they saw him rioting on Friday. Murray claims he is being set up by Cameron and that he did not kill anyone.[30] But so far there have been no reports of deaths among police or strikers as a result of the violence; so, is Murray fearful that his iron bar caused more damage than intended or have rumours begun to spread which the journalists have yet to hear?

In such a volatile situation rumours are dangerous. The city has been quiet all weekend but competing use of 'Tsarist' and 'Bolshevik' references will keep tempers boiling for a while longer. Still adamant the strike will continue, the *Strike Bulletin* accuses the Government of 'Tsarist' strategies to crush the workers, while Glasgow's letter-writing citizens express their anger at a 'Bolshevik' strike appealing to the less well-informed elements of the workforce.[31] Nationally, the opinion is expressed that the striking engineers are the puppets of intellectuals engaged in a wider project to emulate Lenin and Trotsky.[32]

When the call came for military assistance last week, the army reacted as quickly as possible. Troops began to arrive only hours after the worst of the violence, but it has taken until Monday morning for the heavy equipment to arrive. Tanks are difficult to transport, particularly over very long distances. There is lively interest from Glaswegians more used to turning out to view these iron monsters during War Bond fund-raising events, such as 'Tank Week' which happened here a few weeks ago. The particular noise of caterpillar tracks trundling over Glasgow's roads to reach the Cattle Market is quite familiar to the city's residents, but today it is a sound only heard once because the six tanks are driven to the Cattle Market and stay there. Only the truly inquisitive and press photographers visit them where they slumber.[33] They will remain in the Cattle Market sheds, tended by soldiers but undriven, unused, until they depart for their new base in Edinburgh.[34] Last Friday, to army commanders far from Glasgow, the tanks probably seemed a reasonable precaution, but three days later they are a barely visible embarrassment which is quietly forgotten during the first week of February.[35]

Despite the strike committee's leaders languishing in the imposing brick-built Duke Street prison and a steady resumption of work, which some attribute to fewer pickets molesting and intimidating those who wish to work, the strike is not collapsing. In fact, further ballots on whether to take action are planned among industries yet to come out, although it is increasingly clear the shortage of money in households across Glasgow may be the hurdle that causes the strike to falter. A week without wages for families which make do from pay-packet to pay-packet will fray any resolve they have at the start of the strike's second week. They do not have the cash reserves discovered in some of the strike leaders' pockets on arrest. No one wants to suffer as the municipal workers at Coplawhill tramworks did yesterday when the Corporation employees who walked out last Wednesday, 29 January, were dismissed and handed their insurance books – a definite signal their labour is permanently no longer required.[36] In a contracting labour market, those jobs are likely to be filled quickly as men demobilize, but those newly unemployed Coplawhill men will not find new jobs so readily – they have marked characters. However, the Lord Provost, James Stewart, is very unlikely to lose his job. If anyone is considering a vote to remove him, then his plans to publish a lengthy statement concerning events last week should, he hopes, rebuff any opposition. It will take him until tomorrow to compose his speech, to get his thoughts in order, his argument straight and his reputation suitably polished.

On Thursday 6 February, Shinwell, Kirkwood and Gallacher attend the Central Police Court where they are formally charged with inciting a riot. Gallacher's case is heard first. The stipendiary magistrate informs him he will remain in jail for the next four days for his case to be compiled. Gallacher is incensed; he too has a case to put together. He has only been allowed to see his wife for fifteen minutes since his incarceration on Friday, his cell is four paces by four, he is allowed forty-five minutes exercise and he is not a criminal. The stipendiary is unmoved and remits him to the sheriff as his prisoner. Kirkwood is next. He listens to the same charge and asks for bail. The stipendiary says only the sheriff is competent to agree bail. Kirkwood's next sentence is cut short. He is asking about improvements to his prison conditions when he is removed from court. Shinwell is similarly charged and also wishes to see more of his wife and preferably not through bars. The stipendiary directs his complaint to the prison commissioners. George Ebury is last and the outcome is the same.[37]

Nearby at the City Chambers, the town council meets; the Lord Provost presides. It is his moment, as the victor-presumptive, to commence writing his personal history. His speech is measured, conciliatory, complimentary but ultimately self-exculpatory. It is also inaccurate and unreliable. He begins by declaring he has no interest whatever in the strike, its political or economic aims. His sole purpose in office is to maintain law and order. He recounts the details of the week, highlighting his gratitude to Wednesday's delegation for declaring their intentions; he holds no grievance against them, but he is at pains to explain that his agreement to send the telegram to London allowed the Government to understand the critical nature of the situation in Glasgow and the city's need for reinforcements to aid the civilian force in any emergency that might occur. He receives applause. He shifts responsibility for the despatching of the military to Westminster.

His argument reaches a crescendo when, finally, he reaches Friday. He claims the telegram bought him time to obtain military aid but, in his view, the Government's early publication of their response ahead of Friday morning probably allowed the malcontents among the crowd to organize themselves, thus instigating the riot. Then he says something very important. The period of disorder on Friday lasted less than twelve hours and, had it not been for the army's arrival, the violence may have attained greater dimensions. James Stewart continues emphasizing his role as chief magistrate surrounded by advisors, which include the Sheriff of Lanarkshire, and it is the sheriff who has the main authority to deal with incidents like Friday's, he alone who has the power to request military assistance. He shifts responsibility to one of his closest advisors for the decision to call for military aid.

He praises the police for their loyalty, efficiency and their bravery in the face of danger. He criticizes the editor of the *Glasgow Herald* who took him to task publicly in his newspaper earlier in the week by questioning his acceptance of Wednesday's delegation, which the editor considers opened the door for violence. Then he draws the councillors closer into his circle by thanking them for their kindness and sympathy and assures them of the gratitude of Glasgow's citizens.

Baillie John Wheatley, who counselled restraint last Friday, has listened carefully and is the first to respond. He begins by emphasizing the Lord Provost's role as father of the city, his sense of fair play last week with the citizenry and the strikers; he offers his strong opinion that the police acted brutally, which will be debated hotly in the coming months, but most importantly he picks up on the Lord Provost's estimate: the worst of the violence was over within twelve hours. Why then are the military still occupying the city? By what authority is the city under military control? James Stewart replies very cautiously. The city is not under military control and the local authority, that is the men in this room, remains in power.

However, the military will stay for as long as the disturbance continues. But it is now Thursday 6 February and there has been no violence or disorder for six days.[38]

The editor of the city's leading broadsheet newspaper does not take the Lord Provost's criticisms lightly. Friday's edition contains a robust response to James Stewart and accuses him of a mis-statement of facts: the editor did not query his behaviour towards the delegation, only that he had become their instrument in conceding their demand for a telegram to the Prime Minister. The Lord Provost portrays himself as wise as a snake yet as harmless as a dove. He wasted his chance to delay the strike leaders' actions to a time more convenient to himself, a delay in which he could have strengthened Glasgow's forces of law and order, instead of blundering feebly into Friday's maelstrom.[39] It is all a matter of opinion depending on which side of the argument one sits and for anyone reading today's *Glasgow Herald*, they are clearly getting the message that this particular spat is personal. Even letters to the editor in other publications have had time to respond to one another as the week after the 'Battle' progresses. By this evening Mr Klint agrees with 'Apercu' that Glasgow is no more a hotbed of lawlessness than any other big city but 'Truth Stands', writing from America, is fearful of 'Bolsheviki' – his collective noun for anyone politically left-of-centre and non-Christian – and 'One who witnessed part of the riot' refutes claims of a boy killed and another with a broken arm.[40] One enduring truth is that passionately held beliefs will always colour perceptions, irrespective of their basis in real events.

However, when giving a statement of facts to the city's procurator fiscal, the man responsible for gathering all the evidence for last week's events, telling the truth as one witnessed it is paramount. Memory can be unreliable, even a week after the event, but embellishing one's eye-witness account with personal opinion, insinuation and interpretation risks undermining the fairness of the judicial process. The first precognition statements, the depositions which will become the working papers to build the prosecution case, are taken on Friday 7 February. Ordinarily, the procurator fiscal is directed to precognosce witnesses as soon as possible after a crime has been committed, which usually is carried out within three days, and he is instructed not to make the evidence stronger than the witness will attest to if called to court.[41] But in this instance, John Drummond Strathern, Glasgow's procurator fiscal, is perhaps delayed by the overwhelming number of witnesses he must interview. By the time the case reaches trial, Strathern will have taken over 170 prosecution precognitions, most of them from the police on duty throughout the week.[42]

A handful of police have already been precognosced when the Town Clerk, Sir John Lindsay, sits down with Strathern to provide his statement on Saturday 8 February. Sir John's precognition is clear, factual and offers details of meetings he attended throughout the week and what he saw from the City Chambers' windows last Friday. The same day, Sergeant Robert Thomson of Central District with sixteen years' service describes what he saw on Monday, Wednesday and Friday while on duty; he tells Strathern that, in his opinion, the violence was deliberately instigated by threats of drastic action earlier in the week.[43] Across the following fortnight, numerous officers, tram inspectors, drivers and conductors and people uninvolved directly in the strike or demonstration give their precognitions. Largely, police from a single office are precognosced on the same day, some giving lengthy statements while others simply state they corroborate the previous officer's version of events having been standing beside him at the time. Precognitions are conducted as private interviews, to discourage collusion or any facts or circumstances being leaked to the public before a trial; this protects the jury's integrity and impartiality. Likewise, newspaper reporting is supposed to be kept to a minimum.[44] However, the newspapers have not only reported daily throughout the strike, but they have also published sometimes strident opinion and the likelihood of finding a witness who has not read a newspaper this week is slim. Among the police, of course, they have spoken together in the muster halls and on duty about what happened, supporting one another and, as human nature will, apportioning blame.

Sergeant David Murdoch of Central District reckons Shinwell and Gallacher whipped up the mob earlier in the week and believe that this led directly to the violence on Friday; Sergeant McDonald also from Central District corroborates the parts of Murdoch's statement when they were on duty together on 29 and 31 January. Detective Sergeant Wilson, who was on duty on Wednesday, considers the fiery tone of the speeches he heard that day indicated that violence was intended for Thursday but the riot was delayed until Friday by the Lord Provost's intervention. Some, like Detective Inspector Noble, are precognosced twice, first on 18 February and again on 8 March when he has something to add. Noble refrains from expressing an opinion on who said what and what those words might have meant, choosing instead to interpret Kirkwood's 'rally round boys and rush them' as an invitation to charge the police.[45]

The gathering of precognitions and other evidence will take until the end of February, but on what proves effectively to be the penultimate day of the strike, a note of humour appears on the front page of *The Worker* on Saturday 8 February. Like the Lord Provost's speech, it may have taken some days to write but this comedic moral drama is a work of satire and sarcasm. The skit plays on a completely invisible and inaudible disruption of the wildest kind camouflaging Bolsheviks in George Square, with Gillie Wallacher and Cave Dirkwood fomenting mischief which will surely lead to anarchy; Sir Lynn Johnsay and old Wartstew, the barely disguised character of the Lord Provost, make an appearance although Shinbad disappears in this version too. However, the inside page reverts to exclamations about unarmed peaceful citizens being attacked and justifies any violence as retaliation against an unprovoked assault by police. Infamous historical riots such as Peterloo, Tonypandy and Belfast prefix what has now occurred on the Clyde.[46] Yet, Councillor Battersby who has listened to the Lord Provost's self-serving statement in the City Chambers declares he remembers the riots of 1848 and the humanity shown during last week compares favourably with his reminiscences as a very much younger man.[47]

In the small hours of Sunday 9 February Harry Hopkins is woken and arrested by Chief Detective Inspectors Keith and Weir. Not instrumental in the events of last week but certainly a key figure during the wartime strikes, Hopkins is one of the last to be charged with incitement to riot. He makes no reply as they march him to the Central Police Office.[48] There is nothing more to be said. The strike is over.

By Monday the men who have stuck it out all week are drifting back to work. It has been the chilliest of weeks to have sat idle and this morning they are taking breakfast at home at a reasonable hour in order to warm up before walking and taking the tram to work in time to clock on at the unusually leisurely hour of 8.00 am. A meeting of the strike committee this afternoon recommends a resumption of work from the coming Wednesday, 12 February, and asks for sub-committees at each works to put it to their men and to respond in good time. Their plan is to return to work while they become better organized so they can push harder for the Forty-Hours campaign across the whole nation. However, it appears the men could not wait for an official declaration. It is not quite what they struck for, but in the intervening week the employers have confirmed a national settlement for a forty-seven-hour week with no reduction in wages. It is a small but welcome victory and not so bad as *The Worker* describes: this is not a return to work on the old terms. However, the *Strike Bulletin* is adamant that the early resumption of work is due to the dastardly machinations of the *Evening News* which yesterday erroneously published the strike committee's supposed recommendation as an immediate return to work.

Whoever is writing the *Strike Bulletin*'s copy is grasping at straws, inserting a paragraph describing the success of women pickets at Govan now the men are going back; descriptions of women with children in their arms joining picket lines were more plausible last week than this.[49] Any hopes of a forty-hour working-week are dashed; as Harry McShane will recall in later years, forty hours did not happen until after the Second World War.[50]

Today's other big news is the strike leaders' appearance before Sheriff Fyfe and a packed Sheriff Court. Fyfe would prefer to clear the public gallery, but these are exceptional times, so he relents. Shinwell, Kirkwood, Gallacher, Ebury, Hopkins are the key strike leaders, along with Loudon and Alexander who were arrested in the Square for interfering with reading the Riot Act and Gallacher's arrest, respectively. A handful of men who were involved in Friday's mobbing and rioting stand beside them. They are looters, Herbert Strange and four others, part of a larger riotous mob, who engaged in a smashing and grabbing tour of Argyle and Queen Streets later on that Friday evening. In the course of their ill-disposed adventures, they also assaulted two policemen and held up trams. They will be tried separately. The charges against the strike leaders and those participating in the events in the Square are lengthy and involve numerous permutations of who appeared where on certain dates who said what in which location and where and when individuals incited their audiences to riot in George Square. Effectively, the charge accuses them of causing, instigating and inciting to assemble in George Square a mob of 20,000 or thereby rioters, and inciting them to rush the police in a tumultuous manner.[51] With so many men charged and such a complex labyrinth of dates, times and places, this will not be an easy case to prosecute or defend.

The men stand listening to the charges against them and then their legal representatives request bail. That will not be possible. This hearing has requested that they are re-committed for further examination and the procurator fiscal is totally opposed to granting bail because of the serious nature of the charges. Is he fearful they may start causing trouble again if they are released back into their workshops?[52] Being refused bail is frustrating, but members of the *Strike Bulletin*'s reporting team in the public gallery are keen to keep their readers' enthusiasm buoyant. They describe the defendants being in good spirits and keen to continue the strike campaign. It is a disappointment, but plans are already afoot to apply for bail again next week. As Shinwell, Gallacher, Kirkwood and the others prepare to leave court, one law agent steps forward to request that at least they are allowed newspapers to read. The general public is discussing the case freely and there are opinions being aired which may be prejudicial to the case. Although they probably wish they could, neither the sheriff nor the procurator fiscal can prevent the press from speculating before the trial, but they can avoid making a decision whether to allow this request; they pass the matter to the prison commissioners to decide. The only reading material Gallacher has had since his incarceration is a short note from Siegfried Sassoon, special correspondent for the *Nation,* who apologizes for not having visited. Evidently, they do have friends outside prepared to put their side of the case, until they have their day in court.[53]

After ten days off work to recover from his injuries and shock, Lawrence Hunter returns to his jewellery shop today. It is the first time he has felt well enough to venture back.[54] At the moment, only one of several robbers grabbing his stock is known and in custody. Once his windows are repaired, something Hunter has not managed to arrange in his absence, his business can return to normal.

The Executive Committee of the Clyde Shipbuilders' Association is also resuming normal meetings. They are pleased to report a general resumption of work, except at Beardmore's where the electricians continue to agitate and are holding the works to ransom by demanding the assistant foremen and pay-rate fixers stop work and join their union. The electricians' strike had the same effect last week and this will prevent the operation of the entire workshop where there are apprentices and journeymen eager to work. The committee endorses any support Beardmore wishes to afford the men prepared to resume.[55] They would appear to be back in control of their businesses. As the representatives at their joint meeting a few days later note, the irregular strike is presumed a failure due to the arrest of its leaders. There is very little other comment on last week's disturbances and discussions continue on a number of issues: the implementation of a pay rise for women workers in the shipyards; overtime for clerical staff and penalties for men arriving late for their shift. It really is the minutiae of business-as-usual, except for debate concerning the possible illegality of last week's mass picketing. This pivots on the interpretation of the Trades Disputes Act, but it is reported the town council and sheriff are contemplating further 'legislation' to prevent any such recurrence.[56] It is time to promote a more favourable view of the employers' part in the recent agitation to Glasgow's citizens.

Since declaring their intention to strike the Glasgow Trades Council has not met but, like the employers' organizations, they resume business once the first hearings are finished. Shinwell has been temporarily replaced in the chair while he awaits the outcome of another request for bail.[57]

By Monday 17 February the strike leaders' lawyers are in action again presenting petitions for bail to the Sheriff of Lanarkshire. Their various appeals state their clients' innocence of the crimes of inciting to riot, mobbing, rioting and assault. Given time to consider his response, two days later, the procurator fiscal again opposes bail. So, they appeal to the High Court of Justiciary in Edinburgh. The strike's leaders spend a further uncomfortable and hungry four days in Duke Street prison. They want to be released to build their case and to be seen by their supporters; also, there are monies to be raised to fund their defence.[58]

Having also lived in difficult circumstances since their arrival in Glasgow, the troops stationed around the city have been dispersing over the last few days and tonight the remaining soldiers leave. Their departure warrants barely six lines of type in the *Glasgow Herald* and a photograph in the *Daily Mail*. Hostilities continue across Europe, but here in Glasgow restrictions on margarine are lifted, the flour-mill workers are back grinding flour under their previous working conditions and the theatre critics brim with praise for the opera and light musical performances now showing to sell-out audiences. Those eager to see the news from the Continent can visit an exhibition at St Andrew's Hall of the official pictures of the surrender of the German fleet in the Firth of Forth, supplied by the French news and film company Gaumont. Identifying whose ships are whose is not easy for the uneducated eye, but there can be no confusing the German fleet sailing between serried ranks of Allied ships.[59] This victory display unashamedly shows Germany's total subjugation. Surely, no one would consider mixing up these images to tell another, less glorious story?

They have waited another five days to hear their fate and on Saturday 22 February the High Court agrees to bail all those arrested after the George Square riots. Bail bonds are issued over the following days. Samuel Shinwell stands £300 for Manny on 23 February. Baillie John Wheatley rescues his friend and protégé Kirkwood with £300 and Gallacher's lawyer provides a further £300 bond to free him. Harry Hopkins, who took little part in Friday's uproar, is also bailed for £300. The high price of their bailed freedom reflects the seriousness of their alleged offences and perhaps even concerns over their possible flight. By comparison, Loudon and Alexander, who were witnessed snatching the Riot Act from the sheriff's hands and attempting to prevent Gallacher's arrest, are bailed at £120 each, while window-smasher and ex-policeman Murray is freed on £80. Their alleged crimes were violent and unlawful, but they are unlikely to cause further disturbance. And so George Ebury, orator and socialist, is also bailed for £80; perhaps the judicial authorities consider his brand of vocal rabble-rousing for a thirty-hour week deflated by the recent confirmation of a forty-seven-hour week.[60]

Under Scots Law, an accused must be got to trial and the case concluded within 110 days of their first commitment if they remain incarcerated: the strike's leaders are, however, now free. Preparation for their trial begins in earnest and at pace.[61] The need for speed is set by the Lord Advocate, Scotland's most senior law officer, who presses for an early trial. Is the Lord Advocate applying pressure to prevent the defence mounting its strongest case? Or is he himself under pressure from above to conclude the prosecution and get the leaders back in custody? There are so many witnesses for both sides to be precognosced, their evidence collated and an articulate argument mounted. There are a dozen accused to defend on so many different permutations of a single theme: incitement to riot, mobbing and assault.

In London Arthur Henderson, Labour MP, tries to keep up with matters in Glasgow, but is clearly hampered by the postal service. He has been informed by members of the Glasgow Trades Council of a refusal of bail – it is old news. However, he sends a telegram to Robert Munro to complain that this is against the men's civil rights since none of the accused are murderers, one of only two charges on which bail may be refused, the other being treason. Such refusal is delaying their ability to mount a case. By return, Munro dictates emollient words to his aide; under the Bail Act of 1888 etcetera, etcetera. The magistrate has simply done his job invoking Section 2 of the Act which allows him the discretion to refuse bail, and the accused have used Section 4 permitting them to appeal to the High Court of Justiciary. It is a process, that's all; there is nothing to be read into it.[62] The following day the Secretary for Scotland continues to peruse the calendar for suitable dates for the trial; he settles on 18 March, the date he first hoped to secure.[63]

With such little notice to be ready for court, today, 8 March should be the first pleading diet before the sheriff, but there is no way they can proceed. The accuseds' agents are having trouble securing the services of counsel for the full trial and they are considering leaving the accused unrepresented. In Shinwell's absence, the secretary of the Glasgow Trades Council, William Shaw, writes to Sir Thomas Munro at the Ministry of Labour complaining that the defence has barely enough time to examine all 108 current prosecution witnesses and they have 700 non-police defence witnesses to wrangle. He asks Sir Thomas to employ whatever influence he has with the Prime Minister, Lloyd George, or his deputy, Andrew Bonar Law, to give them at least a fortnight's extension. He appeals to justice and fair play, implying there may be more trouble otherwise. Trying to bolster the defendants' case, Shaw prints a poster seeking witnesses to the key events in the last week of January which he also places in the local newspapers: if you were at the Star Picture House on 30 January or George Square on 27, 29 or 31 January, please visit at his headquarters, 95 Bath Street, Glasgow.[64] He arranges for posters to be strategically pasted up around Glasgow's working-class districts, and on the same day Glasgow's procurator fiscal writes to the Crown Agent in Edinburgh to warn him that strike action about the trial may be taken. He warns that news of the defence's disgruntlement at the date for the trial has been spread to nearly every trade union branch in the country, the implication being that this could escalate into the national strike threatened only a few weeks ago.[65] Shaw drafts another letter to Robert Smillie, Labour MP, stating it is felt strongly that the men are being denied ordinary justice. He repeats the claim that the men are contemplating cancelling instructions to their legal agents, which means they would not have legal representation in court – there would be no cross-examination of crown witnesses nor any address to the jury. It would be a mockery of justice. And at a time when the lawyers' staffs are depleted by men still on war service and others sick during the 'flu pandemic.[66]

A reprieve is won and next the lawyers receive a letter asking them to consider an extension until 1 April, which they reject because it is still too soon, or 7 April, which would put too much pressure on them, or 14 April, which they agree would be acceptable. Meanwhile, in Edinburgh the Lord Advocate addresses the senior judiciary; he really wants the trial to commence on 7 April. He does not give a reason. Two days later a telegram arrives authorizing the trial's delay by just a fortnight. It is not what they asked for, but at least they have a date on which to focus – by 7 April they must be ready.[67]

But they require funds, which is where Shaw steps up again. At a meeting of the Trades Council on 10 March a finance committee is voted in. They decide to open a subscription column in *Forward* to reach as many supporters as possible and any monies raised will be placed in a bank account which Edith Hughes, treasurer, will administer.[68] There are too many men requiring legal representation and their families are without a breadwinner while the defence case is prepared, and ultimately no one can predict the outcome once they reach court. This is likely to be an expensive few weeks and, should it go against them, sentences for inciting a riot are not usually brief sojourns in jail.

The imperative to prepare the case leads to some potentially time-saving sharp practice. Councillor Rosslyn Mitchell, who is the legal agent for some of the key accused, has tried to obtain the prosecution's precognition statements rather than make an appointment with some of their witnesses to precognosce them himself. Since time is pressing and funds are short, arguably it is a pragmatic strategy. However, Procurator Fiscal Strathern's personal investigation into how Mitchell managed to obtain some of these papers reveals that he telephoned the Lord Provost, Sheriff MacKenzie, the chief constable and Sir John Lindsay stating he had permission to see their depositions. He did not have the procurator fiscal's authorization and only Sir John is duped into handing his over by mistake.[69] Why the procurator fiscal may not wish Mitchell to see the prosecution precognitions remains a matter of conjecture: has he asked questions beyond the scope of the trial which he is loath for Mitchell to read? In London a request is made to secure the latest version of the indictment. There are plans to raise the matter in the House of Commons tonight, 19 March. A telegram arrives from Edinburgh making the request which elicits a note back: the Speaker of the House has refused to allow the matter to be raised since the case is *sub judice*; the Crown Agent is urged to send the new indictment anyway.[70]

With the trial now a fortnight away the finer details of the indictment are finalized. If any detail can be successfully challenged, then the case may be thrown out, or at least postponed. Much rests on the connection between the act of incitement to riot and actual rioting. Procurator Fiscal Strathern makes the distinction between incitement to riot as a substantive crime in itself or as a piece of narrative leading up to the riot: unless incitement to commit violence results in violence, the crime of incitement is not indictable. Strathern believes this to be the situation with the current wording of the charges. Whereas by instructing a mob to congregate in George Square, where violence most certainly occurred, this could be interpreted to have been a direct result of the incitements to riot allegedly committed earlier in the week. He does not wish the incitements to riot to lose their impact if not connected directly to the violence. Legal nuance is the order of the day. Next, his forensic attention to detail turns to Sheriff MacKenzie who now states that it was not the Riot Act, which was snatched from him, but the Proclamation from the Riot Act which was torn from his hands.[71] It is a fine distinction, but the gimlet-eyed defence will spot it if Strathern had not done so first.

Strathern is kept even busier as witnesses begin to revise their original statements. A Scottish trial is more inquisitorial than adversarial; it is a trial of the evidence, not the opposing counsels' argumentative and oratorical skills. Thus, forensic attention to fine details in witnesses' statements and correct interpretation of the law are critical to a fair trial.[72] It has been a little over a month since the first week of the strike and now Constable Turner is no longer sure he saw Kirkwood in the Square on the Monday or Harry

126

Hopkins in the Square on the Friday, despite corroborating evidence from several other policemen. Inspector Gillies cannot be certain Hopkins was on the Gladstone statue on 29 January because he was not familiar with him in person, although he heard the crowd refer to him as Hopkins; but he is definite he saw him at the Pinkston Power Station on the Wednesday. And now Sir John is not as clear as he'd like to be that Hopkins was one of Wednesday's delegation to see the Lord Provost (he wasn't). Sir John is making further enquiries and will get back to Strathern.[73]

With ten days to go until everyone must appear at the High Court of Justiciary in Edinburgh, the first pleading diet takes place at which defence counsel file special defences for their key clients. Kirkwood was not in George Square on 27 January but was in the Empire Picture House; he was also not in James Watt Lane on 30 January nor West Street nor the Star Picture House, nor Mechan's Engineering but was at various other addresses around Glasgow, notably 95 Bath Street, the Trades Council offices. Shinwell was also at the Trades Council offices rather than present where others allege he was involved in making fiery speeches. Harry Hopkins cannot recall where he was precisely, either his office, at home or elsewhere in Glasgow, but most certainly he was not where they think he was.[74] In fact, by their own admission, no one appears to have been where they were first thought to have been. In addition, Rosslyn Mitchell raises objections to the relevancy of the indictments, which Strathern finds a flimsy argument and asks the sheriff to reject them. Probably unwilling to be responsible for further legal battles, the sheriff defers any decision to the High Court on whether to admit the special defences and therefore the accused are not asked to plead until the second diet. At this point, the legal rules stipulate there can now be no fewer than nine days until the full trial.[75]

With only a few days to go solicitors acting for some of the defence, Gardiner and MacFie, inform the Crown Agent their clients desire to have all the prosecution's witnesses examined, either by the Crown or at least to make them available in court so that defence counsel may examine them. With everyone travelling from Glasgow to Edinburgh for the trial, with some potentially having to stay overnight in the capital, this could make the prosecution case very expensive. Two days later Gardiner and MacFie inform the Crown Agent they have run out of time to precognosce all of the defence witnesses and instead submit an extensive list of their proposed witnesses.[76] Without prior intimation, these witnesses cannot be called to testify in court. Such a lengthy list gives prosecution counsel advance warning of the possibility the Court might have to hear everything from everyone they can possibly summon. Does it also suggest that defence counsel have not been able to precognosce everyone they have named? If so, it means both counsel may be busking it if an unprecognosced witness is called.

Gardiner and MacFie are also keen to ensure their clients are well-rested and comfortable before the trial begins and so they make one last request: will those currently out on bail be able to remain at liberty each night once the trial begins and until the court reaches its final verdict? Either their polite request goes unnoticed, or the judiciary has more pressing matters to deal with, because Gardiner and MacFie ask again on Thursday 3 April. There are just two clear working days before the accused will appear in Edinburgh.[77]

Chapter 8

7 to 18 April 1919

The Trial

Preparation for Monday's trial becomes frenetic in the remaining days. The defence solicitors, Gardiner and MacFie, inform the Crown Agent that they have failed to trace everyone they would like to bring as defence witnesses, but they are offering to provide three days' notice of new names to be added to their list during the trial. They hope this can be accommodated by the prosecution. Then they make one last attempt to find out which of their clients are accused of what part in January's demonstrations and violence. They anticipate the prosecution does not propose to establish each of their client's presence at all the events and times cited. If they can be informed of the prosecution's approach, they may be able to limit the number of defence witnesses they will need to call to speak to every possible accusation. However, there is one witness who will not be able to attend. Inspector MacDonald, who was badly beaten by the crowd in Cathedral Street on 31 January, remains on sick leave as a direct result of his injuries and, on the police force's physician's advice, has returned to the Highlands to recuperate. Procurator Fiscal Strathern took Inspector MacDonald's precognition statement himself and, having witnessed how unwell he was back in February, believes it would be a risk to his health to ask him to attend court.[1]

Holding off for as long as he can to decide how to manage an unfolding situation, on Friday 4 April at 3.15 pm, the Town Clerk, Sir John Lindsay, sends a telegram informing the Crown Agent that the Lord Provost has only just returned to business after several weeks' convalescence from influenza. Is there any possibility his evidence can be taken on Monday to avoid staying overnight or making a return journey the following day? And might the same also be arranged for himself; it would be in the public interest not to spend money unnecessarily.[2] The legal officers for both sides are working through the weekend because on Saturday a letter is sent from the Crown Agent to Gardiner and MacFie finally stipulating which of their clients is being charged with which elements of the range of dates and locations cited. The only date for which they have alleged common culpability is 31 January.[3] With just one day to go, Sunday is unlikely to be a day of rest. It is the last opportunity for both sides to shuffle their papers, prepare their question lists and order their suits. If the defence team has had insufficient time to prepare their case, will there also be lacunae in the prosecution's case?

Outside the High Court of Justiciary in Edinburgh, situated on the Royal Mile, the police are prepared if trouble breaks out. Edinburgh's chief constable was instructed last week to ensure there would be adequate men on duty.[4] If further disturbances are anticipated during the trial, the choice of Edinburgh for this prosecution will deter spectators from attending; fewer will bother to take the train from Glasgow than if the case were heard in its home city. The High Court is a ten-minute walk from Waverley Station which is very convenient for everyone arriving for the start of today's trial. This is the highest court in Scotland, hearing the most serious criminal cases, a fact that is impressed upon everyone – whether defendant, witness or spectator – who steps across its granite threshold. Whatever is decided in court here is final: there is no criminal appellate court in Scotland and there will not be for another seven years.[5] The freedom of twelve men depends on what is said here over the coming days.

It is a basic tenet of the legal system that everyone requested to give evidence today, and any day in the past or future, will give 'the truth, the whole truth and nothing but the truth'. But there have been so many column inches of press reporting ever since the strike was announced, so many pamphlets printed, meetings fraught with discussion and gossip, how is anyone expected to provide an unembellished, unembroidered, cool and clear account of what they saw? Or think they saw? How can any member of the jury possibly set aside personal opinion reinforced by their choice of newspaper, their background and class, and consider the evidence impartially? No one knows how long the trial will take at this stage, but the jury may have a tough time ahead of them. They will have to concentrate very hard to decipher the semantics of certain phrases allegedly employed by the leaders, to unravel conflicting eyewitness accounts of the same event, to turn a deaf ear to pejorative opinions on what strikers or police intended. As the crowds mill outside the court, in Glasgow the agent for the accused makes a last-minute attempt to advise potential defence witnesses that it is a requirement to give a statement to the procurator fiscal or his representative.[6] Either he has already tried unsuccessfully – after all Neil Maclean will attest that he is unaware it is his duty to provide the police with information if asked – or there has been a general avoidance of this duty, but on the first day of the trial time has almost run out.[7] The defence team furiously seeks every last witness with credible and compelling evidence they can find.

The mood and décor are sombre. The dark wood panelling of the court room focuses the spotlight on the key characters appearing on the dais. Unforgiving wooden seating is provided in the public gallery. The court is crowded and so is the dock. It is unusual to have to accommodate twelve men, but Emanuel Shinwell, William Gallacher, David Kirkwood, Joseph Brennan, George Ebury, Harry Hopkins, David McKenzie, Robert Loudon, Neil Alexander, James Murray, Daniel Stewart Oliver and William McCartney squeeze into the dock and overspill onto the press benches. There are so many journalists attending, they too require more seating.[8] Presiding is the Lord Justice Clerk, Charles Scott Dickson, who has risen through the legal ranks to become the second most senior judge in Scotland. He begins this morning's trial with four years' experience in his current role.[9]

First, he must digest which defence counsel represent which individual or group accused. Shinwell and Hopkins have the same team; Kirkwood, Brennan and McKenzie another team; Ebury, Loudon, Alexander and Murray are represented separately from Oliver and McCartney, while Gallacher has decided to conduct his own defence. This maverick approach may appear foolhardy; it does not allow him to benefit from the concerted approach from all counsel such a complicated case requires and Gallacher is known to be unpredictable. Experienced King's Counsel do not need a rebel in their midst. The shorthand writer engaged only on Thursday last week is poised to start transcribing the trial.[10] He has a front-row seat and will witness every frown, smile or moment of exasperation, but none of that can be noted; just the words, every single word: verbatim.[11]

In the jurors' hall over 100 men await the result of the clerk's ballot to discover whether they will be selected for jury service. The clerk's papers note 120 names with annotations for those absent and one whose summons was sent to the wrong address. There are twenty-four 'special jurors' and fifty common jurors from Edinburgh sitting alongside four special and ten common jurors from Leith, the capital's teeming port. Further jurors have travelled from Midlothian, Linlithgow (now West Lothian), Haddington (East Lothian) and Peebles.[12] The jurors' special and common status depends on a property qualification and their tax status; also, they must be aged between 21 and 60 years. The ballot is completely random and will select fifteen men as jurors – five special and ten common – the normal cohort for a Scottish court, which means those awaiting the ballot have a one-in-seven chance of carrying out their civic duty to Crown and community. They will receive no payment for attending court, not even reimbursement of their travel expenses: money would dirty the high regard in which their service is held.[13]

Before the trial can commence, defence counsel enter a number of objections to the relevancy of the charges. The most serious objection concerns the connection between instigating a riot and the riot itself. The procurator fiscal had anticipated this weeks ago and now the Lord Chief Justice must decide whether individual actions by several people on different days did indeed result in the collective action of numerous people in the riot on the Friday. He rejects the objection and believes the case is sufficiently precisely worded for him and the jury to proceed. He has removed any legal imprecision on which the defence can hang an argument. However, an objection on behalf of Oliver and McCartney is allowed: they were involved in robbing, not rioting, although the judge notes the proximity of the streets cited for their actions to George Square. Gallacher enters his own objection, similarly differentiating what happened before the riot and afterwards as two separate contentions. He continues: the crowds which he and others addressed during the week and on Friday may not have been the same people who participated in the riot – that could have been a religious mob or discharged soldiers; how is anyone to know? Originally, he was charged with assaulting the chief constable with a stick and, having appeared in court, he spent three weeks in jail. The judge questions the relevance of this fact; Gallacher is getting to that. He cannot see how all of them can be charged with every crime levelled at them – he alone was charged on Friday evening 31 January with hitting the chief constable, no one else. He illustrates their general argument that they should not all be charged with the entire list of crimes indicted. The judge can see his point, but he would prefer to listen to the evidence and let the jury decide if their actions incited the riot or not.[14]

The fifteen men selected for the jury are shown to their seats. The special jurors are a grocer, butcher, merchant, manager and bank agent, while among the common jurors are a gardener, commercial traveller and, interestingly, a tramcar driver.[15] An initial list of over 1,000 witnesses for the defence has been whittled down to 744 civilian witnesses which includes the Prime Minister Lloyd George and Secretary for War and Air Churchill and a further list naming every policeman who was on duty throughout the week; some or all could be called to give evidence. The Crown has just over 100 witnesses selected. Because no one in Scots Law can be convicted on the testimony of a single witness, every fact of the prosecution must

132

be corroborated.[16] There is no risk of a lack of corroboration with this trial, although the veracity of each contribution will have to be carefully scrutinized. If called, witnesses are expected to rely upon the evidence as given in their precognition and counsel will question them to confirm the facts of their precognition; deviation from their original testimony could lead to searching questions in cross-examination.[17]

The prosecution can now open its case. The Lord Advocate calls his first witness, Lieutenant Lawrence Gray of Central District police. Gray was second-in-command in George Square operating under Superintendent Williamson who is not called. The Lord Advocate asks Gray if he was on duty on Monday 27 January at the corner of Renfield Street and St Vincent Street, did he see a procession of strikers: yes to both. He asks about Shinwell's and Gallacher's positions in George Square later that afternoon and repeats phrases concerning 'oily magnates' supping in the North British Hotel. Together, they run through the entire week's events, the Lord Advocate's questions being lengthy and Gray's responses often only a one-word confirmation. Gray is cross-examined by defence counsel in a similar fashion, and then Gallacher takes his turn.

Now Gray's answers become longer, refuting the statements encapsulated within Gallacher's questions. A verbal skirmish ensues concerning Gallacher's presence on the plinth of the Gladstone statue. He requires Gray to confirm whether he saw him return to the plinth; Gray does not remember except to recall that Gallacher climbed off it just before the meeting broke up. But Gallacher presses him, that he distinctly remembers him addressing the crowd. Yes, that was an outstanding thing, but whether words about the hotel were uttered then or later Gray cannot recollect. What Gallacher tries to prove is Gray's inability to recall if he climbed the plinth once or twice and, if he cannot remember that how can he remember exactly what he said? Then they argue whether a piece of red cloth is a flag; a flag is a piece of cloth, a distinct article. But Gray adheres to the terminology he used in his precognition: a red piece of cloth; infer from that what you will. They return to Gallacher's mention of the hotel and his stated intention to remove control from its manager, which Gray admits was not necessarily what he meant, but nevertheless it was a wrong thing to say to the type of men he was addressing. Gallacher accuses him of being evasive when the evidence put is favourable to Shinwell and yet appears to have heard everything said when the evidence is unfavourable to him. Is it coincidence or intentional? They move on to the police use of batons, which Gray could not see from where he stood, but he is sure the mob rushed the police. And then the stoppage of the trams: whether it was deliberate or not; did it warrant a 'brutal' police baton charge? Gray confirms his belief the crowd stopped the trams on purpose, but he prevaricates when pressed to answer whether a baton charge is a reasonable response. Gallacher expands on the issue of trams always blocking Labour processions in Glasgow; after all it happened last May Day, and for the Lifeboats and a Meat Trades procession. The Lord Justice Clerk interjects: there is enough to understand about this January without going into details about previous years' processions.

Next, Gallacher's assault on the chief constable, about which he muses: if he had wished to succeed it might have been wiser to assault him when not surrounded by police. Gray confirms he has never known Gallacher previously to use violence. They conclude by returning again to the trams which Gray reconsiders: they might have been able to move on if the crowd had allowed them. Day one of the trial has only heard from its first witness. They adjourn until 10.00 am tomorrow.[18] And, as requested earlier, the defendants are allowed to return home overnight.[19] When reported in the labour press, Gray will be ridiculed for his inconsistency under cross-examination.[20]

On the second day, after the Lord Justice Clerk welcomes everyone with a hearty good morning, further police witnesses are called. Again, they are led through the details of the week. Cross-examining counsel attempt to persuade the police that, had their forbearance with the crowd continued until after Friday's deputation to the Lord Provost had returned to speak to the gathered masses, then the baton charges and riot would not have occurred. The police will not budge: they responded to violence; they did not start it. In cross-examination, Sergeant Murdoch admits generally he relies more on memory than the sporadic notes he jots down. This is a perfect crevice into which the cross-examining counsel can drive a wedge. If the Crown has admitted that Kirkwood was not in the procession on the Monday, how can Murdoch so adamantly confirm he was? Murdoch also explains that in the presence of a superior officer, he would defer to him even in matters concerning taking notice of an incitement to riot, so on certain points he is unclear because his officer was taking the notes. Gallacher asks how only one window of the City Chambers was broken with so many missiles flying. He offers no corroboration for this unlikely assertion, and Murdoch can offer no explanation.[21]

They have made it to lunchtime and it is apparent to the Lord Justice Clerk that the fine details which they will need to examine will make this a longer trial than he anticipated; he apologizes for not heeding the advice he received from the Lord Advocate or the defence. He proposes to sit on Saturday if the jury will agree. They adjourn for lunch, after which the foreman of the jury explains that, much as they are content to fulfil their civic duty, they also have other commitments. They agree to attend on Saturday morning only. Now they can pick up where they left off and everyone except the defendants can breathe more easily.[22]

James Cummings, the produce merchant riding Margaret Buchanan's tram on 31 January, confirms the police perspective that the trams were wilfully held up and he adds that cries from the men that they were being run over brought the crowd running, which frightened the police. Tram Inspector David Cree recounts the crowd's anger and abusive language towards the police and adds that the crowds fled when the police drew their batons. He confirms he heard members of the crowd tell him they were out to stop the trams. Inspector Sutherland, who gave the order to use batons, recalls how hostile the crowd was and he is sure his men only struck any miscreants over the shoulder, not about the head or body.[23]

When it comes to his appearance in the witness box, Town Clerk Sir John Lindsay is more matter-of-fact but he, too, maintains the crowd deliberately stopped the trams in the south-east and north-east corners of the Square. Being led through the evidence contained in his precognition, Sir John's answers return largely to single word 'yes' and 'no' responses. He is clear that Kirkwood and Gallacher did not instruct the crowd to further violence when they were asked to appear on the balcony, but his recollections of Wednesday's delegation in the Lord Provost's room indicate his belief that the delegation's main purpose was to secure the stoppage of the trams the next morning or by Friday. The Lord Advocate presses him to explain what the men meant on the Wednesday by threatening to use 'unconstitutional methods'. He desires the jury to understand this phrase as an incitement to riot.

Defence counsel refers to the wording of the telegram sent to London that night, which Sir John agrees did not say anything about trams because of Neil Maclean's last-minute suggestion to remove any mention of them. Defence counsel and Sir John agree that the telegram's main purpose was to request the Government's intervention in the Forty-Hour campaign. It is the end of day two, but Sir John's turn in the box is not finished. Despite attempts to avoid another journey, he will have to return tomorrow to complete giving evidence, when the Lord Provost will accompany him.

Last night, someone writing a supporting article for the defence believed the case was proceeding favourably due to the degree of inconsistency in the prosecution's evidence. The article also claimed a tram inspector was unaware of negotiations among his staff for a forty-seven-hour week and a policeman on duty in George Square was oblivious to any ongoing strike.[24]

135

This is a biased interpretation of what has been said so far, but cracks are indeed appearing in the evidence.

Curiosity is waning as the trial enters day three and only the most interested and involved occupy the public gallery. Of course, much depends on the quality of those being questioned and today Sir John concludes his evidence and is followed by the Lord Provost, James Stewart, who has had a few more days to improve – his health and his evidence. Sir John closes his testimony with details of the conversation with Wednesday's deputation before recounting what he saw on Friday from the windows of the Municipal Buildings. He is at pains to explain that the city council was not responsible for the publication of the telegram in the press; he personally considered the Government's response a private matter. But, when questioned on the urgency of seeing the deputation at noon on Friday so that the crowd might be dispersed as quickly as possible, he cannot explain the Lord Provost's actions.[25]

Sir John is replaced in the witness box by the Lord Provost, who is sworn in and the debate about who said what and who said it first among Wednesday's deputation continues. It is becoming increasingly apparent how confused that meeting was, although he also maintains that the meeting began with a demand to take the trams off the rails. He expands on his understanding of Shinwell's threat to use 'unconstitutional methods' if their so far constitutional actions were not heeded. He moves on to the telegram and confirms Neil Maclean's request for the deletion of any mention of the trams from the draft. James Stewart explains how troubled he was by the publication in full of his telegram and the Government's response in Friday's morning papers. He acknowledges how worried he was that there would be trouble but exonerates himself from any instructions given to the police to stop anyone attempting to obstruct the trams. And he denies any knowledge whatever of a deputation having agreed to visit him at noon on the Friday.[26]

So much dry detail and nuance demands some light relief, which Inspector Duncan Weir provides under cross-examination by Gallacher. Together they cover the key dates, locations and opinions on what happened, but then Weir tells Gallacher he searched his home while the latter was in Duke Street prison. He found nothing pertinent to the strike but did uncover a bank book. Gallacher plays to the gallery: he will have to look for that book when he goes home. The journalists watching every expression, catching every subtlety, note the laughter that follows, but the shorthand writer only pauses; his version of the trial will include no levity.[27]

This morning there is a queue of police witnesses waiting to give evidence. Their testimony concentrates on the minutiae of what they saw and where they were positioned during the week and around the Square on Friday. Both prosecution and defence counsel seek clarity on what caused the riot: did the police start it, or did they respond with a baton charge? Today's evidence focuses on anticipation of behaviour, the intentions of the strikers and responsibility for the tram obstruction which some believe caused the riot, and bottle-throwing in the north-east corner which others allege did not involve strikers. The few friends of the prisoners still attending court daily listen to similar questions and often alarmingly similar answers from each policeman. The time delay between the first week of the strike, taking their precognition statements in mid-February, the opportunity to discuss events and read the newspapers and now appearing in court may have allowed some policemen to polish their evidence. Sergeant Steele injects his opinions among his factual answers and implies the crowd in front of the Municipal Buildings on the Friday was intent on taking possession; his recall of the police using batons to repel the crowds is robust and, when he describes his altercation with Kirkwood, he moves swiftly from 'Kirkwood had his hands raised' to Kirkwood told him 'to hell with you' and then he batoned him. Steele's evidence is closely repeated by his colleague Constable Ritchie. If Steele's evidence in court could be compared with his precognition statement, then small discrepancies would appear.[28] The jury is not privy to the content of the precognitions; they do not know if any of the witnesses in court are changing or mis-remembering their original testimony. And if they hear conflicting evidence from one witness to another, they must decide if one or both have mis-remembered, if any have slanted their evidence, or have they become confused or colluded with others.

On 10 April the chief constable gives evidence. He explains what he witnessed personally, which was not the disturbance by the south-east corner of the Square, which he maintains elicited the first police baton charge, because he was elsewhere at the time. However, he can properly attest to the assault he suffered by the Gladstone statue. He describes the crowd being in a fluid state, implying there was sufficient space for people to move around the Square. He describes a man approaching him, angry and excited, who he thought wanted to speak to him but instead gave him an uppercut blow to the cheek. As the blood welled from his face, he noticed two constables arrest the man. He makes no mention of the policemen using their batons on their prisoner. Once recovered from the assault, Stevenson explains how he moved from the statue to the corner of North Frederick Street where he had a good view of the ensuing bottle-throwing, which he considered was made more dangerous for the police approaching from the bottom of the hill as the bottles' trajectory was aided by the downward slope.

As the commanding officer for Glasgow's police, cross-examining counsel is keen to understand what information Stevenson had gleaned as the week progressed and, therefore, what had this experienced police officer anticipated might happen on Friday? Defence counsel rewinds to the week running up to that fateful last day. Did the reports he received throughout the week indicate the crowd intended to hold up the traffic, intimidate the police and forcibly occupy the Municipal Buildings and North British Hotel on Friday? Stevenson is not sure what their purpose was, but he is clear that, on previous occasions when processions have trailed through Glasgow's streets, the police have always tried to keep the crowds to the left to allow the trams to continue running in the centre of the roads. He admits there is always some friction between the crowds and trams during processions, but this week the crowds' actions had been intentional; he also confirms that Friday's crowd was anticipated to be the biggest of the week. This leaves a gap for defence counsel to insinuate that responsibility for the violence in the south-east corner should lie at the police's door. If the chief constable had witnessed the growing density of the crowd and their reported belligerence, as he confirms by his own evidence, why did he insist on the maintenance of regular tramway traffic? Stevenson maintains that if the crowd had obeyed the police's instructions which he had issued the previous Sunday to prevent the strikers from delaying the trams, there would have been no obstruction to the trams and therefore no disturbance nor violence. Again, defence counsel presses the point: surely if the police had only agreed to suspend the trams until the deputation emerged from the Lord Provost's rooms the lamentable riot would have been avoided? Stevenson refuses to agree to any inference that the police started the riot, although he acknowledges that a police baton charge raises the possibility of a disturbance spreading outwards and he admits innocent people can get hurt.

Whether the missile-throwing was a response to the second baton charge or its cause takes several minutes to resolve, but the cross-examination has wended its way to its next key point: were those missiles coming from the south-east or north-east corner? It is the first proper attempt by the defence to present the argument that two distinct groups were in the Square: peaceful strikers who became angry and admittedly threw clods of earth, and opportunistic looters and rioters who seized bottles from the stricken lorry in North Frederick Street. If the defence can insinuate a difference between the two cohorts, they may convince anyone on the jury who perceives strikers in general as a riotous bunch that in this instance they were not. The point is left to hang in the air as counsel returns to policing numbers on the day.

Either already on duty, escorting processions or drawn from reserves, only 140 men were in the Square to police what the chief constable admits he understood would be a very big crowd. And how many on Glasgow's entire force? Amazingly, Stevenson is recorded as stating he commands 14,000 men; in reality, with so many police still in the armed forces, it is nearer 1,400 out of an establishment of just under 2,000. He had no expectation the crowd would become riotous, otherwise of course he would have deployed more men, although there were few elsewhere he might call on. His 140 officers and constables were only intended to protect the front of the Municipal Buildings, not to cope with a riot among 20,000 or more demonstrators. Gallacher poses the last few cross-examination questions. He faces the chief constable standing in front of him in the witness box and enquires: could the chief constable identify the man who assaulted him? No.[29]

The Crown's evidence concludes at 3.30 pm on Friday 11 April after five days of intense concentration on repeated and minutely differing evidence and interpretations. There is just sufficient time left to hear from the first defence witness before the court closes for the day. Town councillor, Rosslyn Mitchell, defence solicitor for Harry Hopkins but witness too, takes the stand. His analysis of Friday's riot follows the argument that the police overreacted and he can see no reason why they led a baton charge. He adheres to the claim that the density of people in the south-east corner caused the pushing and shoving which manoeuvred the police against the trams. This happened not because there was insufficient space in the Square, but because the people behind did not understand what was happening closer to the trams; essentially there was a localized and confused bottleneck which contributed to the mayhem. He holds that the trams came to a halt in the south-east corner only because it is where they have a scheduled stop and he believes there was no intention by the crowd wilfully to obstruct them. He saw women and children scuttle out of the Square when the trouble began and those men climbing on the trams did so to escape danger. He claims he saw no one remove the ropes from the trolleys or smash any tram windows.[30] His evidence attempts to redefine what other witnesses describe as fifteen or twenty minutes of struggle and growing violence as a few moments of misunderstanding.

Throughout the first week of the trial newspaper reports have dwindled from several columns over two pages to three columns at most on a single page, progressing further towards the back pages. The repetitive minute details are difficult material to conjure into engaging copy, but Saturday's press coverage showed renewed interest as the defence case tried increasingly to paint a picture of police culpability for the 'brutal' violence. Now, as the second week gets underway, it looks as though the trial may conclude soon, but there is a surprising and ironic adjournment. Joseph Brennan, who was expected to make a re-appearance in the dock this morning, arriving in time to start by 10.00 am has been delayed; he will now be late departing Glasgow Queen Street station because a blockage on the trams has caused him to miss the earlier train.[31]

The defence case must also dissect each event of that tumultuous last week of January, hear evidence and opinions from eyewitnesses and participants and re-construct everything the jury has heard so far from a different perspective, one more favourable to their clients. There have been very few women asked to give evidence so far. The tram conductor Mary Beattie appeared last week and now it is Edith Hughes' turn, the Glasgow Trades Council's treasurer and member of numerous labour executives and organisations. Hughes' testimony is concise: Shinwell conducted all meetings as a purely industrial not political movement; Kirkwood would never be party to inciting a mob to violence; on Friday the crowd was orderly and yes, some trams were halted; the crowd did not provoke the police; she saw no missiles thrown, heard no threats and, in her opinion, if the police had waited until the deputation had returned with some answers, the demonstrators would have dispersed peaceably, which to her recollection they have done at past gatherings. Her evidence places her in the centre of the Square from 12.15 pm until the second baton charge when she decides to observe events in Cathedral Street before returning to the Square and then going home. Edith Hughes neither sees nor hears things other witnesses for both sides attest to.

Describing Hughes' credentials on so many left-wing committees may be a defence strategy to elevate her status as a witness although, from a prosecution point of view, the list of councils and executives she sits on may prejudice her evidence if the jury is politically unsympathetic. She has remained loyal to Shinwell, who will fail to reciprocate in future years; he will make the disgraceful and unfounded accusation to his biographer that Edith Hughes was a police spy and informant. But today, she has proved to be an unexcitable and dependable defence witness under cross-examination.[32]

But the comic-turn for the defence must be Isaac Sim, demobilized soldier, delegate member and, according to himself, lead negotiator with the Lord Provost. His evidence is heard on the penultimate day of the trial. Sim credits Shinwell and Kirkwood for getting them through the Municipal Buildings' doors when his own leadership did not win any recognition, but, once in the Lord Provost's library and after Shinwell introduced everyone, Sim claims he was the first to speak. He remembers launching into an account of the Forty-Hours movement and a lengthy statement about his involvement with the strikers. According to him, the discussion concerning the trams did not happen until well into the meeting, despite others saying it was the first item they talked about and, when it was discussed, it was the anonymous seventh man, whose identity no one can recall, who first mentioned the trams. He alone demanded their removal from the entire city by Thursday morning, which is contrary to what the town clerk and Lord Provost state. When the prosecution challenges him that it was Shinwell and Kirkwood who controlled the meeting, indignantly Sim responds that is not correct. According to this demobilized soldier, who was as anonymous to the crowd as the seventh man until after his first visit to the Lord Provost, a lot of what was discussed was said by him. As confusing as the evidence is for Wednesday's delegation, Sim's account rarely coincides with anyone else's. And, on Friday, Sim claims to have been at the centre of everything when they returned to speak to the Lord Provost. He's on the balcony when the men below shouted up for Kirkwood to join them; he's a few feet behind Kirkwood when he was knocked to the ground and, handily, he had a notebook with him in which he jotted down the offending constable's number. By the time Sim is asked to clarify again Kirkwood's alleged threat to the Lord Provost that he would be held responsible for any untoward occurrences if the trams were not removed, the Lord Justice Clerk is so confused he admits he is no longer able to follow Sim. It appears, according to Sim, the discussion about the trams and the decision not to include their mention in the telegram happened before the Lord Provost read his first draft to the deputation and yet, responding to the next question, Sim can think of no explanation why the Lord Provost included a sentence in that first draft concerning the trams. By the time prosecution counsel and Sim have spun through several cycles of what came first, the telegram or the trams, Sim is also forced to admit: I do not follow. It is a brave prosecutor who proceeds with questions to ascertain the meaning of constitutional and unconstitutional methods being employed if the strikers' demands were not met.[33]

The first witness was a respected lieutenant of police, the last is defence witness Neil Maclean, MP for Govan. His evidence is generally and personally exculpatory. His main contribution is evidence concerning

Wednesday's delegation. Neither Shinwell nor Kirkwood, nor himself for that matter, intended to join the delegation; his presence was pure chance when the delegation was held up at the door to the Municipal Buildings. No one had any idea what they might say once inside and his version of the discussion, who said what and in what order, confirms the general understanding by now that this was a very confused moment in the proceedings. However, he claims he was the one to object to the first line of the draft telegram: if it had gone with its original wording the issue of the trams would have amounted to a threat to remove the trams by violence. To Maclean, it did not represent the true feelings of the deputation. Throughout, he has offered a very particular interpretation on the week's events and concludes by accusing the sheriff of twisting Kirkwood's words delivered from the City Chambers' balcony as proof of a premeditated attempt to take the Buildings: 'Your time will come later on.' It never did.

How to sum up? The Lord Advocate takes nearly two hours to summarize his case. The trial has been wearisome and complicated, he admits, but the events described for Friday 31 January amount to the gravest imaginable menace to the public. Events stemming from Monday 27 January onwards were steeped in illegality and anyone interpreting the threat to take the North British Hotel or the Municipal Buildings as a jest should realize it was no joke. The deputation had threatened the Lord Provost and by extension the city with outrage and, by evaporating into the Square when things turned ugly, Shinwell had not evaded responsibility for all the alleged incitements made throughout the week. He is ultimately culpable. Acknowledging the amount of press coverage over the intervening weeks and during the trial, prosecution counsel asks the jury to cast anything they may have heard or read from their minds and offer their verdict on an assessment of the facts as presented to them over the preceding ten days. The Lord Advocate urges them to consider why the crowd would arrive in George Square intent on mischief and, if they had not, then why had the day descended into violence? What and who were the causes?

Summing up the defence case, similar questions are posed concerning the crowd's intentions and counsel asks the jury to consider: if they believe the crowd did not arrive with preconceived ideas of enacting violence, then how can Shinwell and friends be charged with having incited a riot? The defence suggests the prosecution case has broken down. Then Gallacher steps forward to draw his personal conclusions. By conducting his own defence, he has not benefited from the collective approach the professional lawyers have shared. He tells the jury he brought his wife with him to the

Square because he did not foresee trouble. He was clubbed by eight or ten batons. Yes, he did discuss the North British Hotel, but he has done nothing unlawful at any point, and whether he sleeps tonight at home or in a prison cell his conscience is clear.[34]

There has been no time for the judge to commence his summing up this afternoon. He jests with the fifteen men of the jury that any delay after he has offered his guidance will be their own fault because, once he has completed his address, the next stage of the trial is for them to debate.[35]

This morning, 18 April, however, will not be a swift affair. Before the jury can depart to consider their verdict, Lord Justice Clerk Scott Dickson offers them more than a few words of direction. By the time the court shorthand writer's hieroglyphics are typed up, it amounts to eighty-seven pages of thoughts, guidance and a compliment to Gallacher for conducting his own defence so admirably, possibly not so polished as his defence colleagues, but most definitely quite fairly done. The jury must consider all the evidence, not press opinion, and if they labour under any reasonable doubt then the accused are entitled to benefit from that doubt. They must consider the key dates of Monday 27, Wednesday 29 and Thursday 30 January, because these are the days on which the incitements to riot are alleged to have taken place. However, he directs them to reject the flying of a red flag on Monday; it may be a political symbol, but it is immaterial to the case and the accused have been quoted as having asked for its removal from their meetings because they were industrial gatherings and nothing to do with political flags.

Throughout his direction to the jury, Scott Dickson reminds them frequently they are supreme in deciding the verdict for these men. His role is to give legal direction where necessary, but in this instance the law is not in dispute by either side; rather it is the great weight of facts on which they must concentrate. He is clear: the jury should not convict Shinwell, Brennan and Ebury of actual rioting; Hopkins cannot be found guilty of incitement to riot, there is insufficient evidence and he should be discharged; no one at the Star Picture House can be found guilty of incitement to riot because the Lord Advocate led no evidence on that point despite its inclusion in the indictment; there cannot have been an incitement on Monday 27 January because there was yet to be an arrangement for a demonstration on Friday, and by extension any inclusion of Monday's 'taking the North British Hotel' within the incitement charge is invalid. And there is conflicting evidence concerning Kirkwood. The photograph of him being batoned over the shoulders is a production in court and will assist the jury in their final verdict.

In the judge's opinion, the weight given to either the prosecution or defence case has been equal, but he would like to give the police a special mention: they have no one to represent them, they are largely recruited from the humbler classes and he would ask consideration for their evidence to be viewed as likely to be truthful and as honest as any other witness whether born high or low. The testimony of one unsympathetic constable, whose words have lodged in the judge's mind, is not representative of the whole force and he marks out Detective Inspector Louis Noble as one officer who took notes throughout the week.

The Lord Justice Clerk, who has sat patiently at the front of the court for over a week, interjecting where evidence became too dense even for him to comprehend, acknowledges the great quantity of conflicting testimony but encourages the jury to use their intelligence as men untrammelled by legal technicalities and niceties to search for the truth within it. Whether Shinwell and the delegation requested the removal of the trams before Friday or else, whether they said certain words in a particular manner, whether any intention to disrupt the trams on Friday would have been better achieved at an alternative and busier junction; all this evidence will help inform their decision: did the accused incite the riot, and who among them was involved in rioting and mobbing? These are extremely serious charges, Scott Dickson explains, only one notch below a capital offence. But let's remind ourselves, when these events occurred unwise things were said and done, some of which may have been criminal, but it was only a few weeks after the Armistice was declared and everyone was still so very upset after four years of hostilities. The strike may have been aggravated by that heightened tension. Let's adjourn for lunch.

Charles Scott Dickson has been speaking for two hours and the break is likely welcomed by everyone. When the court returns there are only the men charged with mobbing and rioting left to address, the type of participants whom Scott Dickson this morning called unimportant members when discussing Wednesday's deputation. If Isaac Sim is fuming, he does so unnoticed. He makes it explicit there is no evidence against Oliver, the jewellery thief, for the more serious charge of rioting and, as the specific charge of robbing the jewellery shop was removed from the indictment the jury would do well not to convict him. Despite being found with stolen jewellery on his person, Oliver has got away with it on a technicality.[36] After four hours summing up, by early afternoon the jury leaves to deliberate.[37]

A Scottish jury has three verdicts available to them. Guilty and not guilty are defined and used the same in Scotland as every jurisdiction, but the third verdict under Scots Law, 'not proven', is another verdict of acquittal. It does not suggest the jury believes the accused is innocent of the charge, but it indicates a deficiency in the evidence enabling them to convict.[38] If the jury returns a not proven verdict, the accused will walk free, even if a shadow of doubt remains over him. In such a complex case, with so many protagonists involved, it might be anticipated that doubt would creep into the jury's deliberations. They depart the court room at 1.53 pm and return at 4.40 pm.[39] Taking into consideration time to settle into their seats, pour a glass of water, ask the clerk a handful of questions, they reach their verdict in under three hours. In Scots Law, their decision is not required to be unanimous or even carried by a large majority; a jury division of eight in favour to seven against will suffice to carry their decision. When the jury re-appears, they have reached a black-and-white verdict.

The press reporters have their pencils poised, but none of them notes the atmosphere in the courtroom. Does anyone hold their breath? Are there sweaty palms clenched together in the dock? The press, like all the spectators and accused, are only interested in the verdict. The clerk asks the foreman of the jury have they reached a decision? Yes, they have. By a majority of fourteen to one, they find Shinwell and Gallacher guilty of incitement to riot only; Murray who enjoyed his hooligan spree in Cathedral Street and elsewhere and McCartney, accused of smashing the tram window and rioting in Paisley Road, are found guilty of mobbing and rioting. Everyone else can walk free: Alexander, who went to help Gallacher; Loudon the man accused of stopping Assistant Chief Constable Mennie arresting a man, Kirkwood, Ebury, Brennan and McKenzie are all 'not guilty'.

After ten long days of intense and, as the *Glasgow Herald*'s leader writer confirms, tedious evidence, a single juror disagreed whether the accused were guilty or not. The Lord Advocate may not have managed to get all his men, but the Crown has at least won against four of them: two looters and rioters and two of the strike's leaders. Shinwell and Gallacher are going down. Only not for long.

The jury decides the verdict but the judge determines the length of sentence. The Lord Justice Clerk sends both Murray and McCartney down for three months' imprisonment each. It is a short sentence bearing in mind the damage and mayhem they have perpetrated. When considering Gallacher's sentence, the jury asks for leniency in light of his attempts to disperse the crowd peacefully from the balcony on the Friday. However, Gallacher is not happy to let his case rest. He informs the judge he is surprised by the verdict and thus regrets nothing, nor does he feel any shame. Shinwell's defence counsel takes an equally startling approach, considering the verdict is absolute. His counsel admits he does not understand the jury's decision and attempts to argue as though the case were not closed. Scott Dickson dismisses his pleas.

Tomorrow morning the press will describe how, on that fateful Friday, the strikers and their supporters were knocked down like ninepins, how only days earlier Gallacher made a manly address to the jury. Other journalists will depict the events of the last week in January as a squalid attempt at Bolshevism with impossible demands attached and they will encourage the men involved to realize how close they brought Scotland, and indeed the United Kingdom, to the political horrors now unfolding in Europe.[40] It all depends for which side of the political divide one writes. Lord Justice Clerk Charles Scott Dickson possesses no political adherence when wearing his judicial wig. Any personal opinions are kept tucked away as he pronounces sentence. Taking into consideration the three weeks already spent in prison in February, he sentences Emanuel Shinwell to five months' imprisonment. Shinwell's crime of incitement to riot is just short of a capital offence in the judge's eyes, yet deftly Scott Dickson expresses his personal view of the Crown's case so succinctly. Then, for anyone still in doubt on his stance towards the prosecution's case, he pronounces sentence on the only other strike leader found guilty. William Gallacher, who could not have cared whether he was going home tonight or to a cold cell, is sentenced to three months alone with his clear conscience.[41]

Chapter 9

April 1919 and beyond

Interwar Leaders

As the trial opened in Edinburgh, at Westminster that day there could be no mention of the proceedings. Discussion of cases *sub judice* was prohibited but related topics could be raised in the House of Commons. Mr J. Jones MP questioned the First Lord of the Admiralty on the suspension of Naval shipbuilding on the Clyde. Work had been ordered to stop on four W- and Y-class destroyers – *Yeoman*, *Zealous*, *Zebra* and *Zodiac* – potentially an economically devastating cancellation of orders already underway with men committed to them. Did the First Lord feel the suspension of work on the four ships had caused the unemployment and unrest on the Clyde? Would he consider reinstating the contracts? The Parliamentary Secretary to the Admiralty replied: he was still waiting for a date from the shipbuilding firms when they could cease work without a sudden dislocation of all the men currently employed, but the honourable gentleman must understand it was unnecessary for the Government to continue building ships they did not need. It was a valid point, but Mr Noel Pemberton Billing, MP for Hertford, then enquired: would it not be financially preferable to keep the men on short time, to continue to build the ships and keep the men in jobs rather than have them claim on the unemployment fund and spend their days loafing the streets?[1]

On the second day of the trial, the cost of housing was debated in the House of Commons. Surely, the expense of the new housing proposals was preferable to the cost to the country of Bolshevism and revolution? Expenditure on one was insurance against the other. The time had come to address the findings of a recent Royal Commission on Scotland's housing problems and provide the 'homes fit for heroes' which had been promised.[2] Evidently, the fear of a politicized uprising among the working classes continues to exercise those in government into spring 1919.

At Thursday's summing up at the trial, the Lord Advocate for the prosecution connected the threat of socialism to the socialists standing in the dock awaiting their fate. Some observers on the left interpreted his words to mean that the Forty-Hours campaign had threatened capitalism itself and there could be no greater crime. When his turn came, William Gallacher framed this trial as the prosecution's attempt to cover up police brutality by blaming what happened on that critical day in January on the strike leaders.[3] What was loosely discussed in Parliament during the trial's first week, arguably, might have been better debated six months earlier in preparation for the end of the war and a return to normal civilian life, not after the eruption of discontent that Glasgow had endured. Some in power realize they have come too close to political disaster with recent events across the United Kingdom and on Clydeside; those on the shopfloor must now confront the failure of their Forty-Hours movement, regroup and decide how to proceed with their campaign.

The first task for the Clyde Workers' Defence Committee is to raise money to pay for the trial and to continue to agitate for workers' rights. Unbeknownst to many, there was almost a cessation of the trial because funds promised to Edinburgh solicitors Gardiner and MacFie to pay the defence counsel dried up. As the first witness for the defence was called on Monday 14 April, Gardiner and MacFie had written to the Clyde Defence Fund expressing their disappointment that they had not received payment of their fees. It was not what they agreed. Before the trial was over, Gardiner and MacFie received their money, but now the Clyde Defence Fund must be replenished. Established back in February, the Clyde Workers' Defence Committee struggles to balance its books as the monies dribbling into their coffers do not match the sums outstanding. Mr Donnelly has collected £1 5s 0d while Alexander Rose has forwarded £2 15s 0d, both from Dumbarton Road, just north of the river. These are sizeable sums of money from families facing economic hardship in a declining job market, but they will hardly pay off the fees now due to the defendants' legal advisors, some of which remain outstanding at the end of May.[4]

Monies received and monies spent, when audited on 8 May, are the same. Every penny of £2,552 19s 1d raised so far from subscriptions, individuals, and the proceeds of the sale of the *Strike Bulletin* are accounted for, the vast majority having been paid to Glaswegian solicitor John Crosthwaite who used it to pay defence counsel attending the High Court in Edinburgh. Now he requires a further settlement of £1,400 for his own firm's work in preparing the case. The worrying size of their account reflects the enormous amount of work which went into precognoscing so many witnesses and the many letters sent back and forth between different parties' solicitors, the Crown Agent in Edinburgh, and the accused. They are desperately seeking donations from every union branch and executive to relieve the accused of this responsibility. A subscription slip is appended to their generic letter to all union branches. From his prison cell, Emanuel Shinwell is demanding a public inquiry, which might be a further expense to the Clyde Defence Fund if he succeeds.[5]

To force a public inquiry into events in George Square, the Glasgow Trades Council decides to organize a petition, which begins in early May. The broadsheets with space for hundreds of signatures and the aims of the petition printed on top are circulated to Independent Labour Party and British Socialist Party meetings, labour meetings of every type and individuals at railway stations and other public places are stopped by workers canvassing supporters. If these sheets can be filled in completely, two columns of names and addresses to every page, it will be delivered to the Secretary for Scotland while he considers the inquiry. Gardiner and MacFie are also part of the plan. They write to Robert Munro directly, explaining their personal assessment of Shinwell's and Gallacher's performances at the trial, indicating their disappointment in the jury's inattention to both men's attempts to impose orderly behaviour on the processions and at the various strike meetings. Their every intention was for the meetings and demonstrations to be law abiding. Their letter crosses with another from Crosthwaite to William Shaw at the Glasgow Trades Council. Crosthwaite explains he has requested his Edinburgh-based colleagues to approach Munro whom they have employed when he was formerly an advocate. The lawyers have done all they can to assist any possible inquiry. Keeping the men's political activities separate from the finances, Crosthwaite writes again the following day to William Shaw, urging payment of his fees. By the end of May he is also chasing news of the Glasgow Trades Council's progress with exerting political influence at the Scottish Office.[6]

When it is presented the petition demands the release of Shinwell, and Gallacher, and the two men charged with mobbing and rioting and the cancellation of their sentences. The petition states that the mobbing and rioting was caused by the unwarranted attack from the police and that, of the twelve men tried, only two were found guilty of violence when proof of the involvement of more of them was given in court. There are nine reasons given in total.[7] However, having already spent six weeks in jail, the petition may run out of steam before the men's sentences are served, but other disputes are also breaking out, this time among different unions.

On a local level, the district secretary of the National Amalgamated Workers' Union takes umbrage with a complaint lodged at the Glasgow Trades Council that his men at the Pinkston and Dundas power stations did not come out in support of the Forty-Hours campaign. They reply that they did strike, except the handful of men kept on to maintain power to the city.[8] Nationally, at the Scottish Trades' Union Congress in May, disagreement concerning the parliamentary committee's support for a strike which their national executive had not condoned becomes heated.[9] Strikes are exhausting for the workforce and they require cohesion among their leaders: otherwise, collective successful negotiation might never happen. And if government's attitude towards the trade unions changes, then progress for the working man will grind to a halt. By July there are a few union leaders who believe the Government is attempting to confound the Triple Alliance of rail, transport and miners' unions and confront them with troops. If this is true, it reverses the Minister of Labour, Sir Robert Horne's, advice to Cabinet in February this year that, to prevent further fragmented and unofficial strikes like the ones in Glasgow, Government should encourage centralized unionization.[10]

Secretary for Scotland, Robert Munro, rejects the Trades' Council's petition to cancel the strikers' sentences and in August, now a free man, Gallacher's desire to see the police on strike comes true. It is not the first time the police have struck, but it is the most tumultuous. A year ago London's police walked out for better pay and conditions, marching on Downing Street beneath their banned union standard. Now, a year later, a police strike is called again and, this time, only in Liverpool and Birkenhead does it have any success, where it is estimated half of the city's police force is out. In essence, this is an industrial strike, although the police are unsupported by the wider workforce. So, with insufficient police to patrol the city, hundreds of opportunist looters and rioters take to Liverpool's streets over the August bank holiday. This time it is Liverpool's lord mayor who calls for military and naval assistance.[11] Apart from who is on strike, what makes this different from Glasgow seven months earlier is the involvement of the armed forces. This time they are needed on the streets – with tanks sitting in the city square – to maintain order, assisted by plain-clothes detectives with truncheons. The authorities are more concerned by the wider societal ramifications of striking police than shipbuilding engineers whose services to the country are no longer as crucial as they were during the war. Nine hundred soldiers are deployed who open fire on the rampaging crowds, killing a rioter and wounding another.[12] The Government has spent months managing industrial strife, with smaller and larger strikes breaking out across the country in many different industries and workplaces. They had been able to rely on Glasgow's police when needed, but for the English police forces to strike again within a year should be a warning to anyone in authority that something needs to change.

However, industrial unrest is not restricted to Britain or limited to Europe because the call for workers to unite spans the Atlantic. In February it was reported that 65,000 men employed in the textile industries in Seattle were out campaigning for shorter hours along with shipyard workers on the Eastern seaboard. Yarrow's of Scotstoun to the west of Glasgow also has a shipyard in Vancouver and news of their Scottish brothers' recent stoppage is alarming Yarrow's Canadian manager. A strike here could cripple operations on both continents.[13] Even if the western world's workforce has not managed a full-blown revolution, it appears the world may be ripe for its milder cousin: widespread agitation. Attempting to promote workers' rights and create solidarity between America's workforce and the working class in her husband's domicile, journalist Crystal Eastman requests interviews from January's key protagonists. Crystal has experience writing for radical publications with her brother before and during the war. Now she has married an Englishman with similar sympathies to her own and she is in Britain to listen to Clydeside's leading voices.

Crystal meets Arthur McManus, a fellow journalist and a deportee during 1916's arrests. He bemoans the failure of the Clyde Strike Committee's leaders and the workers to realize the potential they possessed back in January when they might have started a revolution. She is impressed by the 4,000 votes McManus won in December's general election, especially because he stood for the Socialist Labour Party. But she is not sufficiently beguiled by him not to recognize the distance he places between himself and any liability for the failure of January's strikes to achieve their goal. After all, he too was a member of the Clyde Workers' Committee. However, she is charmed by William Gallacher, a 'revolutionist' to the core, but one able to admit his part in January's defeat. She speaks to Neil Maclean MP, who is keen to attach himself to John Maclean's socialist reputation and finds the latter, who until recently was Bolshevik Consul for Scotland, to be cheery despite his years in prison for the cause during the war.[14] She paints a picture of revolutionary rosy health on Clydeside but, despite ongoing antagonism between workers and employers, the energetic spirit required to foment a general strike appears to have dissipated.

It may not be active policy, but to the men on the shopfloor it seems the most vociferous socialists are being weeded from the workforce and so anyone wishing to keep their job keeps their head down.[15] Indeed, being seen in Gallacher's presence in the workplace can prompt immediate dismissal. Looking back on these weeks immediately after his release from prison, he will claim that he cannot get work and, when he does, within a week the managers have spotted him and ousted him from the premises, in one instance along with the foreman who was audacious enough to employ him.[16] Stories of their leaders' victimization fly around the Clyde and, without the kind of work they were accustomed to during the war, the group of leaders seek other paths. While Gallacher heads to Moscow to begin his communist career, David Kirkwood becomes an unofficial community lawyer.

Remaining a free man after the trial, Kirkwood's leadership skills have already been recognized by election to the national administrative council of the Independent Labour Party. It is a fulltime job when combined with his local obligations. He has also embraced a new role as secretary of the Scottish Women's Housing Committee. As an eventful 1919 closes and the first months of 1920 begin, Kirkwood spends his days in the Summary Ejection Court of Lanarkshire, witnessing family after family pleading their woes; unable to pay their rent they are being evicted from their homes. Without a full welfare state to support them, Glasgow's families lean on Kirkwood to speak a few kind words on their behalf. His great oratory is reduced to hasty words spoken before the housing factor can enter his proceedings before the judge: will he accept a few shillings? Can the family re-negotiate?[17] They are desperate to keep a roof over their heads as unemployment rises. His involvement in local politics, officially and unofficially, increases Kirkwood's reputation among his once fellow workers. Yet, while they remain his fellow citizens, clearly his career is moving beyond the shopfloor and local council chambers. He has come to the notice of Ramsay MacDonald and Philip Snowden who are currently vying for leadership of Britain's Labour Party.[18]

Ever comfortable with extremes, William Gallacher is dissatisfied with middle-ground left-wing politics but, like Kirkwood in early 1920, he also comes to the notice of a great man. Without a passport or much logistical planning, Gallacher arrives in St Petersburg late for the second congress of the Communist Internationale. He falls under Lenin's spell and, no matter his loyalty to Glasgow's working men, his horizons expand. By the time he returns to Scotland, he has spoken personally to Lenin and agrees to join the newly-formed Communist Party of Great Britain, pledging to do his utmost to promote the party to his Scottish comrades. Less than a year ago, he explained to Crystal Eastman how much he preferred to agitate from the shopfloor and had no political ambition beyond leading his men, how the forces pitched against working men are subtle and ruthless and how he urged his comrades in America to play their part.[19] From 1920 Gallacher's political allegiance faces east, while Kirkwood, Shinwell and others realize that for anything to change properly in Glasgow, their experiences in

January 1919 might now be used to campaign via constitutional politics on a national platform. Their electioneering for Parliament commences.

After the last general election in December 1918, Shinwell was described as a socialist speaker and failed parliamentary candidate for Linlithgow, but now in 1922, in his late thirties, his experience as chairman of the Glasgow Trades Council and town councillor stands him in good stead for another attempt at Westminster. Also seeking better representation for his native Glasgow is David Kirkwood, a decade older than Shinwell and just as experienced in a general election: in 1918 he failed to win in Clydebank.[20] Their hopes for success are greater this time. In December 1918 calling a general election two weeks after the Armistice was opportunistic on two counts. Lloyd George had won the war for the nation and loyalty to this Liberal Party leader and wily personality remained strong. Further, there was no alternative party representing the needs of the newly-enfranchised men and some qualifying women. Their choice was Liberal or Conservative, while the Labour movement resolved its internal issues to become a viable party of government or at least one of opposition.[21] However, in Glasgow the Left has always been strong and it is now four years later and unemployment is rising. Glasgow's reliance on a select few heavy industries has hit hard now that the munitions factories are obsolete and short-term re-stocking of ships and military materiél is no longer required.[22] The general election in November 1922 is a chance to put Glasgow at the centre of government if the people are with them. Which they are.

On the day before the working men are due to vote in their second national election since gaining the franchise, the industrial court determining whether His Majesty's Dockyard workers might have an advance on their wages of twelve shillings per week rejects their claim. Despite the deprivation caused by the current high cost of living, it is thought that a pay rise for government employees would be ill-considered when men employed in similar trades in commercial firms earn less. They cannot interfere with the free-market economy. The court provides a statement alluding to some future point when His Majesty's shipbuilding establishments may review its wages policy.[23] Timing is everything in politics. Disappointing Glasgow's shipyard workers on the morning they are due to vote may not risk the entire general election, although it could cause a local revolt.

In January almost four years ago, success might have come with an immediate capitulation by Glasgow's shipbuilding employers to Shinwell's and Kirkwood's demands for a forty-hour week. None of their aims were agreed, but the slow burn, patiently waiting for the rewards of their efforts, has finally come to fruition. Of just over half a million eligible voters on

Wednesday 15 November 1922, 76 per cent of Glaswegians turn out at the ballot box. They wake the following day to hear Labour has polled 33 per cent of the vote and, in Glasgow's city centre, the results look especially promising for Labour.[24] Baillie John Wheatley is returned as Member of Parliament for Shettleston with a majority of over 4,000; Neil Maclean retains Govan with a 6,000 majority and James Maxton, left-wing educator and activist, wins Bridgeton.[25] Of fifteen seats available in Glasgow, Labour has won ten. Finally, the results for Linlithgow and Dumbarton Burghs are in; Shinwell wins on his second attempt as does Kirkwood.

Rosslyn Mitchell, unsuccessful Labour candidate and solicitor at the trial in April 1919, writes a messianic declaration to send the city's new Members of Parliament to Westminster. Gathering once again in St Andrew's Hall before an audience of thousands, the ten new Members of Parliament pledge their zeal for humanity and prosperity of all people; they will address unemployment and workplace conditions; they will pay pensions for war widows and aid the sick, and they will reject self-promotion as servants of the people.[26] Across the whole of Scotland the people have returned thirty Labour MPs to Parliament. As part of Labour's total of 142 newly-elected members, they form His Majesty's opposition for the first time. The 'Clyde Brigade' is heading to London.[27]

There is a tremendous send off as the Clyde's leaders catch the night train from St Enoch Station in Glasgow to the centre of British government. On arrival, their political impatience and parliamentary inexperience are immediately apparent. On 21 November the *Manchester Guardian*'s reporter hears a distinctly Scottish accent yelling from the gallery as the House of Lords take their seats: we'll smash that lot. Having been sworn into the House of Commons, two days later John Wheatley explains more eloquently how the citizens of the second city of empire have sent their representatives south to prove how thoroughly capitalism has failed. Showing his customary confidence in front of an attentive audience, next David Kirkwood speaks his maiden words to the House. Everyone concentrates hard as he recounts his meetings with Lloyd George in 1916 and how he and his fellow Clyde men are here to bring the prevailing system to an end; he predicts the doom of the ruling classes and tells his honourable colleagues the writing is on the wall. He raises a laugh. This is all very novel for the House of Commons' more practised members who are unaccustomed to being referred to as 'friends' and the accents of the new honourable gentlemen will take some fathoming. However, Labour's Scottish contingent has made its mark in the opening days of this new Parliament.[28]

From winter 1922 Glasgow's representatives, once strike leaders of a regional campaign for a reduced working week and better conditions at work and at home, live in London hundreds of miles distant from the men, women and children who once populated their daily routine. The dislocation does nothing to weaken their resolve. Within a week of admittance to the Commons, Wheatley interrupts the business of the House on the topic of unemployment while Kirkwood disrupts debate with minor factual corrections. Kirkwood interjects again a week later when an honourable colleague mentions land ownership in Britain and the misapprehension held by so many that land is owned by those who inherited it. Kirkwood snipes, 'by those who stole it'.[29] These are small steps on the path to learning the ropes of opposition government.

However, a year later in December 1923, Labour is returned in coalition with the Liberals. Glasgow's MPs help to form the first-ever Labour government in the United Kingdom. It is a short-lived opportunity to put into practice the ideas honed during years of speechifying, but it is a start. Labour comes to Westminster in the 1920s intent on rectifying inequalities in British society that had become entrenched before the war.[30] Success proves to be an insurmountable challenge. An unemployed and hungry workforce will be pushed to the limits as is witnessed in 1926 during the General Strike, but it is no political nor social revolution and quickly peters out. Labour will have to wait until 1929 to return as the party in government.

Throughout the 'Clyde Brigade's' first decade at Westminster, Scotland's unemployment never drops below 10 per cent, rising to 20 per cent in the early 1930s; figures quadruple for unemployed men in the West of Scotland. Among the skilled workers of the Clyde's shipbuilding industry, many are deflated by unrelenting poverty and indolence; it is no good for a man, once a hard worker and head of his household, to be idle on the streets.[31] These are desperate times for Scotland, whose Labour leaders now represent all unemployed struggling Britons. Their focus remains on social improvements for the working classes in the face of increasing global economic collapse. Throughout the 1920s Kirkwood rises in the House of Commons to discuss the pressing issue of unemployment on numerous occasions; in 1927 he calls into question the need to fund the Duke and Duchess of York's voyage to Australia at what he equates to be the same expense as removing 6,000 men from the government's unemployment insurance scheme. Would it change anything in Britain if the Yorks didn't return? Kirkwood is called to order by the deputy chairman of the House for his disrespect towards the royal family. From castigating royals to supporting miners, Kirkwood and his fellow Glaswegians are a thorn in the side of Parliament; their speeches are hardly polished and their incisive interjections make for uncomfortable listening.[32] The rough edges of a working life in the Clyde's shipyards are hard to erase.

When they arrived at Westminster over a decade ago, Glasgow's MPs were local minor celebrities, men of the people who had worked shoulder-to-shoulder with their followers during the war, attending meetings and forming policies in their spare time. They were family men who gave of themselves to change the working world one shopfloor at a time. They came to Parliament to make an impact through policy, not personality, yet their ideological difference makes them remarkable among their Westminster peers. During the 1920s the 'Clyde Brigade' assimilates into the Labour Party while remaining a readily identifiable group. As the calendar notches up another decade of leadership, Clydeside's rabble-rousers turn their spare energies to reminiscence. Is their purpose to remember as precisely as the passage of time will allow or to re-claim a past which is fading as they become increasingly part of the establishment at Westminster?

David Kirkwood is the first to publish. All those years ago when she interviewed him, Crystal was right about him. Kirkwood's colleagues described him to her as a man no good in a strike, too excitable and liable to strike an attitude, but the man she met in late 1919 spoke with a mellifluous tongue, still narrating the tale of the Forty-Hour campaign full of fire and passion.[33] When his book is published in 1935 he remains all of those things as well as having become a respected Member of Parliament. His style is more establishment than revolution; after all his onetime opponent during the war – Winston Churchill – writes the foreword. Immediately, Churchill recognizes the swirling typhoon of emotions in constant motion inside this pugnacious yet friendly man. Kirkwood recounts a personal life of hardship from birth to marriage, his fervent desire to improve his own as well as his fellow man's life, but when it comes to details the intervening years have eroded and reframed his memories. Clydeside's working men are the chorus to this very personal tale, even Friday 31 January's deputation to speak to the Lord Provost is reduced to himself and three others – Neil Maclean and Manny Shinwell, and Harry Hopkins who was never there – set against a backdrop of mayhem in George Square.[34] When he hears the uproar outside, he confesses he smashes a window to reach the balcony where he shouts to the police below to stop batoning the workers. It is not a detail anyone else noted at the time or since. As defence counsel attempted to argue at the trial, Kirkwood blames the rioting into Friday evening on a gang of unruly men, and yet when he recalls the days attending the trial he declares it a weary experience. Every night he returns to Glasgow where he continues to speak at meetings, heading back to Edinburgh the following morning on little sleep. David Kirkwood elides his own version of that fraught fortnight into a single page.[35] Perhaps if he had been found guilty, a prison sentence might have destroyed this big man, as Gallacher suggests the following year when he publishes.

William Gallacher spends the late 1920s supporting and agitating among the miners. He publishes several pamphlets and books about the Left, gradually progressing his arguments towards a rejection of working-class emancipation through the ballot box. Personally, he moves beyond democracy in its British form, yet, by 1935, his political ambitions and his promise to Lenin all those years ago to build a communist party in Great Britain finds success when he is returned to Westminster as the Communist Member of Parliament for West Fife.[36] By 1936 he sets pen to paper for his first memoir. Perhaps the notion was first seeded in his consciousness when he read Crystal Eastman's interview with Arthur McManus nearly seventeen years ago. Should January 1919 have really been the start of the revolution? Gallacher has had time to toy with the idea: the workers might have anticipated a revolution in the same way much of the establishment press did at the time, but the Clyde's leaders hadn't considered it.[37] He now views it as a missed opportunity for the people. His memoir describes his role in events of the last week of January 1919. His recollections in 1936 conform to his current and more extreme left-wing politics, adding fresh colour to aspects of what happened in George Square. He most certainly gave the chief constable a violent punch, but he now claims it was in retaliation for being batoned (rather than being batoned because he assaulted the chief constable). It is a detail not recorded in the precognitions, nor at the trial. As he writes, he conjures women and children milling around him in George Square, one woman in particular with a muddy boot print on her face lying on the ground. None of the police so closely huddled around him that day, nor anyone giving evidence in court, noticed her. However, his interpretation of police brutality has not altered since the trial; they caused the riot and they coshed a defenceless Kirkwood in the most cowardly act he has ever witnessed. That may be so, but his claim that there was a signal for the police to start an assault on the rear of the crowds will become one of the most contested elements of the events of January 1919 for the coming century.

He says he finds it inexplicable that of the long line of windows fronting the Municipal Chambers not one was broken either by Kirkwood, or in the mêlée despite police statements describing a hail of missiles. Clearly, he has not considered other more reliable witnesses' evidence before writing. He was in custody from the afternoon of 31 January 1919 but is sure the troops who arrived that night were young raw recruits transported from outside Glasgow because the veteran soldiers stationed in Maryhill Barracks were locked inside, their loyalty in their home city questioned. He is right; the soldiers he did not see in Glasgow came from beyond the city because that is army policy, to bring in outsiders, but he invents the situation at Maryhill Barracks.[38] It was not even occupied by a Glasgow regiment.[39] By making unfounded claims about the Maryhill Barracks, he creates a myth that will become an unshakeable 'fact' in the catechism of the Battle of George Square.

The night before April's trial begins John Wheatley visits him to ask if there is anything he can do for Kirkwood if the verdict goes against him. It is a private conversation which no one can corroborate. Kirkwood is a big man who needs an audience to survive; his hatred of capitalism requires an outlet. Gallacher promises to do what he can for Kirkwood in prison if they are all found guilty. Remarkably, he recounts the deliberations of the jury at the end of the trial, a matter discussed behind closed doors without notes ever reaching the public gaze. Apparently, the jury discusses him at length and only decides to find him guilty because he struck the chief constable.[40]

Emanuel Shinwell has always bided his time to see how the wind blows. He waited until the Clyde Workers' Committee was determining whether to vote for a thirty-hour or forty-hour week before he contributed his thoughts, and he waits until the 1950s to write his memoirs. When he does, he publishes three versions of his autobiography, followed by a fourth 'conversation' and gives permission for an authorized biography.[41] As distance from 1919 increases, Shinwell might be allowed some licence, but his behaviour on Bloody Friday belies a vacillating and convenient relationship with the 'truth'. In his 1973 account he claims Churchill sends 'troops, machine guns and tanks' to Glasgow, a populist accusation that sticks fast before changing his mind in subsequent versions of his life to blame Lloyd George instead.[42] At the age of 96, as the sole survivor of the Forty-Hours campaign's leadership, Shinwell writes his last autobiography in 1981, by when the events of January 1919 fill just seven pages. Whether he is being modest or not when he describes how he declines their proposal, his election as chairman of the Clyde Workers' Committee proves his standing among the men. Yet, he skims over the week's meetings and marches, dismissing every demonstration as unsuccessful until Friday's gathering in George Square. By now, the crowd has swelled from contemporary reports of 20,000 to a crushed 80,000 and Gallacher is already a member of the Communist Party, an organization yet to be established. The vandalism and violence in North Frederick Street are blamed on the crowd running to escape police brutality who now number in their hundreds. By the time he is found guilty of incitement to riot, he attributes his lengthy sentence to his position as chairman of the Clyde Workers' Committee; the Government manipulated this labour trouble to divert attention from their inability to do anything for the unemployed. His five months in Edinburgh's Calton gaol merits more description than the entire trial.[43]

Can we ever by happy with how our past turned out? When they come to write their recollections and interpretations of what happened in Glasgow in January 1919, while William Gallacher wishes a revolution might have been, David Kirkwood matures with age yet his fire remains undampened, and Emanuel Shinwell waits until he is the last man standing to have the final say. Apart from their precognitions and the trial transcript of every word said in court, none of the police writes a personal account; neither does the Lord Provost James Stewart, nor the Town Clerk, Sir John Lindsay, Chief Constable Stevenson, nor Sheriff MacKenzie. Why would they? Their lives have moved on; the strike for them is not a defining moment. But for the Red Clydesiders it is.

The men and women of Clydeside's heavy industries are required to pull out all the stops once again as Britain and the world lurches towards another global conflict. They have faced unemployment before and will do so again; they will strike and walk out, and they will lock themselves in to protect their jobs. And thus, the legend of a red and possibly revolutionary, but far from Bolshevik, Clydeside begins.

Chapter 10

The most mythologized event in twentieth-century Scottish history?

'soon after the race riots [Shinwell] had faced down an army
tank in George Square'.[1]

When we have spoken about our research publicly, we have described the
'Battle of George Square' as the most mythologized event in twentieth-
century Scottish history, and no one has yet contradicted us. How did
this happen? In this final chapter we look at the mythology: how it has
developed and how it continues to be used. We also look at some aspects
of the mythology that couldn't easily be dealt with in the narrative chapters
and, as part of this, explore some of the odd avenues down which research
into the 'Battle' and its aftermath has taken us.

The main elements of the myths as they are now used by historians,
in school textbooks, newspaper articles and social media can be listed
thus:

- the riot was deliberately provoked;
- the army was on the move before the riot began;
- the government/Churchill/'the English' sent the army;
- the army was sent to crush the strike;
- a revolution/'Bolshevik rising' was under way or possible;
- the troops were raw recruits;
- the troops were all English;
- there were tanks in George Square;
- martial law was declared;
- the deployment was illegal;
- Scottish troops were locked in their barracks in case they joined the
  strikers;
- there was a howitzer in the Square/on the roof of the City Chambers;

- machine-gun nests were set up round George Square;
- there were orders to shoot to kill and the army injured or killed people.

None of these claims is true. And this is why.

How did we get to a situation where the mythology has so replaced reality? The mythologizing started at about 1.00 pm on Friday 31 January. It gained momentum as the case for the defence was prepared and presented in court. And it was cemented in place by about fifteen pamphlets, books and articles, written over a period of sixty years by seven men closely associated with the Forty-Hours strike.

John Maclean	Socialist leader and supporter of the strike	1919	Pamphlet. *Sack Dalrymple, Sack Stevenson. Let Labour revenge Bloody Friday*
D.S. Morton	Joint Secretary, Strike Committee	1919	Pamphlet. *The 40 hours strike: an historic survey of the first General Strike in Scotland*
Kirkwood	Strike leader	1935	*My Life of Revolt*
Gallacher	Strike leader	1936	*Revolt on the Clyde*
Tom Bell	Union leader & shop steward	1941	*Pioneering Days*
Tom Bell		1944	*John Maclean, a fighter for freedom*
Shinwell	Chair of Strike Committee	1955	*Conflict without Malice*
P. Dollan	Editor, *Strike Bulletin*	1957	Memoir. *Sunday Mail*, 6 October 1957
Gallacher		1966	*The Last Memoirs of William Gallacher*
Shinwell		1973	*I've lived through it all*
H. McShane	Follower of Maclean	1978a	*Harry McShane: no mean fighter*
McShane		1978b	*Glasgow 1919: the story of the 40 hours strike*
Shinwell		1981	*Lead with the left: my first ninety-six years*

Shinwell		1984	*Shinwell Talking: a conversational biography to celebrate his hundredth birthday*
Shinwell, via Peter Slowe		1993	Slowe's *Manny Shinwell: an authorised biography*. Shinwell seems to have been Slowe's main source

Together with the version of events presented at the trial – 'an unprovoked attack on a peaceful crowd by savage, out of control police' – and in the pages of the *Strike Bulletin*, these created the basic 'catechism' of the 'Battle', forming the dominant narrative.

The prosecution's version of events, recorded only in the press coverage of the trial, together with the rather overheated coverage in newspapers like the *Glasgow Herald* in January and February – 'Bolshevik Terrorists!' – sank from view quite quickly once the trial verdict was delivered. The prosecution no longer had to make a case – more pressing concerns absorbed the government. That 'side's' account never formed part of a bourgeoning identity: that of Red Clydeside.

We were surprised to find that the transcript of the trial and the precognitions were open to researchers without restriction until 2003. As data protection legislation began to have effect, first the precognition file was closed for 100 years and then the same happened with the trial transcript in 2017. The War Cabinet minutes were opened in 1969. Even access to the *Strike Bulletin* has been problematic for researchers – we had to consult three separate archives in Edinburgh, Glasgow and London to see the whole run of fourteen issues. So, in the early years of research into Red Clydeside, when archive catalogues were card-based and thoroughly analogue, a historian would need to make a speculative visit to the archives and possibly seek the help of the resident archivist to ascertain if materials useful to the topic were available and accessible. Therefore, unless a historian was willing to sit for days to read the thousand-plus pages of trial evidence or some contemporary newspapers (which would have to be physically examined rather than viewed online), the only sources available were these fifteen publications.

This is fair enough, but these publications have been treated as reliable historical sources: they weren't entirely reliable, nor are they really history. The first two, apparently written before the trial by D.S. Morton, labour supporter and strike committee pamphleteer, and John Maclean, were part of the effort to shift the blame wholly onto the police. Both indulged in conspiracist thinking, especially Maclean. His *Sack Dalrymple, Sack Stevenson* blamed the manager of the tram system and the chief constable for deliberately fomenting the riot by driving trams into the crowd. Tom Bell, member of the Clyde Workers' Committee, repeated and elaborated upon Maclean's accusations and later authors have accepted this as the truth.[2] Maclean wasn't even in Glasgow on 31 January 1919 and no evidence at all for Morton's and Maclean's accusation has ever been offered.

Iain McLean was the first to use the War Cabinet minutes, as one of the strands of evidence in his magisterial reconsideration of Red Clydeside. Unfortunately, a misunderstanding carried over from his thesis into the subsequent book, about the location and direction of the baton charges, divorced the charges from the source of the unrest in the south-east corner. This unfortunately led him to conclude that 'These charges can therefore only be regarded as unprovoked attacks by the police designed to intimidate or scatter the crowd ...', giving renewed vigour to the story of 'the police-provoked riot'.[3] Other writers have used the War Cabinet minutes less scrupulously, going so far as to edit them subtly to put blame on Churchill's shoulders.[4]

The personal memoirs make good reading, but they can be self-exculpatory, especially when recounting the events of January 1919. Gallacher and the other memoirists weren't writing history; they were trying to establish their place *in history*, occasionally at the expense of their contemporaries: both Gallacher and Shinwell (via his biographer Slowe) indulged in this sport, Gallacher describing John Maclean as 'a mentally unstable, historically marginal, Scottish socialist' – Special Branch had used the phrase 'mentally unstable' in their reports to London and 'Scottish socialist' is true, but marginal is insulting. In his authorized biography, Shinwell blamed Kirkwood for the unfortunate outcome of the meeting with the Lord Provost on 29 January and accused Edith Hughes of being a police spy.[5] Through their memoirs, Gallacher and Shinwell aimed, more than anything else, to shift blame for the violence or even the failure of the strike, onto the police, the government or, in Shinwell's case, onto his fellow strike leaders. Kirkwood isn't blameless, but less blameworthy in this respect.

Shinwell's memoirs have been described as 'entertaining but unreliable', a polite understatement.[6] He invented Churchill's responsibility for the military deployment in his 1973 memoir, *I've lived through it all*, having blamed 'Whitehall' in an earlier book, and 'Lloyd George' in two subsequent volumes.[7] Shinwell also contributed lavishly to the mythology in his recorded interviews, memorably claiming angrily that 'there was no riot' in George Square in an interview included in a 1984 television documentary.[8]

The result is that the hitherto unchallenged, dominant narrative of the 'Battle' is as reliable as a history of the General Strike of 1926 written using only Churchill's memoirs and the government's propaganda sheet the *British Gazette*.

How has this happened?

The historian Richard Evans has described Labour history from the 1970s onwards as an explicitly committed form of historical writing and research, written from the point of view of the industrial working class to recover their history as a means of strengthening the class-consciousness and political commitment of the working class. As a consequence, he suggests, labour history has lost any claim to objectivity.[9]

We can see that, in writing about the 'Battle', authors sympathetic to the struggle of working people to achieve better working conditions have perhaps been less than dispassionate in their choice of sources and their presentation of the story. If one is writing history, rather than a rousing call to the barricades, if one's heart is too firmly 'in the left place', this may be a problem, if it leads to a lack of sceptical scrutiny and an unwillingness to listen to all the 'voices' from the past.[10]

Historians and authors of more general books on Red Clydeside, and twentieth-century Scottish history, and of school textbooks have accepted the version told in the fifteen publications, or in most cases have merely followed other writers who have previously relied upon them; errors and myths are passed from one text to another. The depressing fact though is that much of the mythology could be dismissed by any author taking time to read the *Glasgow Herald*'s coverage for late January and early February 1919. Yes, that newspaper was hostile to the strike, but that bias appeared largely in its fulminating editorials, not in its reporting of events, which was generally corroborated by other newspapers, including those more in sympathy with the strike, such as the *Manchester Guardian*.

In a popular and academic history and in other media the largely mythologized version of events in January and February 1919 has almost completely displaced the reality. The extent to which the wells of history have been poisoned is shown most clearly by the school history textbook in use in Scotland and approved by the government's Scottish Qualifications Authority between 2013 and 2018.[11] It summarizes the myths succinctly.

In response, the government rushed 12,000 English troops to Glasgow in case a revolution broke out. Scottish troops were locked in their barracks at Maryhill in case they supported the strikers. There were tanks in George Square and machine-gun posts in buildings around the area. Newspapers reported that 90,000 people attended this demonstration … .

The Scottish Government's lead education body, Education Scotland, contributed its own 'alternative facts' in a teaching aid titled *The Road to the Scottish Parliament*.[12] The section on the 'Battle' read:

In an event unique in British history, Winston Churchill dispatched English troops and tanks against a large demonstration in George Square on 31st January 1919. The event became known as The Battle of George Square. Scottish troops already present in Glasgow were locked in Maryhill Barracks for fear that they might join the demonstrators and precipitate a major revolution. Thousands of English troops remained in Scotland for many months.

The nationalist spin being put on the 'Battle' in both these texts became a cause célèbre in 2020 when prominent historians accused the Scottish Government of distributing 'arrant propaganda', 'dangerous nonsense' and a 'perversion of history … frightening as it was blatantly political and clearly designed to support the cause of Scottish independence'.[13]

In these two examples, virtually everything is wrong: Churchill wasn't responsible, nor was the force sent by the government; the force was 10,000 not 12,000 and it was mainly Scots, called in by the sheriff, and they left within three weeks. The Maryhill myth is lifted straight from Gallacher. There were no tanks in George Square nor machine-gun posts in buildings around the Square. The crowd was between 20,000 and 30,000 strong – 90,000 people couldn't physically fit in the Square (below). In responding to enquiries about how Education Scotland could have published such obviously fake history, not only did they claim that their account was 'on the whole factually correct', they invented ten further wholly imaginary armoured vehicles being sent to the city, in addition to the six tanks![14]

Modern writers have not helped the situation and have gone beyond accepting the fifteen publications as reliable sources and have added to the mythology, especially in support of the conspiracy of the kind first floated by John Maclean in the immediate aftermath of the riot. It would have been a conspiracy if troops were being moved to Glasgow before the riot, and some writers have indeed claimed this. For example, in a book published at the centenary the author quoted a newspaper article supposedly published in Edinburgh on the afternoon of 31 January to support his claim that troops were already moving through Edinburgh, the implication being that this was before the sheriff called for help at 1.30 pm. However, his 'evidence' was actually published in Glasgow on the following day (1 February) and described the army arriving in the city late at night on 31 January.[15] Others have argued that the whole deployment had been planned days in advance, 'That Glasgow could have been placed under armed occupation without prior planning and consultation is inconceivable'.[16] Of course, the War Cabinet minutes show that the possibility of military aid was discussed on 30 January. And at the time, the British Army was the most efficiently organized army in the world and a deployment fifty miles from its local HQ in peacetime conditions, in nine to eighteen hours, with approximately eighteen hours' advance notice was entirely feasible.

Some academic historians have taken the conspiracy narrative to heart. One argues that the government deliberately engineered the military intervention in Glasgow to 'simply [provide] the necessary trigger for the anti-strike measures agreed by the cabinet …', and goes further, to claim this was done without involving the local authorities in any way, explicitly denying the clearly-evidenced role of the sheriff.[17] It is notable that not one of the twenty or so modern accounts we have consulted (until 2019) mentions the fact that the army was called for by the sheriff, either implying or stating explicitly that the government was responsible.[18]

The situation became much worse when documentary producers decided that the 'Battle' would make good television. In his book accompanying the 2009 *Making of Modern Britain* television documentary, Andrew Marr claims the tanks and troops were already on their way before the demonstrators in George Square had gathered.[19] Television documentaries like Marr's have played a significant role in the spread of the mythology, in particular the notion that 'there were tanks in George Square' (which we haven't found mentioned before 1994), rather than in the Cattle Market. At least twelve documentaries have included the events in George Square, in wider surveys of Scottish history or accounts of Red Clydeside, from 1965 to (so far) 2017. Starting in about 1980 documentary producers began using archive film of events in other places and other times in such a way as to illustrate clearly, but very misleadingly, that the viewer was seeing events in Glasgow in 1919. That 1980 documentary used an image of a tank sitting in a street in Liverpool in August 1919 to suggest that it was in Glasgow eight months earlier. The misrepresentation has been repeated in at least three subsequent programmes. Could this misuse of the Liverpool tank photograph be one source for the idea that there *were* 'tanks on the streets'? Certainly, the image has been used regularly on social media to 'prove' there were 'tanks in George Square'. The Glasgow tanks, in reality, were driven the short distance from College Goods Station to the Cattle Market and remained there, unused.

It is amazing what can be achieved by using misleading footage: a clip of a crowd roiling around a trapped horse-drawn wagon during the 1911 Dundee Carters' strike was also used in the 1980 documentary and has since been used several times to complement a voice-over about Glasgow in 1919.[20]

The most recent offender as far as the misrepresentation of images and film footage is concerned is the 2017 *Age of Tanks* documentary, in which a wide range of material of other times and other places is used to 'illustrate' events in Glasgow under an ominous narrative of 'revolution' and tanks as tools of 'oppression'. The false claim is made that the citizens of Glasgow were the first civilian population to be faced with tanks (that dubious honour belongs actually to Liverpool in August 1919). The image used here is of 'Julian's Baby' on a fundraising tour of the city in mid-January 1919, but in the *Age of Tanks* it is part of a sequence including the Liverpool tank footage and film from another anonymous fundraising parade: the 'Julian' tank parade from 1918, Glasgow's 'Tank Week'.

One of the strangest statements in any of Shinwell's memoirs was about tanks, which he claimed 'few in Glasgow had ever seen'. He also claimed that tanks were 'ostentatiously parked at strategic points' round the city.[21] If any evidence was needed that he was making things up as he went along, on the basis of a poor memory or his own wishful thinking, these examples would suffice. Glaswegians were not only 'familiar' with tanks, but at two points in the previous year had become quite dotty about them. In January 1918 tank 'Julian' had paraded through the streets between vast crowds, with the result that Glasgow contributed the greatest sum to war bonds of any town or city in Britain. The *Bulletin* newspaper had photographs and cartoons and descriptions of Julian and his sales success on the front and inner pages every single day that week. Such had been the success of the first 'Tank Week' that a second was run in the city in mid-January 1919, only a couple of weeks before the 'Battle'.

This time three tanks – two heavies, 'Haig' and 'Beattie', and a light Whippet tank, 'Julian's Baby' – arrived on 13 January 1919. The tanks paraded through the city and demonstrated their capabilities by climbing obstacles erected on Glasgow Green. Several dignitaries were given rides in 'Haig'. Most of the time the tanks were parked outside the City Chambers, where there were swift sales of Victory Bonds. Were confused memories of these events partly responsible for later claims of 'tanks in George Square'?

We can deal with the fabled 'howitzer' quickly here. No artillery was deployed and none was mentioned until it appeared in Harry McShane's memoir in 1978.[22] Neither the mainstream press nor the *Strike Bulletin,* which gleefully or with outrage respectively listed the military equipment taken to Glasgow, mention artillery. The idea that a 4.5 inch howitzer, weighing 1.3 tonnes, was in fact mounted on the roof of the City Chambers (leading to visions of sweating soldiers manhandling it up the marble staircases of the Chambers) is one of the dafter elements of the mythology. Fortunately, there is an explanation. In October 1918 a German 'trophy' howitzer had been gifted to the city, and it was displayed in George Square. There's even an image of it, festooned with small boys, in the *Daily Record.*[23]

So, what about those thousands of soldiers?

The military deployment to Glasgow is perhaps the event that most firmly cemented the riot into Glasgow's consciousness: 'the net effect of the tanks in the Cattle Market … gave the strike a romantic history which successfully concealed an otherwise ignominious failure'.[24] The deployment is also the event around which much of the mythology revolves: 'English troops'; the 'howitzer'; 'tanks in George Square'; 'machine guns on the roofs of buildings'; 'sent by government to crush the strike'; and even the imposition of martial law. Martial law is poorly defined; even General Robertson, commander of troops in Britain, would write: 'to me the position is still somewhat obscure' when asked to explain the mechanism for martial law coming into effect.[25] In Britain it could only be said to be in force if the general running, and especially the administration of justice, of a town or district was taken over by the military – for example, the replacement of civil courts by courts martial. It has never been in effect in modern times on the British mainland, and only once in the UK – in Ireland in 1920-21 during the independence crisis.[26] We say 'in effect' because, despite what is written about Ireland in 1920-21, in 1919 both senior military commanders and politicians seem not to have known of any formal process by which martial law could be 'declared'.

The suggestion that the military had 'occupied' or taken over the running of Glasgow was first made in the mainstream press and by John Wheatley in his response to the Lord Provost's statement on Thursday 6 February when he asked 'by what authority the city was placed under military control?'.[27]

What actually happened in Glasgow was not 'Martial Law' but the provision of 'Military Aid to the Civil Power'. Although the flawed *Road to the Scottish Parliament* document (above) claims what happened in Glasgow was 'an event unique in British history'; it was emphatically not. Indeed, local police and magistrates called for military aid to keep order so often in the late nineteenth and early twentieth centuries that, in 1908, Parliament appointed a Select Committee on the 'Employment of Military in Cases of Disturbances' to find out why this was so, and to find ways to stop local authorities relying excessively on military assistance.

The conclusions of the Select Committee informed the re-writing of the *King's Regulations for the Army* in 1912, the version still in force in 1919. One of the key principles discussed, in evidence given to the Standing Committee by the Secretary of State for War, Richard Haldane, was that 'the military have no discretion when they are called on' by the civil authorities – that is, they must respond to such a request, the government's approval is not required. Haldane disagreed with this only insofar as a situation might arise where the commander on the ground might decide that the presence of his men was not, in fact, required. This proviso was written into the 1912 edition of the *King's Regulations*.

An oddity of the Select Committee's remit was that it was limited to England and Ireland (although evidence was also given in relation to Wales). Even more surprising is the realization that a great deal of academic writing on the subject of the use of the military in keeping order in Britain works within the same boundaries. The consequence is that, while events in Glasgow are referenced in academic studies (albeit often repeating the mythology), authors seem at a loss to place them in the context of the separate systems of law and public administration that exist between England and Wales on the one hand, and Scotland. Studies of the use of military aid concentrate on the relationships between the Home Office, the Metropolitan Police, local police forces and the magistracy in England and Wales, within a framework of the (English) Common Law and Crown Prerogative. Of these, only the last is relevant to Scotland, where the Home Department responsibilities had been exercised by the Scottish Office since 1885, and where the Metropolitan Police had no locus.

Scotland in the late-nineteenth and early-twentieth centuries saw few episodes when military aid was called for. Amongst the many strikes in 1911, only the Dundee Carters' strike became sufficiently violent, and additional police from Edinburgh and Glasgow were supplied and military aid was called for by Dundee's Lord Provost. Of the thirty Scottish strikes in 1912 only the Leith dock strike required the local authority to call for aid, in this case in the form of the crews of six Royal Navy gunboats sent to the port.[28]

The formal framework for the deployment of military aid was set out solely in *The King's Regulations for the Army*, a document that had no separate legislative foundation. That lack was used by the government in 1911 to claim that the deployment of troops without request from local authorities was not a breach of the law, but only of practice.

Histories of the period and those discussing military aid to the civil power rarely discuss the vast size of the deployment to Glasgow – 10,000 men and six tanks. In the 'Great Unrest' of 1911, when the government in many instances broke the *King's Regulations* by itself deploying troops, rather than responding to requests from local authorities, a total of 58,000 troops was deployed in thirty-five English and Welsh towns and cities, an average deployment of only 1,600 troops. In August 1919, during the police strike in Liverpool, when the city was convulsed by violent non-political rioting and looting over a weekend, only 900 troops and perhaps a similar number of naval personnel were deployed. Why then such a large number of men despatched to Glasgow?

One explanation is that the army, when deciding on the forces to be deployed, and in the absence of reliable intelligence, prepared for the very worst they might face – perhaps a re-run of the Easter Rising in Dublin in 1916.[29] This may be part of the explanation, but perhaps there was another factor: did the particular mix of personalities and political aims of senior figures in the army contribute? At the time there was a struggle for control of troops to be used for internal security duties in Britain.

Throughout the interwar period 'Most military chiefs ... hoped that troops would not be used on a massive scale in policing as they had been before 1914'.[30] But an influential group of reactionary senior army officers was particularly fearful of the possibility of revolution and sought to influence their colleagues and their political masters. The most influential of these was Sir Henry Wilson, 'the worst political general', an inveterate intriguer, deeply conservative and an active Irish Unionist. As Director of Military Operations in 1914 he had supported the officers in the 'Curragh Incident', who made it clear that they would refuse to lead their men to implement the Home Rule Bill in Ulster.[31] He had, nevertheless, become professional head of the British Army in the spring of 1918.

The views of senior army officers who did not share Wilson's perspective were represented by General Macdonogh, the Adjutant General. Part of the struggle between their two positions concerned which part of the army command structure should be responsible for overseeing the provision of military aid to the civil power, the extent to which the army should be actively involved in planning such interventions and the location of troops, because units scattered about the country in case of civil disturbance could not be training and doing their basic job of soldiering. Wilson wanted to move responsibility from the Adjutant General to the operational arm – the Military Operations Directorate, more firmly under his control. Both sides of the argument would have claimed to prefer that soldiers were involved as little as possible in 'aid to the civil power', but Wilson's exaggerated fears of revolution coloured his views and his actions.[32] Wilson went so far in 1920 as to sound out Churchill to be ready to lead a coup against Lloyd George as he (Wilson) feared that Lloyd George was a traitor, because of his policy of rapprochement with the Soviet Union.[33]

Both Wilson and Macdonogh were present at the key War Cabinet meeting on 30 January at which the situation in Glasgow was discussed, but neither was present on 31 January when the sheriff's request was reported upon. However, Major General Romer was at both meetings, a man who had been 'extensively occupied in duties connected with industrial unrest' who Wilson later would want as 'the senior officer … to take over executive command of all troops in Great Britain in the event of a serious internal upheaval'. It was Romer who reported at the 31 January meeting that tanks and 100 lorries would be sent north that night.

Wilson's and Romer's intention in sending such a huge force to Scotland may have been to paint the events in Glasgow as particularly threatening, to convince others that Wilson's view of the risks of revolution were indeed real: a 'great' response must surely indicate a 'great' threat? The presence of the tanks in Glasgow, although not used, may be attributed to Wilson's enthusiasm for the tank arm.[34]

But where has the myth of 'raw recruits' and 'English' troops come from?

The claim that the soldiers arriving in Glasgow were young soldiers, even 'raw recruits', seems to have been Gallacher's in 1936. In reality, the contemporary newspaper reports note mature men returned from France, with medal ribbons and wound stripes. Gallacher, of course, was in prison for the whole time the army was in Glasgow, along with Shinwell and Kirkwood and saw none of the soldiers.

The 'all the troops were English' element is a more recent addition to the mythology of the 'Battle' and has been used, in conjunction with the idea that 'Scots troops were locked in their barracks because they couldn't be trusted', to drive the narrative of an 'English invasion', 'English troops sent by Churchill' to 'crush the Scots/the strike/the revolution'. This part of the myth seems to have grown in fits and starts, from Gallacher's *Revolt on the Clyde*, in which he claimed that the Scots troops weren't used because they might join the strikers. By 1966 this had become the 'fact' that the troops were 'from England'. In 1957 Patrick Dollan, who had edited the *Strike Bulletin* (and had served as Glasgow's first Labour Lord Provost 1939-1941) published a memoir in the *Sunday Mail*. It repeats many of the myths: machine-gun muzzles trained on people in George Square; tanks trundling into the city centre; 50,000 in the Square; and train loads of English troops, although he also mentions 'Highlanders'. By 1973 John Maclean's daughter had reduced this to only the 'trainloads of young English soldiers' in a biography of her father, while another biography of Maclean in the same year claimed 'Significantly most of the soldiers were English'.[35] It is not difficult to see how this aspect of the myth has entered educational materials and mainstream popular history.

The mythology of the 'Battle', especially the 'English invasion', has become one of a number of invented pieces of grievance history centred round Scotland's military, now regularly repeated in support of Scottish independence – what 'the English have done to us'.[36]

Part of the mythology of the 'Battle' – once again courtesy of Gallacher – is that men of the 'local' regiment, the Highland Light Infantry (HLI), were locked into Maryhill Barracks, because it was feared that they might side with the strikers. But the HLI was not based at Maryhill in 1919. The barracks had been occupied since December 1918 by the 4th (Reserve) Battalion of the Royal Scots Fusiliers, the county regiment of Ayrshire and the south-west of Scotland.

These 'Reserve' battalions had become responsible during the war for inducting and training the huge number of men needed to form and reinforce each regiment's many battalions on active service. It was from these reserve battalions that the force was drawn which was deployed to Glasgow, described by General Robertson (Commander-in-Chief Great Britain) at the War Cabinet meeting on 30 January as:

> reserve-finding units, and consisted of all sorts of men, old, young, convalescent, and men with wounds. As regards their officers, these were not very efficient.[37]

By 1919 the reserve battalions were mainly based in vast purpose-built hutted camps and, even in early 1919, the number of men in these units could exceed 3,000 and included large numbers of men who had returned from France ready to be demobbed.[38]

Contemporary newspaper reports list units from seven regiments. Where two locations are mentioned, there were two reserve battalions available: Royal Scots (near Edinburgh); King's Own Scottish Borderers (Dunfermline); East Surrey Regiment (Bridge of Allan); Seaforth Highlanders (Cromarty and Edinburgh); Gordon Highlanders (Aberdeen and Edinburgh); Argyll and Sutherland Highlanders (Dunbar and Galashiels); Durham Light Infantry (South Shields and Seaham Harbour).

The choice of troops, and the weeding out of Glasgow men reported from at least one Seaforth battalion that was sent, clearly conforms to the army's longstanding policy of 'distant locality' – that is only using men originating from outside the affected area when military aid was provided.[39]

With 10,000 troops arriving in Glasgow, what size of turbulent crowd had they been told to expect?

A feature of the development of the story of the 'Battle' is the way that the reported size of the crowd in George Square has continued to grow. At the time of the trial both sides accepted a figure of 20,000-25,000. This range was attested to by seven police witnesses, but outliers as low as 6,000-7,000 (Constable McCormick) and as high as 70,000 were also claimed (Constable Ritchie). An anonymous report in the files of the Ministry of Munitions claimed 60,000.[40] As already noted, in 2013 a Scottish school textbook claimed 90,000 and two general history books of Scotland have put it as high as 100,000 or more.[41] The estimation of crowd size is fraught with difficulties. Even people experienced in crowd management can inflate the size of a crowd by a factor of ten.[42] In an evenly distributed crowd an observer, even in a raised position, will see a more distant part of the crowd as being denser, the 'density perspective illusion'.[43] If the person estimating the size sees advantage in exaggerating or minimizing the crowd size – to enhance or diminish the significance of the event – this will cause further problems.

One thing is clear: no one who has bandied these higher figures about has ever thought about just how many people might fit into the Square, nor considered what the recorded behaviour of the crowd tells us about its density. George Square is, when measured out to the buildings lining it, 19,127 square metres in area; the pedestrian area within the bounding roads is 10,600 square metres. 'Hard' constraints – thirteen statues and a cabman's shelter that stood in the Square in 1919 – reduce these figures by 286 square metres. The 'soft' constraints – ten areas of grass and flower beds (3,618 square metres) – which would normally be avoided by people, were being trampled over even before the riot. Fortunately, the low fences protecting them had been removed at the initiative of defence witness Councillor Mitchell only a few weeks before. It is frightening to think of the greater number of injuries that might have occurred had these trip hazards still been in place during the rapid movements of the crowd later on.

The crowd varied considerably in density in different parts of the Square and at different times during the day as attested to by the police accompanying various processions, who noted different times for their arrival in the Square. People in a crowd that starts as evenly distributed will tend to move towards a centre of attraction, as in the drift towards the east and south-east recorded in George Square. Descriptions at the trial of the crowd's density and the way it moved were coloured by the needs particularly of the defence, who wanted to establish that the people in the south-east corner were on the tram tracks *because of* pressure from a dense crowd behind. Descriptions of the crowd's reaction to the first baton charge show, however, that people had room to move away quickly from the police, but that it was dense enough to set off a movement of people behind, towards the door of the City Chambers, but that the crowd was not sufficiently dense for this sudden and violent movement to lead to falls or crush injuries. The crowd also recoiled rapidly from the second and third baton charges, from in front of the City Chambers, without crush injuries, falls being explained by tripping over obstructions and batoning rather than crowd density. The only newsreel film of the event shows the crowd running freely past the front of the City Chambers.[44] None of the more balanced police reports, either in precognition or at trial, described such difficulties in moving through the Square, in particular Detective Inspector Louis Noble, who observed from several points and described in great detail what he saw, did not include details of difficulty traversing the Square.

Although the defence case was that the obstruction of the tram traffic in the south-east corner was caused by the crowd spilling onto the roadway because of the pressure from behind, the tram traffic ran without hindrance for the rest of the afternoon, once the obstruction had been cleared.

At densities of six or seven people per square metre, individuals are surrounded on all sides and are in physical contact with each other. In this circumstance the energy of a push at one side of the crowd will be transmitted through it as a compression wave or shockwave, gaining momentum as it proceeds, which 'only occurs when the crowd density is such that there is no space between individuals'.[45] In these circumstances individuals cannot move their feet to counter the push, people fall like dominoes, have difficulty rising, and others trip over them and there are crush injuries.[46]

The average area occupied by a person is calculated to be 0.2 square metres, including a small amount of space round each body.[47] Theoretically at least, five people could fit into a metre square, and 500 could fit into 100 square metres, but only if they were static and evenly distributed.[48] At this density someone would find it difficult to move through or leave the crowd; someone falling might find it difficult to stand again. At densities of six or seven people per square metre, people would be in physical contact; this density may have been reached round a speaker on the plinth of the Gladstone statue. Any shock to the crowd – a push on one side – could be transmitted right through the crowd, people could fall, and could be unable to stand up again but there are no reports of this happening. Even at five people per square metre movement is slow and awkward – people have difficulty maintaining balance. What we know about the crowd in George Square, in particular its movement under the stress of the police baton charges, suggests that the crowd was generally not so dense. It recoiled; people ran as Gallacher described from his position on the Gladstone statue plinth.

Using this theoretical 'maximum packing capacity' of 500 people in 100 square metres, one might cram 51,500 people into the pedestrian area of the Square. But this would be an evenly distributed crowd incapable of movement. A crowd of 30,000 would require a density of around four per square metre in the internal area of the Square.

The calculations and the anecdotal evidence suggest strongly that in every part of the Square where the police charged the crowd, the crowd was able to move away rapidly, without any of the problems that such pressure would cause in a tightly packed crowd. This would support the case for the lower (20,000-25,000) estimates for the crowd size used by most contemporaries. Some witnesses report many people in side streets off the Square, and others describe being delayed in these streets as they made their way into the Square. But there is no evidence that the crowds in the side streets were there because of overcrowding in the Square: there were many people there merely as onlookers.

What can we conclude?

> the doctrine that history exists to fulfil a social need … confusing history and mythology. What society calls for – and too often gets – is not history but myth, the cement which holds all society together.[49]

We have endeavoured to present the facts dispassionately, as they can be gleaned from all the sources, with the intention that, for the first time in over

100 years, the history of Bloody Friday can be read by a wider audience without recourse to the thousands of pages of original source material now available.

It has been suggested that our desire to explore the evidence for the events and their proximate causes reflects 'no interest in interpreting the events of Bloody Friday or in discussing its meaning' and, further, that it misses the point that 'the myth is the history' now.[50] But how can anyone 'interpret the events' if the event is not as thoroughly understood as the archival sources allow?

We are strongly of the view that there should be room not only to explore the power and meaning of the mythology, but also to write a history more securely founded on evidence, with which the mythology can be compared. It is surely also worth trying to understand how such a powerful but substantially mythologized history has been created in the teeth of the evidence. But these approaches appear to provoke hostility. We seem to be encouraged to accept the alternative described by Holocaust historian Deborah Lipstadt in which the notion of 'truth' has no validity and in which 'Any truth can be retold. Any fact can be recast'. 'This', writes Lipstadt 'has nothing to do with ideas. This is bigotry'.[51]

Everyone involved in the strikes, riots and trial in 1919 had an agenda, and so it seems now do historians, writers, educators, members of the public and politicians. In 1919 the strike leadership tried to shift blame onto a supposed hooligan element in the crowd; later, when convenient, they celebrated their violent resistance to the police, while presenting it as a 'good fight' by a crowd of thousands facing fewer than 200 policemen.[52] The police and prosecution counsel attempted to paint the strikers as selfish malcontents threatening the citizenry of Glasgow with fears of revolution not far behind.

The court papers require close reading to try to establish what happened in late January 1919. There were no revolutionaries but there were no tanks on the streets either. There were few English troops, and no 'unprovoked attack on a peaceful crowd'.

The most telling conclusion was provided by the Lord Justice Clerk, Scott Dickson, in charging the jury at the trial: in his summing up he showed how limited a threat the establishment by then considered events in Glasgow to have been. He told the jury not to convict half of the accused and sentenced only two men to prison for the major crime of incitement to riot, and, considering the seriousness of the charges, for very short sentences – five and three months.[53] By 18 April 1919 concerns about

Clydeside had been replaced by more pressing matters: strikes elsewhere, housing, employment and health.

The 'heroes' of Bloody Friday would take to constitutional politics and end up knighted, or in the House of Lords, or as an 'uncritical supporter' of Soviet communism.

Sources & Select Bibliography

Archival Sources

National Records of Scotland, High Court of Justiciary papers

AD15/19/11 precognition series
JC26/1919/85 criminal trial papers
JC36/31/01-09 trial transcript

National Archives at Kew

Cabinet Papers: CAB/23/9 and CAB/24/74, 75 and 93 series
War Office Papers: WO 32 and WO 73 series

Mitchell Library, Glasgow City Archives

TD241/1/16-18 miscellaneous papers of Glasgow Trades' Council
TD2020/1/2-3 Clyde Shipbuilders' Association minutes

Contemporary and Primary Sources

Bell, T., *John Maclean: a fighter for freedom*, (Glasgow, 1944)
Gallacher, W., *Revolt on the Clyde*, (Chadwell Heath, 2017)
Johnston, T., *The History of the Working Classes in Scotland*, (Glasgow, 1922)
Keedy, E.R., 'Criminal Procedure in Scotland', *Journal of the American Institute of Criminal Law and Criminology*, volume 3, (1912), pp.728-53

_____, 'Criminal Procedure in Scotland II', *Journal of the American Institute of Criminal Law and Criminology*, volume 3, issue 6, (1913), pp.834-54

Kirkwood, D., *My Life of Revolt*, (London, 1935)

MacGregor Mitchell, R., *A Practical Treatise on the Criminal Law of Scotland, by the late Right Honourable Sir J. H. A. Macdonald*, (Edinburgh, 1929)

McShane, H. & Smith, J., *Harry McShane: No Mean Fighter*, (London, 1978)

Shinwell, E., *Conflict without Malice*, (London, 1955); *I've lived through it all*, (London, 1973); *Lead with the Left: My first Ninety-Six Years*, (London, 1981)

Newspapers & Magazines

Daily Mirror

Daily Record

[Glasgow] *Evening News*

Forward

Glasgow Herald

Manchester Guardian

Strike Bulletin

The Bulletin

The Liberator

The Observer

The Times of London

The Worker

179

Secondary Sources – Books, Chapters & Journal Articles

Baillie, M., 'A New View of Dilution: Women Munitions Workers and Red Clydeside', *Scottish Labour History Society*, volume 39, (2004), pp.32-49

Barclay, G.J., '"Churchill rolled the tanks into the crowd": mythology and reality in the military deployments to Glasgow in 1919', *Scottish Affairs*, (January, 2019), pp.32-62

_____, '"Duties in Aid of the Civil Power"': The Deployment of the Army to Glasgow, 31 January to 17 February 1919', *Journal of Scottish Historical Studies*, volume 38, issue 2, (November, 2018), pp.261-92

_____, '"The evidence has always been there": unreliable narrators and archival sources for the Battle of George Square, Glasgow 31 January 1919', *Scottish Archives*, volume 25/26, (2021), pp.108-22

Bellamy, M., 'Shipbuilding and Cultural Identity on Clydeside', *Journal for Maritime Research*, (January, 2006), pp.1-33

_____, *The Shipbuilders: An Anthology of Scottish Shipyard Life*, (Edinburgh, 2001)

Brown, G., *Maxton*, (Edinburgh, 1986)

Craig, M., *When the Clyde ran Red: a social history of Red Clydeside*, (Edinburgh, 2018)

Damer, S., *Glasgow: Going for a Song*, (London, 1990)

Dickson, T., ed, *Scottish Capitalism: class, state and nation from before the Union to the Present*, (London, 1980)

_____, ed, *Capital and Class in Scotland*, (Edinburgh, 1982)

Donnachie, I. & Whatley, C., eds, *The Manufacture of Scottish History*, (Edinburgh, 1992)

Duncan, R. & McIvor, A., *Militant Workers: Labour and Class Conflict on the Clyde 1900-1950, essays in honour of Harry McShane (1891-1988)*, (Edinburgh, 1992)

Evans, R.J., *In Defence of History*, (London, 1997)

Foster, J., 'The 1919 Forty Hours Strike', *Theory and Struggle*, volume 120, issue 1, (2019), pp.30-40

_____, 'Strike Action and Working-Class Politics on Clydeside 1914-1919', *International Review of Social History*, volume XXXV, (1990), pp.33-70

Fowler, S. & Weinbren, D., *Now the War is Over, Britain 1918-1920*, (Barnsley, 2018)

Goldsmith, A.L., 'The Development of the City of Glasgow Police c. 1800-1939', unpublished PhD thesis, (University of Strathclyde, 2002)

Gordon, P., *Policing Scotland*, (Glasgow, 1980)

Harvie, C., *No Gods and Precious Few Heroes: Scotland since 1914*, (Edinburgh, 1981)

Jackson, L.A., with Davidson, N., Fleming, L., Smale, D.M. & Sparks, R., *Police and Community in Twentieth-Century Scotland*, (Edinburgh, 2020)

Jenkinson, J., 'Black Sailors on Red Clydeside: Rioting, Reactionary Trade Unionism and Conflicting Notions of "Britishness" following the First World War', *Twentieth Century British History*, volume 19, no 1, (2008), pp.29-60

Knox, W., *Industrial Nation: work, culture and society in Scotland, 1800-Present*, (Edinburgh, 1999)

_____, *James Maxton*, (Manchester, 1987)

_____, *Scottish Labour Leaders 1918-1939*, (Edinburgh, 1984)

McLean, I., *The Legend of Red Clydeside*, (Edinburgh, 1999)

Marwick, A., *The Deluge: British Society and the First World War*, (London, 1965)

Middlemas, R.K., *The Clydesiders: a left wing struggle for Parliamentary power*, (London, 1965)

Reynolds, G.W. & Judge, A., *The Night the Police went on Strike*, (London, 1968)

Shiels, R.S., 'The Criminal Trials of John Maclean', *Judicial Review*, volume 1, (2001), pp.1-21

_____, 'The Mid-Victorian Codification of the Practice of Public Prosecution', *The Scottish Historical Review*, vol. 98, supplement no. 248, (October, 2019), pp.410-38

_____, 'The Crown Practice of Precognition in Mid-Victorian Scotland', *Law, Crime and History*, vol. 2, (2015), pp.29-43

Slowe, P., *Manny Shinwell: an authorised biography*, (London, 1993)

Smith, J., 'Labour Tradition in Glasgow and Liverpool', *History Workshop*, no 17, (Spring, 1984), pp.32-56

Smout, T.C., *A Century of the Scottish People 1830-1950*, (London, 1986)

Storch, R., 'The Policeman as domestic missionary: urban discipline and popular culture in Northern England, 1850-1880', *The Journal of Social History*, (1976), pp.481-509

Webb, S., *1919 Britain's Year of Revolution*, (Barnsley, 2016)

Weinberger, B., *The Best Police in the World*, (Cambridge, 1995)

_____, *Keeping the Peace? Policing Strikes in Britain, 1906-1926*, (Oxford, 1991)

Winter, J.M., *Socialism and the Challenge of War: ideas and politics in Britain 1912-18*, (Aldershot, 1993)

Notes

Authors' Foreword

1. Evans, *In Defence of History* (London, 2000), p.121
2. Knox, 'What ever happened to Red Clydeside?', unpublished paper delivered at the Scottish Economic and Social History Conference, Caledonian University, Glasgow (November 1998)
3. Evans, *In Defence*, p.252

Introduction

1. Morton, 'The 40 Hours Strike: An Historic Survey of the First General Strike in Scotland', (Clydebank Branch of Socialist Labour Party, 1919) p.1
2. Kirkwood, *My Life of Revolt*, (London, 1935), p.171
3. Morris, 'Urbanisation and Scotland', eds Fraser & Morris, *People and Society in Scotland, Volume II, 1830-1914*, (Edinburgh, 1990), p.1 Table 1; Gray, *Scottish Population Statistics including Webster's Analysis of Population 1755*, vol. 44, series 3, (Edinburgh, 1952), p.xvii
4. Harvie, *No Gods and Precious Few Heroes: Scotland since 1914*, (Edinburgh, 1981), p.4
5. *Report of the Royal Commission on the House of the Industrial Population of Scotland*, (Edinburgh, 1917), pp.4-5; *Departmental Committee on Sexual Offences against Children and Young Persons in Scotland*, (Edinburgh, 1926), pp.40-2; 10.9% of Glasgow's houses contained over 4 persons per room with 55.7% housing over 2 people per room; comparable figures for England were 0.8% and 9.4 percent.
6. Smout, *A Century of the Scottish People 1830-1950*, (London, 1986), p.50
7. Anderson & Morse, 'The People', eds Fraser & Morris, *People and Society*, p.30 Table 1
8. Brown, *Maxton*, (Edinburgh, 1986), p.88

9. Smout, *Century of the Scottish People,* p.51
10. Crowther & White, *On Soul and Conscience: the medical expert and crime*, (Aberdeen, 1988), p.52
11. Smout, *Century of the Scottish People*, pp.255-6
12. Dickson, *Scottish Capitalism: class, state and nation from before the Union to the Present*, (London, 1980), p.266
13. Marwick, *The Deluge: British Society and the First World War*, (London, 1965), p.70
14. Keedy, 'Criminal Procedure in Scotland II', *Journal of the American Institute for Criminal Law and Criminology*, vol.3, no.6, (1913), pp.835-6; Shiels, 'The Mid-Victorian Codification of the Practice of Public Prosecution' *The Scottish Historical Review*, vol.98, supplement 248, (October, 3019), p.436
15. Gallacher, *Revolt on the Clyde*, (London, 2017), p.164; we invite other researchers to assist in our search for any evidence to support Gallacher's supposed 'quotation'.
16. War Cabinet minute, 523, 31 January 1919, National Archives CAB23/9/, p.2

Chapter 1: Morning, Friday, 31 January 1919

1. *Glasgow Herald*, 28 January 1919, p.5
2. https://digital.nmla.metoffice.gov.uk/IO_07f09c27-1b87-4e38-a7a9-2ac974e66b11/ p.127 accessed January 2022
3. Knox, 'A History of the Scottish People: Urban Housing in Scotland, 1840-1940', SCRAN, chapter 4, p.3; *Royal Commission on the Housing of the Industrial Population of Scotland Rural and Urban*, (Edinburgh, 2017), pp.90-100
4. JC36/31/06 (Wallace)
5. In their precognitions, most policemen provided an estimate of crowd sizes at the events they attended. However, they were wildly different when estimating attendance in George Square itself although the majority of police witnesses estimated between 20,000 and 30,000 (see chapter 10). Police 'District' is used in preference to 'Division' because it is the term most frequently used by the police in their precognitions.
6. AD15/19/11, pp.167-8 (Gillies)
7. AD15/19/11, pp.97-8 (Gallagher)
8. AD15/19/11, pp.55-6 (Steele)
9. JC36/31/06 (Wallace)
10. AD15/19/11, p.57 (Steele); p.168 (Gillies)

11. JC36/31/04 (Stevenson)
12. Gallacher, *Revolt on the Clyde*, (Chadwell Heath, 2017), p.160; Foster, 'Red Clyde, Red Scotland', *The Manufacture of Scottish History*, eds Donnachie & Whatley, (Edinburgh, 1992), p.106; see FN2 for official weather forecast
13. AD15/19/11, p.113 (Gray)
14. The rank of lieutenant equated to that of chief inspector and was used in some Scottish county and burgh forces. It was changed to chief inspector in 1948. In Glasgow in 1919, uniformed lieutenants worked in parallel with plain-clothes chief detective inspectors.
15. JC36/31/09 (Sim)
16. AD15/19/11, p.114 (Gray)
17. AD15/19/11, p.20 (Lindsay); p.66 (Ritchie)
18. AD15/19/11, p.22 (Lindsay)
19. Minutes of a Meeting of the War Cabinet, 30 January 1919; National Archives, CAB23/9/9, p.5
20. Joint Meeting of the Executive Committees of the Engineers' and Shipbuilders' Associations, 30 January 1919, pp.142-3, Mitchell Library, TD241/1/18. The Clyde Federation of Shipbuilders' delegation to the Lord Provost appears to have been an unminuted consultation. However, their official meeting later on 31 January 1919 lists all representatives present at West George Street; the Lord Provost's name is not included. Thus, it appears the delegation met the Lord Provost earlier that morning and his responses were reported at their later meeting, which probably took place before the disturbances in the Square.
21. JC36/31/03 (Stewart) The Lord Provost provides conflicting information concerning his awareness of the time of the strike leaders' arrival. In his precognition statement (AD15/19/11, p.13) he says he received the secretary of the Trades Council, William Shaw's letter indicating the time of the deputation's arrival on Thursday 30 January. In his trial evidence he denies any knowledge of an arranged meeting; JC36/31/03. Either way, it is unlikely he would have been able to cancel the magistrates' meeting at short notice to accommodate the strike leaders' delegation. The *Workers' Dreadnought* claimed that the magistrates telephoned the Lord Provost at 11.30am to request his presence at their meeting; *Workers' Dreadnought*, 15 February 1919, p.1228
22. JC36/31/03 (Stewart)
23. JC36/31/02 (Lindsay); AD15/19/11, pp.1-4 (MacKenzie)

24. In the Minutes of the Corporation of Glasgow, 31 January 1919, Parks, Open Spaces & North of River Clyde sub-committee Mitchell is listed as present. This meeting was held within the Municipal Buildings. In his trial evidence Mitchell also confirms he was working at the Sheriff Court, JC36/31/05 (Mitchell), which he may have been earlier before the parks or finance meeting commenced.
25. JC36/31/05 (Mitchell)
26. JC36/31/08 (Forman)
27. JC36/31/06 (Wallace)
28. AD15/19/11, p.145-6 (Noble); *Glasgow Herald*, 1 February 1919, p.5
29. See Chapter 10 for discussion of crowd density.
30. Gallacher, *Revolt on the Clyde*, p.160
31. AD15/19/11, p.145 (Noble)
32. Kirkwood, *My Life of Revolt*, (London, 1935), p.172
33. AD15/19/11, p.154 (McArthur)
34. AD14/19/11, pp.234-5 (Cummings); p.243 (Buchanan); pp.237-8 (Sutherland)
35. AD15/19/11, p.59 (Ritchie); pp.243-5 (Buchanan); JC36/31/02 (Cree)
36. AD15/19/11, p.122 (Cree); pp.234-5 (Cummings)
37. AD15/19/11, pp.320-1 (Naismith)
38. AD15/19/11, pp.231-2 (McCulloch); JC36/31.09 (Sim & Maclean)
39. AD15/19/11, pp.117-18 (Gray); p.55 (Steele); pp.237-8 (Sutherland); JC36/31/02 (Cree)
40. JC36/31/06 (Wallace)
41. In his memoir, McShane stated the crowd stood its ground at the first baton charge; McShane, *No Mean Fighter*, (London, 1978), p.106. Analysis of the precognitions and trial transcript describe otherwise.
42. AD15/19/11, pp.6 & 22 (MacKenzie & Lindsay)
43. AD15/19/11, p.238 (Sutherland)
44. AD15/19/11, pp.57-8 (Steele)
45. Gallacher, *Revolt on the Clyde*, p.160; AD15/19/11, p.108 (Turner); pp.114-15 (Gray); p.215 (Miller)
46. AD15/19/11, p.83 (Gargan)
47. Kirkwood, *My Life of Revolt*, p.49
48. JC36/31/09 (Maclean) The photograph was produced in court.
49. Kirkwood, *My Life of Revolt*, p.172 Kirkwood's account is unclear whether he was knocked fully unconscious or not. AD15/19/11, pp.58 (Steele); pp.67-8 (Ritchie); p.221 (Melrose); JC36/31/09 (Maclean)
50. JC36/31/07 (Highton)

51. Jackson, Davidson, Fleming, Smale & Sparks, *Police and Community in Twentieth-Century Scotland,* (Edinburgh, 2020), p.57
52. *The Bulletin,* 1 February 1919, p.front
53. AD15/19/11, p.321 (Naismith); Knox & McKinlay, 'Crime, Protest and Policing in Nineteenth-Century Scotland', eds. Griffiths & Morton, *A History of Everyday life in Scotland 1800-1900,* (Edinburgh, 2010), p.222
54. In their precognition statements, MacKenzie says he witnessed the baton charge in front of the Buildings; Lindsay says they were both in the Magistrates' Room at the time and did not see it. AD15/19/11 p.7 (MacKenzie), p.23 (Lindsay)
55. *The London Gazette,* 3 August 1917, p.7914
56. AD15/19/11, p.22 (Lindsay)
57. AD15/19/11, Meeting of the Town Council of the City of Glasgow held within the City Chambers on Thursday, 6 February 1919, p.19
58. JC36/31/06 (Stewart); AD15/19/11, p.22 (Lindsay)
59. It has occasionally been claimed that the sheriff's failure to complete the reading of the Proclamation of the Riot Act invalidated MacKenzie's reading. The Act, however, makes provision for such a failure insisting only that it need be read 'in these words or like effect'; Riot Act 1714, 1 Geo. 1, St.2, c.5
60. AD15/19/11, p.42 (Mennie); p.126 (Keith)
61. JC36/31/06 (Wallace); the rank of chief detective inspector is that given in the individual's precognition statement and trial transcript.
62. JC36/31/04 (Rennie)
63. Kirkwood, *My Life of Revolt,* p.173
64. AD15/19/11, pp.10-11 (MacKenzie); pp.24-6 (Lindsay); p.31 (Stevenson); JC36/31/05 (Mitchell); JC36/31/07 (McBain)

Chapter 2: Monday, 27 January 1919

1. McLean, *The Legend of Red Clydeside,* (Edinburgh, 1983), p.121
2. *Manchester Guardian,* 27 January 1919, p.5
3. *Manchester Guardian,* 27 January 1919, p.5
4. Lloyd George, quoted Foster, 'Red Clyde, Red Scotland', *The Manufacture of Scottish History,* eds Donnachie & Whatley, (Edinburgh, 1992), p.117
5. Marwick, *The Deluge: British Society and the First World War,* (Basingstoke, 1973), pp.69 & 72-3; *Manchester Guardian,* 27 January 1919, p.5

6. *Memorandum on Movements for Reductions in Hours of Labour*, National Archives, CAB24/74/12, p.43; McLean, *Legend*, pp.113-14

7. Eastman, 'The Workers of the Clyde', *The Liberator*, (October 1919), p.31; *Glasgow Herald*, 23 January 1919, p.5

8. Middlemas, *The Clydesiders: a left-wing struggle for Parliamentary Power*, (London, 1965), p.90

9. 'Report No.31', *Fortnightly Report on Revolutionary Organisations in the United Kingdom and Abroad*, National Archives, CAB24/74/13, pp.1-2; War Cabinet 519, *Minutes of a Meeting of the War Cabinet*, 24 January 1919, CAB23/9/6, p.2

10. *The Worker*, 25 January 1919, pp.1-2; 'The Labour Situation', Secret, GT6792, *Report from the Ministry of Labour for the week ending 12th February 1919*, National Archives, CAB24/74/96, p.2

11. *The Bulletin*, 25 January 1919, p.2

12. *Glasgow Herald*, 27 January 1919, p.8

13. *Manchester Guardian*, 27 January 1919, p.5

14. *Glasgow Herald*, 25 January 1919, p.5; *Manchester Guardian*, 27 January 1919, p.5

15. *Glasgow Herald*, 24 January 1919, p.6

16. *Manchester Guardian*, 27 January 1919, p.5; Minutes of the Executive Committee of the Engineers' and Shipbuilders' Association, 20 January 1919, p.25, Mitchell Library, TD24/1/18

17. *Manchester Guardian*, 27 January 1919, p.5; *Glasgow Herald*, 25 January 1919, p.6

18. Foster, 'The 1919 Forty Hours Strike', *Theory and Struggle*, vol.120, issue 1, (2019), p.33

19. *The Bulletin*, 28 January 1919, p.2

20. *Bulletin*, 27 January 1919, p.2

21. Ibid.

22. Kirkwood, *My Life of Revolt*, (London, 1935), p.64-5, 87

23. Middlemas, *Clydesiders*, p.99

24. Kirkwood, *My Life of Revolt*, p.89

25. *Glasgow Herald*, 28 January 1919, p.5

26. Kirkwood, *My Life of Revolt*, pp.100-2; AD15/19/11, p.105 (Board)

27. Smith, 'Labour Tradition in Glasgow and Liverpool', *History Workshop*, no.17, (Spring, 1984), p.38

28. Kirkwood, *My Life of Revolt*, p.106

29. Gallacher, *Revolt on the Clyde*, pp.71-74

30. Marwick, *Deluge*, p.73; Middlemas, *Clydesiders*, p.65

31. *Glasgow Herald*, 28 December 1915, p.4; Gallacher, *Revolt on the Clyde*, p.82-3
32. Middlesmas, *Clydesiders*, p.66-7; Parliamentary Papers 1914-16, XXIX 297
33. Morton, *The 40 Hours Strike: a historic survey of the First General Strike in Scotland*, (February, 1919), p.7; *Glasgow Herald*, 28 January 1919, p.5
34. McShane, *No Mean Fighter*, (London, 1978), p.104
35. JC36/31/08 (Chappell); *Glasgow Herald*, 28 January 1919, pp.5-6
36. AD15/19/11, p.104 (Turner)
37. AD15/19/11, pp.91-2 (Lingard)
38. *Glasgow Herald*, 28 January 1919, p.6; AD15/19/11, p.104 (Turner); p.92 (Gallagher)
39. *Daily News*, 28 January 1919, p.1
40. JC36/31/07 (Highton)
41. *The Scotsman*, 28 January 1919, pp.5-6
42. *Glasgow Herald*, 28 January 1919, pp.5-6
43. Photograph, *The Bulletin*, 28 January 1919, p.9
44. AD15/19/11, p.92 (Gallagher)
45. AD15/19/11, p.110 (Gray)
46. AD15/19/11, p.124 (Keith)
47. AD15/19/11, p.110 (Gray); Andrew Gallagher estimates 7-8,000 (AD15/19/11), p.92
48. *Glasgow Herald*, 28 January 1919, p.6; *The Scotsman*, 28 January 1919, p.5
49. *The Bulletin*, 28 January 1919, p.1
50. AD15/19/11, p.136 (Weir)
51. AD15/19/11, p.93 (Gallacher); p.129 (Thomson); p.118 (Murdoch)
52. AD15/19/11, p.49 (Steele)
53. JC36/31/09 (Maclean); he is not mentioned in any of the police precognitions at this stage.
54. AD15/19/11, p.118 (Murdoch); p.104 (Turner)
55. AD15/19/11, p.94 (Gallagher); p.104 (Turner)
56. JC36/31/04 (Stevenson)
57. AD15/19/11, attachment to precognition (Stevenson)
58. AD15/19/11, p.27 (Stevenson)
59. Webb, *1919: Britain's Year of Revolution*, (Barnsley, 2016), pp.29-32
60. Gallacher, *Revolt on the Clyde*, p.156
61. *Glasgow Herald*, 28 January 1919, p.6
62. Gallacher, *Revolt on the Clyde*, p.85-8

63. Hansard, 28 March 1916, Fifth series, vol.81, cc.564-67
64. Hansard, 28 March 1916, Fifth series, vol.81, cc.564-67
65. JC36/31/04 (Keith)
66. Knox, *James Maxton*, (Manchester, 1987), pp.22-3; Shiels, 'The Prosecution of James Maxton', *Scottish Law Gazette*, vol.73, (2005), pp.92-3; Middlemas, *Clydesiders*, pp.67-9; Brown, *Maxton*, (Edinburgh, 1986), pp.71-2; Kirkwood, *My Life of Revolt*, pp.116-31; *Glasgow Herald*, 12 May 1916, p.7
67. Kirkwood, *My Life of Revolt*, pp.140-62
68. Foster, 'Strike Action and Working-Class Politics on Clydeside 1914-1919', *International Review of Social History*, vol.XXXV, (1991), p.36
69. Foster, 'Strike Action', p.62
70. Dickson, *Scottish Capitalism: Class, State and Nation from before the Union to the Present*, (London, 1980), p.273
71. *The Times*, 28 January 1919, p.8
72. Foster, 'Strike Action', p.53
73. *The Times*, 28 January 1919, p.6
74. Dickson, *Scottish Capitalism*, p.267; *Glasgow Herald*, 28 January 1919, p.6
75. JC36/31/09 (Maclean)
76. *The Times*, 28 January 1919, pp.8 & 10

Chapter 3: Tuesday, 28 January 1919

1. *Glasgow Herald*, 19 June 1915, p.11
2. Marwick, *The Deluge: British Society and the First World War*, (London, 1965), p.89
3. *Glasgow Herald*, 19 June 1915, p.11
4. Kirkwood, *My Life of Revolt*, (London, 1935), p.94; Hansard, 28 March 1916, Fifth series, vol. 81, cc.564-67
5. McLean, *The Legend of Red Clydeside*, (Edinburgh, 1983), pp.80-1
6. Foster, 'Strike Action and Working-Class Politics on Clydeside 1914-1919', *International Review of Social History*, vol.XXXV, (1990), p.55
7. *The Bulletin*, 29 January 1919, p.3
8. *Manchester Guardian*, 28 January 1919, p.5
9. *Glasgow Herald*, 29 January 1919, p.7; AD15/19/11, p.79 (Johnston)
10. *Glasgow Herald*, 29 January 1919, p.7
11. *Manchester Guardian*, 30 January 1919, p.5
12. *Glasgow Herald*, 29 January 1919, p.7

13. Gordon & Robb, 'Small-scale Residential Differentiation in Nineteenth Century Scottish Cities', *Scottish Geographical Magazine*, vol.97, vol.2, (1981), p.81
14. *Report of the Royal Commission on the Housing of the Industrial Population of Scotland, Rural and Urban*, (Edinburgh, 1917), pp.4-5
15. Middlemas, *The Clydesiders: a left wing struggle for Parliamentary Power*, (London, 1965), p.19
16. AD15/20/75 provides an example of the re-arrangements required when a lodger is taken in.
17. *Glasgow Herald*, 27 October 1915, p.12
18. *Glasgow Herald*, 7 June 1915, p.5
19. McLean, *Legend*, p.21
20. Melling, 'Scottish Industrialists and the Changing Character of Class Relations in the Clyde Region c. 1880-1918', ed Dickson, *Capital and Class in Scotland*, (Edinburgh, 1982), p.110
21. McLean, *Legend*, p.21-2
22. Gallacher, *Revolt on the Clyde*, (Chadwell Heath, 2017), pp.55-6; Eastman, 'The Workers of the Clyde', *The Liberator* (October 1919), p.28-9
23. *Glasgow Herald*, 27 October 1915, p.12
24. Knox, *Industrial Nation: Work, Culture and Society in Scotland, 1800-Present*, (Edinburgh, 1999), pp.176-7; Oakley, *The Second City*, (Glasgow, 1946), pp.250-1; Melling, 'Scottish Industrialists', p.96
25. McLean, *Legend*, p.20
26. *Glasgow Herald*, 27 October 1915, p.12
27. Melling, 'Scottish Industrialists', p.127
28. McLean, *Legend*, p.22
29. Foster, 'Strike Action', pp.48-9
30. Bell, *John Maclean: a fighter for freedom*, (Glasgow, 1944), pp.50-2
31. McLean, *Legend*, pp.22-3
32. Craig, *When the Clyde Ran Red*, (Edinburgh, 2018), p.41-2
33. Morton, *The 40 Hours Strike: a historic survey of the First General Strike in Scotland*, (February, 1919), p.7
34. *Glasgow Herald*, 29 January 1919, p.8
35. *The Bulletin*, 29 January 1919, p.3
36. McLean, *Legend*, p.113
37. *Evening Times*, 29 January 1919, front page
38. *The Bulletin*, 29 January 1919, p.3
39. Melling, 'Scottish Industrialists', p.119
40. McLean, *Legend*, p.70

41. Association of Clyde Shipbuilders Minute Book 9, 21 March 1916, pp.172-4; Mitchell Library, TD241/1/16
42. Glasgow Labour History Workshop, 'Roots of Red Clydeside: The Labour Unrest in West Scotland, 1910-14', eds Duncan & McIvor, *Militant Workers: labour and class conflict on the Clyde 1900-1950, essays in honour of Harry McShane, 1891-1988,* (Edinburgh, 1992), p.92
43. Gallacher, *Revolt,* pp.83-4; M Baillie, 'A New View of Dilution: Women Munitions Workers and Red Clydeside', *Scottish Labour History Society,* vol.39, (2004), p.39
44. Baillie, 'Dilution', p.35
45. *Partick and Maryhill Press,* 22 October 1915, p.1
46. McShane, *No Mean Fighter,* (London, 1978), pp.31-2, 35
47. *Glasgow Herald,* 2 May 1917, pp.6 & 7; Burmah [sic]
48. *Glasgow Herald,* 26 May 1917, p.6
49. Glasgow Labour History Workshop, 'Roots of Red Clydeside', p.99
50. Bambery, *A People's History of* Scotland, (London, 2014), p.153; Foster, 'Red Clyde, Red Scotland', eds Donnachie & Whatley, *The Manufacture of Scottish History,* (Edinburgh, 1992), p.112
51. Baillie, 'Dilution', pp.41-3
52. *Glasgow Herald,* 19 January 1918, p.5
53. Ibid., p.6
54. *Glasgow Herald,* 19 January 1918, p.6
55. *The Times,* 24 January 1918, p.6
56. War Cabinet minute, 521, 28 January 1919, National Archives CAB23/9, p.8
57. *Fortnightly Report on Revolutionary Organisations in the United Kingdom and Morale Abroad,* 28 January 1919, pp.48-50; National Archives, CAB24/74/13
58. *Report from the Ministry of Labour for the Week ending 29th January 1919,* National Archives, CAB 24/74/21, p.4

Chapter 4: Wednesday, 29 January 1919

1. AD15/19/11, p.196 (Ross); *Strike Bulletin,* 30 January 1919, p.3
2. Gallacher & Campbell, *Direct Action: An Outline of Workshop and Social Organisation,* (London, 1972), p.13
3. McShane, *No Mean Fighter,* (London, 1978), p.105
4. Foster, 'Strike Action and Working-Class Politics on Clydeside 1914-1919', *International Review of History,* vol.xxxv, (1990), pp.38-41

5. Damer, *Glasgow: Going for a Song*, (London, 1990), p.110
6. Knox, *Scottish Labour Leaders 1918-1939*, (Edinburgh, 1984), p.167
7. Foster, 'Strike Action', p.34; *Glasgow Herald*, 30 January 1919, pp.4-7
8. Eastman, 'The Workers of the Clyde', *The Liberator*, (October 1919), p.31
9. *Glasgow Herald*, 30 January 1919, p.4
10. *Glasgow Herald*, 30 January 1919, p.6; AD15/19/11, p.50 (Steele)
11. *Bulletin*, 30 January 1919, p.3
12. *Glasgow Herald*, 30 January 1919, p.6
13. JC36/31/07 (Highton)
14. *Glasgow Herald*, 30 January 1919, p.6; *Evening Times*, 29 January 1919, p.front
15. JC36/31/08 (Angus)
16. AD15/19/11, p.61, (Ritchie); pp.50-1 (Steele)
17. AD15/19/11, p.52 (Steele)
18. Harvie, *No Gods and Precious Few Heroes: Scotland since 1914*, (Edinburgh, 1981), p.11
19. AD15/19/11, pp.94-5 (Baillie); pp.97-8 (Wilson)
20. McShane, *No Mean Fighter*, (London, 1978), p.104; AD15/19/11, p.105 (Board)
21. *Manchester Guardian*, 30 January 1919, p.5
22. Eastman, 'Workers of the Clyde', pp.31-2, p.28
23. AD15/19/11, pp.51-2 (Steele, precognition taken 7 February 1919)
24. AD15/19/11, pp.62-3 (Ritchie, precognition taken 11 February 1919); pp.160-1 (Wilson)
25. Minutes of the Corporation of Glasgow, 30 January 1919, p.572; Mitchell Library
26. Gallacher, *Revolt on the Clyde*, (Chadwell Heath, 2017), p.157
27. *The Bulletin*, 30 January 1919, p.2 photo
28. *Glasgow Herald*, 30 January 1919, p.6
29. AD15/19/11, p.95 (Constable Gallagher); p.36 (Florence)
30. *Glasgow Herald*, 30 January 1919, p.6
31. AD15/19/11, p.37 (Florence)
32. AD15/19/11, pp.18-19 (McDonald); p.40 (Campbell)
33. *The Times*, 6 October 1902, p.10; *Glasgow Herald*, 24 January 1919, p.6; Aspinwall, 'Glasgow Trams and American Politics, 1894-1914', *Scottish Historical Review*, vol.54, no.161, part 1, (April, 1977), p.69
34. Eastman, 'Workers of the Clyde', p.29
35. AD15/19/11, p.20 (McDonald); p.28 (Ramsay)
36. *Scotsman*, 30 January 1919, p.4

37. AD15/19/11, p.22 (Clark)
38. AD15/19/11, p.96 (Constable Gallagher)
39. AD15/19/11, p.112 (Lawrence)
40. AD15/19/11, p.129 (Thomson); p.142 (Noble); p.170 (Beaton)
41. JC36/31/09 (Maclean); AD15/19/11, pp.142-3 (Noble); Slowe, *Manny Shinwell: an authorised biography*, (London, 1993), p.81
42. JC36/31/09 (Sim & Kennedy)
43. *Glasgow Herald*, 30 January 1919, p.6
44. JC36/31/09 (Maclean)
45. JC36/31/09 (Maclean); JC36/31/08 (Maloney & Harvey)
46. AD15/19/11 Lord Provost to Town Council, 6 February 1919, p.2
47. JC36/31/02 (Lindsay)
48. JC36/31/08 (Harvey)
49. JC36/31/03 (Stewart)
50. JC36/31/03 (Stewart)
51. JC36/31/09 (MacLean)
52. JC36/31/09 (Kennedy, Sim & Harvey)
53. AD15/19/11 (Lindsay); Lindsay's population figure for Glasgow must include outlying districts.
54. JC36/31/03 (Stewart)
55. Slowe, *Manny Shinwell,* p.82
56. JC36/31/08 (Harvey)
57. JC36/31/09 (Sim)
58. *Dominion,* vol.4, issue 1206, 15 August 1915, p.5; Smith & Anderson, *Glasgow's Trams: The Twilight Years*, (Clophill, 1998), p.12
59. AD15/19/11 (Lindsay)
60. AD15/19/11, p.18 (Lindsay)
61. JC36/31/09 (Maclean & Stewart)
62. AD15/19/11, p.18 (Lindsay)
63. JC36/31/02 (Lindsay); AD15/19/11, p.18-19 (Lindsay); Slowe, *Manny Shinwell*, p.82
64. AD15/19/11, p.19 (Lindsay)
65. JC36/31/03 (Lindsay)
66. JC36/31/02 (Lindsay)
67. JC36/31/08 (Harvey)
68. War Cabinet minute, 522, 30 January 1919, National Archives CAB23/9, p.2
69. JC36/31/03 (Lindsay)
70. War Cabinet minute, 522, 30 January 1919, National Archives CAB23/9, p.2

71. JC36/31/09 (Sim) Despite Sim's unreliability, others state similarly.
72. *Evening Times*, 29 January 1919, p.1
73. AD15/11/19 p.19 (Lindsay)
74. AD15/19/11, p.144 (Noble)
75. AD15/19/11, p.138 (Weir); JC36/31/05 (Mitchell)
76. AD15/19/11, p.113 (Gray)
77. AD15/19/11, p.143 (Noble)
78. *Glasgow Herald*, 30 January 1919, p.6; AD15/19/11, p.113 (Gray)
79. *Strike Bulletin*, 30 January 1919, p.4
80. AD15/19/11, p. 144 (Noble)
81. Melling, 'Scottish Industrialists and the Changing Character of Class Relations in the Clyde Region c. 1880-1918', ed Dickson, *Capital and Class in Scotland*, (Edinburgh, 1982), pp.95 & 104
82. Glasgow Labour History Workshop, 'Roots of Red Clydeside: The Labour Unrest in West Scotland, 1910-14', eds Duncan & McIvor, *Militant Workers: Labour and Class Conflict on the Clyde 1900-1950*, (Edinburgh, 1992), p.94
83. Foster, 'Strike Action', p.47-8
84. Minutes of the War Cabinet 28th January 1919, 521, National Archives, CAB 23/9/8, p.7
85. Joint Meeting of the Executive Committees of the Engineers' and Shipbuilders' Associations, 28 January 1919, pp.136-9; Mitchell Library, TD241/1/18
86. Joint Meeting of the Executive Committees of the Engineers' and Shipbuilders' Associations, 30 January 1919, pp.141-2; Mitchell Library, TD241/1/18
87. Melling, 'Scottish Industrialists', p.118
88. Report from the Ministry of Labour for the week ending 29th January 1919, National Archives, CAB24/74/21, p.7
89. Report from the Ministry of Labour, pp.1-3
90. AD15/19/11, pp.92-3 (Lingard)

Chapter 5: Thursday, 30 January 1919

1. Foster, 'The 1919 Forty Hours Strike: a turning point for class mobilisation in Britain', *Theory and Struggle*, vol.120 (i), (August 2019), p.33; *Glasgow Herald*, 31 January 1919, p.7
2. *Strike Bulletin*, 30 January 1919, p.3
3. https://digital.nmla.metoffice.gov.uk/IO_07f09c27-1b87-4e38-a7a9-2ac974e66b11/ p.123 accessed April 2022

4. AD15/19/11, pp.97-8 (Wilson), pp.94-5 (Baillie)

5. Middlemas, *The Clydesiders: a left wing struggle for Parliamentary Power,* (London, 1965), p.92; Slowe, *Manny Shinwell: an authorised biography*, (London, 1993), p.85

6. *Glasgow Herald*, 31 January 1919, p.7

7. AD15/19/11, pp.85-6 (Henderson)

8. *Strike Bulletin*, 30 January 1919, p.3

9. Jackson, Davidson, Fleming, Smale & Sparks, *Police and Community in Twentieth-Century Scotland*, (Edinburgh, 2020), pp.54-5

10. Goldsmith, 'The Development of the City of Glasgow Police, 1800 – c.1939', unpublished PhD thesis, (University of Strathclyde, 2002), table VII p.85; appendix VI p.400

11. *Glasgow Herald*, 30 January 1919, p.6; *Strike Bulletin*, 30 January 1919, p.4; *Bulletin*, 30 January 1919, p.3

12. Jackson et al, *Police and Community*, p.23

13. Gordon, *Policing Scotland*, (Glasgow, 1980), pp.25-6

14. AD15/19/11, p.53 (Steele)

15. AD15/19/11, p.53 (Steele); Jenkinson, 'Black Sailors on Red Clydeside: Rioting, Reactionary Trade Unionism and Conflicting Notions of 'Britishness' following the First World War', *Twentieth Century British History*, vol.19, no.1, (2008). Steele notes the riot on 23 January originally began as white and black sailors against the Chinese, before turning white sailors against black seamen.

16. AD15/19/11, pp.53-4 (Steele). He notes the riot on 23 January started as white and black sailors against Chinese before becoming black versus white seamen; *Evening Times*, 23 January 1919, p.1 quoted in Jenkinson, 'The 1919 Race Riots in Britain: their background and consequences', PhD thesis, (University of Edinburgh, 1987), p.65

17. *Glasgow Herald*, 24 January 1919, p.8; *Bulletin*, 24 January 1919, p.2; *Manchester Guardian*, 24 January 1919, p.8

18. Jenkinson, 'Black Sailors', p.41

19. JC36/31/09 (Kennedy & Blamires)

20. AD15/19/11, pp.53-4 (Steele)

21. AD15/19/11, p.197 (Ross)

22. https://web.archive.org/web/20080330022316/http://www.nahste. ac.uk/cgi-bin/view_isad.pl?id=GB-0248-UGD-295&view=basic accessed 13 April 2022

23. *Strike Bulletin*, 30 January 1919, p.2

24. AD15/11/19, p.191 (McLennan)

25. AD15/11/19, pp.199-200 (Gordon); pp.196-8 (Ross)

26. AD15/19/11, p.47 (McKeown)
27. AD15/11/19, pp.192-4 (McLennan)
28. Minutes of the War Cabinet 30th January 1919, 522, National Archives, CAB 23/9/9, p.1
29. Goldsmith, 'City of Glasgow Police', pp.87-8
30. JC36/31/04 (MacKenzie)
31. Weinberger, *Keeping the Peace?: Policing Strikes in Britain 1906-1926*, (Oxford, 1991), p.134, quoted in Jackson et al, *Police and Community*, p.17; *The London Gazette*, 1 September 1914, pp.6968-9
32. Lamb would go on to become Permanent Under Secretary, the senior civil servant in the Scottish Office.
33. War Cabinet, 522, p.5
34. Jackson et al, *Police and Community*, p.18
35. War Cabinet, 522, pp.1-5
36. *The Scotsman*, 31 January 1919, p.4
37. AD15/11/19, pp.33-7 (Stevenson)
38. AD15/19/11, pp.175-6 (Ferguson)
39. AD15/19/11, p.183 (Wishart), p.181 (Sellars)
40. AD15/19/11, pp.185-6 (Moffat)
41. AD15/19/11, p.176 (Ferguson)
42. *Bulletin*, 30 January 1919, p.3
43. *Glasgow Herald*, 30 January 1919, p.6
44. Bellamy, 'Shipbuilding and Cultural Identity on Clydeside', *Journal for Maritime Research*, (January, 2006), p.10
45. Jackson et al, *Police and Community*, p.218 table A.1
46. Jackson et al, *Police and Community*, p.56
47. Goldsmith, *City of Glasgow Police*, p.408 Table XII 'Wages Comparison – Constables with other workers' weekly wages in shillings'
48. Jackson et al, *Police and Community*, p.218 table A.1
49. Jackson et al, *Police and Community*, pp.27-8, 45, 55
50. AD15/11/19, pp.4-6 (Mulherrin)
51. Knox, 'James Dunlop MacDougall 1891-1963, activist', *Scottish Labour Leaders 1918-1939*, ed Knox, (Edinburgh, 1984), pp.170-3
52. There is no evidence for this claim.
53. AD15/11/19, pp.10-11 (McGlachan)
54. AD15/11/19, pp.6-7 (MacDougall; MacFarlane corroborates without detail)
55. *The Scotsman*, 31 January 1919, p4
56. JC36/31/08 (Moir); JC36/31/09 (Maclean)

57. AD15/19/54 – miscellaneous court papers & precognitions; *Glasgow Herald*, 1 May 1919, p.9
58. Joint Meeting of the Executive Committees of the Engineers' and Shipbuilders' Associations, 30 January 1919, pp.141-3; Mitchell Library, TD241/1/18
59. *Strike Bulletin*, 30 January 1919, p.4

Chapter 6: Afternoon, Friday, 31 January 1919

1. Slowe, *Manny Shinwell: an authorised biography*, (London, 1993), p.86
2. AD15/19/11, p.87 (Gargan)
3. AD15/19/11, p.247 (McQuade); pp.251-2 (Binnie)
4. AD15/19/11, p.255-7 (McKendrick)
5. AD15/19/11, pp.247-8 (McQuade)
6. AD15/19/11, pp.87-8 (Gargan)
7. AD15/19/11, p.90 (Blackhall)
8. AD15/19/11, pp.251-2 (Binnie)
9. AD15/19/11, p.116 (Gray)
10. AD15/19/11, p.116 (Gray); p.218 (Ross)
11. AD15/19/11, p.145 (Noble); *The Scotsman*, 31 January 1919, p.4
12. AD15/19/11, p.147 (Noble), p.140 (Weir)
13. AD15/19/11, p.267 (McGowan)
14. AD15/19/11, pp.158-9 (Wilson); p.268 (McGowan)
15. AD15/19/11, p.239 (Sutherland); p.171-3 (Cameron)
16. AD15/19/11, p.90 (Blackhall); p.102 (Smith); p.100 (Gallagher); p.176 (Cochran); pp.260-1 (MacDonald); pp.265-6 (Graham); p.147a (Noble); pp.269-70 (Smart); p.272 (Beaton)
17. *Glasgow Herald*, 1 February 1919, p.5
18. AD15/19/11, pp.312-4 (Halliday); *Glasgow Herald*, 1 February 1919, p.5; *Evening News*, 31 January 1919, p.2
19. JC36/31/05 (Mitchell)
20. JC36/31/07 (Highton)
21. AD15/19/11, p.281-2 (Beattie)
22. AD15/19/11, pp.273-5 (McNair); p.276 (Orr)
23. AD15/19/11, pp.277-8 (Player)
24. AD15/19/11, p.134-5 (Erskine)
25. AD15/19/11, p.279 (Quail)
26. AD15/19/11, pp.176f-i (Innes/Ferguson). Inspector Innes dies at some point before the trial and his precognition taken on 13 February 1919

has his name crossed out and replaced by Sergeant Ferguson who was one of his team at these events.

27. AD15/19/11, p.278 (Player)
28. AD15/19/11, pp.176j-k (Innes/Ferguson); p.304 (Gray, driver)
29. *Glasgow Herald*, 1 February 1919, p.5
30. AD15/19/11, p.11 (MacKenzie)
31. WO32/8466, 1908-1912, *King's Regulations for the Army*, paragraph 955
32. War Cabinet minute, 523, 31 January 1919, National Archives CAB23/9, p.1. Without other evidence to support some form of written communication from Glasgow to London, we have assumed that the message was conveyed by telephone to the War Cabinet.
33. War Cabinet minute, 523, 31 January 1919, National Archives CAB23/9, p.2
34. *Glasgow Herald*, 16 November 1918, pp.4-5 & 31 January 1919, p.5
35. Middlemas, *The Clydesiders: A left-wing struggle for Parliamentary power*, (London, 1965), p.87
36. Pittock, *Scottish Nationality*, (London, 2001), p.103; see chapter 10 for discussion of troop numbers. The Easter Rising in Dublin 1916 is also referred to as the Easter Rebellion.
37. War Cabinet minute 523, 31 January 1919, National Archives CAB23/9, pp.2-3
38. AD15/19/11, pp.286-7 (Hunter); pp.294-5 (Stewart); pp.292-3 (MacFarlane)
39. AD15/19/11, p.90 (Blackhall); p.219 (Ross)
40. AD15/19/11, p.135 (Erskine)
41. AD15/19/11, p.147 (Noble)
42. AD15/19/11, p.47 (Imrie)
43. AD15/19/11, p.140 (Weir)
44. *Daily Record*, 3 February 1919, p.1; *The Observer*, 2 February 1919, p.9; *Glasgow Herald*, 3 February 1919, p.5; *Daily Mirror*, 3 February 1919, p.3
45. Blake, *Civil Disorder in Britain, 1910-1939: the roles of civil government and military authority*, DPhil, (University of Sussex, 1979), p.85
46. AD15/19/11, p.169 (Gillies)
47. *The Bulletin*, 3 February 1919
48. Middlemas, *The Clydesiders*, p.92; Slowe, *Manny Shinwell*, p.85
49. *Glasgow Herald*, 1 February 1919, p.5

Chapter 7: 1 February to 6 April 1919

1. AD15/19/11, p.302 (Storrar); p.308 (Coulter); Shinwell, *Lead with the Left: my first ninety-six years*, (London, 1981), p.64
2. *Evening Times*, 31 January 1919, p.4
3. *Strike Bulletin*, 1 February 1919, p.1; *Glasgow Herald*, 1 February 1919, p.5
4. Middlemas, *The Clydesiders: a left wing struggle for Parliamentary Power,* (London, 1965), p.92; P Slowe, *Manny Shinwell: an authorised biography*, (London, 1993), p.85
5. Shinwell, *Lead with the Left*, pp.63-4; *Strike Bulletin*, 1 February 1919, p.4; Slowe, *Manny Shinwell*, pp.85-6
6. AD15/19/11, p.108 (Turner)
7. AD15/19/11, pp.302-3 (Storrar)
8. AD15/19/11, City of Glasgow Police Criminal Investigation Department. Additional Information against Emmanuel [sic] Shinwell and Others, 1 March 1919, p.72; AD15/19/11, p.306 (Mair); p.307 (McIntyre)
9. AD15/19/55 miscellaneous High Court criminal papers & precognitions for case: Strange *et al*
10. *Glasgow Herald*, 1 February 1919, p.5
11. AD15/19/11, p.249 (McQuade)
12. *The Observer*, 2 February 1919, p.9
13. *Daily Record and Mail*, 1 February 1919, p.1
14. Ash, *The Lost Dictator,* (Worthing, 1968), chapter 19
15. *Daily Sketch*, 3 February 1919, p.1
16. *Manchester Guardian*, 3 February 1919, p.7; *Glasgow Herald*, 3 February 1919, p.5
17. Letter marked 'secret', 8 April 1919, General Roberston to Winston Churchill, National Archives, WO32/18920, explains that the rules concerning martial law are 'obscure'; even the authorities are unclear of the process.
18. *Daily Record*, 1 February 1919, p.1
19. *Glasgow Herald*, 1 February 1919, p.6
20. *The Worker*, 1 February 1919, p.1
21. *Strike Bulletin*, 1 February 1919, pp.1 & 4
22. *The Observer*, 2 February 1919, p.9
23. *Guardian*, 3 February 1919, p.7
24. Morton, *The Forty Hours Strike: an Historic Survey of the First General Strike in Scotland*, (February, 1919), p.13
25. AD15/19/11, p.303 (Storrar)

26. AD15/19/11, p.288 (Hunter); p.301 (Storrar)
27. https://digital.nmla.metoffice.gov.uk/IO_f85659cb-61f4-4f3d-9309-34e9ad145245/ accessed May 2022
28. AD15/19/11, p.264 (Smith)
29. AD15/19/11, p.187 (Lobban); *Evening Times*, 3 February 1919, p.1
30. AD15/19/11, pp.173-4 (Cameron); p.175 (Smillie); p.309 (Barbour)
31. *Guardian,* 3 February 1919, p.7; *Glasgow Herald,* 1 February 1919, p.7
32. *The Times*, 1 February 1919, p.9
33. *Glasgow Herald*, 4 February 1919, p.5; *Guardian*, 4 February 1919, p.5; *Bulletin*, 4 February 1919, p.9
34. WO32/18920 18 March 1919 National Archives
35. The issue of the tanks has become a key contention in the ensuing 100 years. For clarity, no one rode a tank in George Square on Friday 31 January 1919 because the tanks had not arrived; thus, it was impossible for anyone to be injured by one in George Square and no tanks patrolled Glasgow's streets at any time after their arrival on Monday 3 February 1919 when they were driven directly to the Cattle Market. Statements including any of these notions serve a purpose that is not historical.
36. *Guardian*, 4 February 1919, pp.4-5; *Glasgow Herald,* 4 February 1919, p.5
37. *Glasgow Herald*, 7 February 1919, p.8
38. AD15/19/11, Meeting of the Town Council of the City of Glasgow held within the City Chambers on Thursday, 6 February 1919, pp.1-26 (page numbers used are centre top); *Glasgow Herald*, 7 February 1919, pp.7-8; *The Worker*, 15 February 1919, p.1
39. *Glasgow Herald*, 7 February 1919, p.6
40. *Evening Times*, 6 February 1919, p.3
41. Shiels, 'The Mid-Victorian Codification of the Practice of Public Prosecution', *The Scottish Historical Review*, vol.98, supplement 248, (October, 2019), p.419
42. Defence or exculpatory precognitions were paid for by the defence. Over 700 defence witnesses were listed in the trial papers, but none of their precognitions has survived as far as we are aware.
43. AD15/19/11, p.132 (Thomson)
44. Keedy, 'Criminal Procedure in Scotland', *Journal of the American Institute of Criminal Law and Criminology*, vol.3, no.5, (1912), p.747
45. AD15/19/11, pp.118a-g (Murdoch); p.119 (McDonald); pp.157-62 (Wilson); pp.142-7a (Noble)
46. *The Worker*, 8 February 1919, pp.1-2
47. AD15/19/11, Meeting of the Town Council, p.24

48. AD15/19/11, p.127 (Keith); p.141 (Weir)
49. *Evening Times*, 3 February 1919, p.1; *Strike Bulletin*, 11 February 1919, pp.4-5; *Glasgow Herald*, 11 February 1919, p.6; *The Worker*, 15 February 1919, p.2
50. McShane, *No Mean Fighter*, (London, 1978), p.108-9
51. JC26/1919/85 contains both the draft charge sheet and final indictment among other court papers and correspondence.
52. At this stage of the process, the accused could be refused bail on several counts: regarding the nature of the crime; the accused's previous record and the attitude of the Crown. There may be a risk of tampering with evidence if liberated on bail or intimidation of witnesses. Also, while in custody, it is recognized that preparation of the case is impeded. Smith, 'Bail Before Trial: Reflections of a Scottish Lawyer', *University of Pennsylvania Law Review*, vol.108, no.3, (January, 1960), pp.318 & 321
53. *Glasgow Herald*, 11 February 1919, p.6; *Strike Bulletin*, 11 February 1919, p.4; Gallacher, *Revolt on the Clyde*, (London, 1978), p.165
54. AD15/19/11, p.287 (Hunter)
55. Meeting of the Executive Committee of the Clyde Shipbuilders' Association, 11 February 1919, pp.36-7, Mitchell Library, Minute Book 12, TD241/1/18
56. Joint Meeting of the Executive Committees of the Engineers and Shipbuilders Associations, 14 February 1919, pp.150-9, Mitchell Library, Minute Book 12, TD241/1/18 We do not understand the reference to 'legislation' because, beyond by-laws, the city council could not pass 'laws'.
57. General Committee of the Glasgow Trades Council Minutes, 14 February 1919 (pages unnumbered), Mitchell Library, TD2020/1/3/2
58. AD15/19/11, Bail Petitions, pp.1-38
59. *Glasgow Herald*, 18 February 1919, p.6
60. AD15/19/11, Bail Bonds pp.73-82, 85-8, 101-2
61. MacGregor Mitchell, *A Practical Treatise on the Criminal Law of Scotland*, (Edinburgh, 1929), pp.310-11
62. HH16/147 Correspondence Henderson to Munro, 28 February 1919; Munro refers to Bail (Scotland) Act 1888 which should be viewed in conjunction with Criminal Procedure (Scotland) Act 1887
63. AD15/19/11, handwritten note Secretary for Scotland, 1 March 1919
64. AD15/19/11, *Citizen*, 4 March 1919
65. AD15/19/11, Letter procurator fiscal to Crown Agent; Letter William Shaw to Sir Thomas Munro; Letter procurator fiscal to Crown Agent; Public Notice by William Shaw, all dated 8 March 1919

66. Letter from Trades Council to Robert Smillie MP, undated and unknown if sent; Mitchell Library, TD2020/1/2/2/1
67. JC26/1919/85, Letter Crown Office to the Right Honourable the Lords Commissioners of Justiciary, 13 March 1919; AD15/19/11, Telegram to Gardiner & MacFie solicitors, 15 March 1919
68. Joint Finance Committee, Minutes of Meetings of Glasgow Trades & Labour Council, 10 and 17 March 1919, Mitchell Library, TD2020/1/2/2/1
69. AD15/19/11, Letter procurator fiscal to Crown Agent, 21 March 1919; Shiels e-mail to author Heren, 7 November 2019
70. AD15/19/11, telegram from solicitor general to Crown Agent, 19 March 1919; handwritten note solicitor general to Crown Agent, 20/21 March 1919
71. AD15/19/11, Letter Procurator Fiscal to Crown Agent, 17 March 1919
72. Keedy, 'Criminal Procedure in Scotland II', *Journal of the American Institute for Criminal Law and Criminology*, vol.3, no.6, (1913), pp.835-6; Shiels, 'Mid-Victorian Codification', p.436
73. AD15/19/11, Letter procurator fiscal to Crown Agent, 22 March 1919
74. AD15/19/11, Special Defences, pp.1-26
75. AD15/19/11, Letter procurator fiscal to Crown Agent, 28 March 1919; Mitchell, *Criminal Law*, p.458
76. AD15/19/11, Letters Gardiner & MacFie to Crown Agent, 1 and 3 April 1919
77. AD15/19/11, Letter Gardiner & MacFie to Crown Agent, 28 March 1919; Letter Gardiner & MacFie to Crown Agent, 3 April 1919

Chapter 8: 7 to 18 April 1919

1. AD15/19/11, Letters Gardiner & MacFie to Crown Agent, 3 April 1919; Letters Dr Halliday to Procurator Fiscal, Procurator Fiscal to Crown Agent, 2 April 1919
2. AD15/19/11, Telegram Lindsay to Crown Agent, 4 April 1919
3. JC26/1919/85, Copy letter Crown Agent to Gardiner & MacFie, 5 April 1919
4. JC26/1919/85, Letter Chief Constable to Clerk of Justiciary, 2 April 1919
5. The Appellate Court for criminal cases in Scotland was established in 1926.
6. Letter Crosthwaite to miscellaneous, 7 April 1919; Mitchell Library, TD1/2/2/1

7. JC36/31/09 (Maclean)
8. *Glasgow Herald*, 8 April 1919, p.7
9. *The Edinburgh Gazette,* 20 October 1903, issue 11560, p.1061; *The London Gazette*, 20 October 1903, issue 27607, p.6368
10. JC26/1919/85, Letter Hodge & Co. to Clerk of Justiciary, 3 April 1919
11. The complete trial transcript is available at the National Records of Scotland, JC36/31/01-10, approximately 1,600 pages of type.
12. JC26/1919/85, List of Assize
13. Keedy, 'Criminal Procedure in Scotland', *Journal of the American Institute of Criminal Law and Criminology*, vol.3, no.5, (1912), pp.752-3. Women became eligible for jury service in late December 1919 after the Sex Disqualification (Removal) Act received royal assent. In reality, the first female jurors in Scotland began service on criminal proceedings in Spring 1921; Heren, *Sex and Violence in 1920s Scotland*, (London, 2023), in preparation
14. JC36/31/01, Ruling, 7 April 1919, pp.1-5; *Glasgow Herald*, 8 April 1919, p.7
15. JC26/1919/85, List of Assize – pencil numbers in the left-hand margin denote those balloted
16. Keedy, 'Criminal Procedure in Scotland', *Journal of Criminal Law and Criminology,* vol.3, issue 6, (1913), p.837
17. AD15/19/11, List of Defence Witnesses, pp.1-48
18. JC36/31/01 (Gray); *Glasgow Herald*, 8 April 1919, p.7
19. *Glasgow Herald*, 9 April 1919, p.7
20. *The Worker*, 12 April 1919, pp.1-2
21. JC36//32/02 (Murdoch); *Glasgow Herald*, 9 April 1919, pp.7-8
22. *Glasgow Herald*, 9 April 1919, p.7
23. *Glasgow Herald*, 9 April 1919, p.8
24. *The Worker*, 12 April 1919, p.2
25. *Glasgow Herald*, 10 April 1919, p.7
26. JC36/31/03 (Stewart); *Glasgow Herald*, 10 April 1919, pp.7-8
27. JC36/31/03 (Weir); *Glasgow Herald*, 10 April 1919, p.8
28. JC36/31/03 (Steele & Ritchie)
29. JC36/31/04 (Stevenson)
30. JC36/31/05 (Mitchell); *Glasgow Herald*, 12 April 1919, p.8
31. *Glasgow Herald*, 15 April 1919, p.5
32. JC36/31/07 (Hughes); *Glasgow Herald*, 15 April 1919, p.5; Slowe, *Manny Shinwell: an authorised biography*, (London, 1993), p.84
33. JC36/31/09 (Sim)
34. *Glasgow Herald*, 18 April 1919, p.8

35. *Glasgow Herald*, 18 April 1919, p.8
36. JC26/31/10 (Scott Dickson)
37. *The Worker*, 26 April 1919, p.4
38. Hume, *Commentaries on the Law of Scotland in Matters Criminal*, (1884), ii, p.422; quoted in Gane, 'The Scottish Jury', *Revue International de droit penal*, vol.72, no.1, (2001), p.269
39. *Forward*, 26 April 1919, p.11
40. *Forward*, 19 April 1919, pp.1-10; *Glasgow Herald*, 19 April 1919, p.4
41. JC36/31/10 (Scott Dickson)

Chapter 9: April 1919 and Beyond

1. House of Commons Sessional Papers, *Hansard,* 7 April 1919, Fifth Series, vol.114, cc.1663-1664
2. Parliamentary Debates 1919, cxiv, col.1956, 8 April 1919; *Report of the Royal Commission on the Housing of the Industrial Population of Scotland, rural and urban*, (Edinburgh, 1917)
3. *The Worker*, 26 April 1919, pp.4-5
4. £1 5s 0d today approximately equals £36 or in 1919, 3 days' wages for a skilled worker; £2 15s 0d equals £80 or in 1919, 8 days' work; the fees owed to Crosthwaite at the end of the trial are the equivalent of £40,680 today; https://www.nationalarchives.gov.uk/currency-converter/ accessed June 2022
5. Letter Gardiner & MacFie to William Shaw, Secretary, Glasgow Trades & Labour Council, 14 April 1919; Letter Clyde Workers' Defence Committee to Shaw, 3 May 1919; Income & Expenditure Account, 18 February to 8 May 1919; Letter Glasgow Trades & Labour Council to Trade Union Executive Committees, 28 May 1919; Letter Crosthwaite to Shaw, 1 May 1919; all Mitchell Library, TC2020/2/2/1
6. Letter Crosthwaite to William Shaw, 12 May 1919; Letter Gardiner & MacFie to Secretary for Scotland, 13 May 1919; Letter Crosthwaite to Shaw, 14 May 1919; Letter Crosthwaite to Shaw, 15 May 1919; Letter Crosthwaite to Shaw, 29 May 1919; all Mitchell Library, TC2020/2/2/1
7. Petition to the Right Honourable Robert Munro, Mitchell Library, TC2020/2/2/1
8. Letter P Campbell NAWU to William Shaw, Glasgow Trades Council, 8 July 1919, Mitchell Library, TC2020/2/2/1
9. McLean, *The Legend of Red Clydeside*, (Edinburgh, 1983), p.129
10. Fowler & Weinbren, *Now the War is Over: Britain 1919-1920*, (Barnsley, 2018), pp.xii & 33; 'The Labour Situation', Report from the

Ministry of Labour for the week ending 12 February 1919, National Archives, CAB24/74/96, p.4

11. Reynolds & Judge, *The Night the Police went on Strike*, (London, 1968), pp.152-60

12. Reynolds & Judge, *The Night the Police*, pp.161-73; J Blake, *Civil Disorder in Britain 1910-1939: The Roles of Civil Government and Military Authority*, DPhil thesis, (University of Sussex, 1979), pp.172-3

13. *The Worker*, 9 February 1919, p.3

14. Eastman, *The Liberator*, (October 1919), pp.29-30

15. McIvor & Patterson, 'Combating the Left: Victimisation and Anti-Labour Activities on Clydeside, 1900-1939', eds Duncan & McIvor, *Labour and Class Conflict on the Clyde 1900-1950, essays in honour of Harry McShane*, (Edinburgh, 1992), p.139

16. Gallacher, *Revolt on the Clyde*, (Chadwell Heath, 2017), p.172

17. Kirkwood, *My Life of Revolt*, (London, 1935), pp.175-7

18. Marwick, *The Deluge: British Society and the First World War*, (London, 1965), p.312

19. Gallacher, *Revolt*, pp.173-5; Eastman, *The Liberator*, p.33

20. AD15/19/11 City of Glasgow Police Criminal Investigation Department, Additional Information against Emmanuel Shinwell and Others, pp.65 & 68-9

21. Middlemas, *The Clydesiders: a left wing struggle for Parliamentary Power*, (London, 1965), pp.84; J M Winter, *Socialism and the Challenge of War: ideas and politics in Britain 1912-18*, (Aldershot, 1974), p.273

22. Knox, *Industrial Nation: work, culture and society in Scotland, 1800-Present*, (Edinburgh, 1999), p.189

23. *Glasgow Herald*, 15 November 1919, p.4

24. *Glasgow Herald*, 17 November 1919, p.11

25. *Glasgow Herald*, 16 November 1919, p.7

26. Middlemass, *The Clydesiders*, pp.111-2

27. Dickson, *Scottish Capitalism: Class, State and Nation from before the Union to the Present*, (London 1980), p.278; Kirkwood, *Revolt*, p.191 – also a formation of the British Army, the 1922 group of Glaswegian MPs became affectionately known as the 'Clyde Brigade' at Westminster.

28. *Manchester Guardian*, 21 November 1922, p.10; 24 November 1922, pp.4 & 8

29. *Hansard*, 29 November 1922, vol.159, cc.775-847 & 5 December 1922, vol.159, cc.1610-97

30. Winter, *Challenge of War*, p.278

31. Knox, *Industrial Nation*, pp.190-1

32. *Hansard*, 4 February 1926, vol.191, cc. 365-480; 17 February 1927, vol.202, cc.1226-48; 6 February 1929, vol.224, cc.1777-89
33. Eastman, *The Liberator*, p.29
34. Town Clerk Sir John Lindsay erroneously stated Hopkins was among the deputation in his precognition, AD15/19/11 p.16
35. Kirkwood, *Revolt*, pp.171-4
36. Knox, *Scottish Labour Leaders 1918-1939*, (Edinburgh, 1984), pp.116-18
37. Eastman, *The Liberator*, p.30; Gallacher, *Revolt on the Clyde*, p.164
38. Barclay, '"Churchill rolled the tanks into the crowd": mythology and reality in the military deployments to Glasgow in 1919', *Scottish Affairs*, (January, 2019), pp.32-62
39. Barclay, 'Churchill rolled the tanks', p.39
40. Gallacher, *Revolt on the Clyde*, pp.160-9
41. Shinwell, *Conflict without Malice*, (London, 1955); *I've lived through it all*, (London,1973); *Lead with the Left: My first Ninety-Six Years*, (London, 1981); Shinwell & Doxat, *Shinwell Talking: a conversational biography to celebrate his hundredth birthday*, (London, 1984); Slowe, *Manny Shinwell: an authorised biography*, (London, 1993)
42. Shinwell, *Malice*, p.64; *Lead with the left*, p.63; *Through it all*, pp.45, 93-4
43. Shinwell, *Lead with the Left*, pp.60-7

Chapter 10: The Mythology of 'Bloody Friday'

1. Naughton, *Glasgow's East End: from Bishops to Barraboys*, (Edinburgh, 2014), p.191. This claim is absurd.
2. Bell, *John Maclean: fighter for freedom*, (Glasgow, 1944), p.85
3. The explanation is to be found in McLean's thesis, in which his map of events (I McLean, 'The Labour Movement in Clydeside Politics, 1914-1922', (DPhil, University of Oxford, 1971, p.213) in the Square shows that he erroneously placed the beginnings of the riot in the south-*west* corner of the Square instead of the south-*east*, with the first baton charge west to east along the south side of the Square, in front of the Post Office, and the second, as noted above, south to north along the front of the City Chambers.
4. Barclay, '"Duties in Aid of the Civil Power": the deployment of the army to Glasgow, 31 January to 17 February 1919', *Journal of Scottish Historical Studies*, volume 38.2 (2018, 261-292), pp.271-2

5. Brotherstone, 'John Maclean and the Russian Revolution: a discussion article', *Scottish Labour History Society Journal,* volume 23, (1988, p.), p.17; Slowe, *Manny Shinwell: an authorised biography,* (London, 1993), pp.81-2

6. Robbins, *The Blackwell biographical dictionary of British political life in the twentieth century,* (Oxford, 1990), p.372

7. Shinwell, *I've Lived through it all,* (London, 1973), p.45; *Lead with the Left: My first Ninety-Six Years,* (London, 1981), p.63; Shinwell & Doxat, *Shinwell Talking: a conversational biography to celebrate his hundredth birthday,* (London, 1984), pp.93-4

8. BBC 1984 TV Documentary, 'Manny at 100: the fighter'

9. Evans, *In Defence of History*, (London, 2000), 2nd ed., p.196

10. Damer, 'And if you know the history', *Scottish Affairs*, volume 28.1, (2019), pp.112-15

11. McGonigle & Wood, *The Era of the Great War*, (Glasgow, 2013), p.84

12. Subsequently removed from the agency's website.

13. Wilson, 'Nationalist propaganda disguised as history for school children is a worrying sign about where Scotland is heading', *The Scotsman,* 12 December 2020, digital edition, https://www.scotsman.com/news/opinion/columnists/nationalist-propaganda-disguised-as-history-for-school-children-is-a-worrying-sign-about-where-scotland-is-heading-brian-wilson-3065384

14. Education Scotland 2021, 'Review of "Timeline to the Scottish Parliament"', https://www.gov.scot/binaries/content/documents/govscot/publications/foi-eir-release/2021/06/foi-202100199983/documents/foi202100199983---annex/foi202100199983---annex/govscot%3Adocument/FOI202100199983%2B-%2BAnnex%2BA.pdf These two problematic organisations are due to be abolished and replaced by 2024.

15. MacAskill, *Glasgow 1919: The Rise of Red Clydeside*, (London, 2019), p.228

16. Kendall, *The Revolutionary Movement in Scotland 1900-21*, (London, 1969), p.139, also quoted in Leopold, 'The Forty Hours Strike,' in Flynn (ed), *We shall be all: recent chapters in the history of working-class struggle in Scotland,* (Glasgow, 1978) pp.34-44 at p.40

17. Weinberger, *Keeping the peace?: policing strikes in Britain, 1906-1926*, (Oxford, 1990), pp.152-62

18. Barclay, '"The evidence has always been there": Unreliable Narrators and Archival Sources for the Battle of George square, Glasgow,

31 January 1919', *Scottish Archives,* volume 25/26, (2021), pp.108-22 at p.117

19. Marr, *The Making of Modern Britain,* (London, 2009), pp.231-2
20. BBC Documentary 1980 'The Revolutionaries: John Maclean'
21. Shinwell, *Conflict without Malice,* pp.62-4; *I've Lived through it all,* p.45
22. McShane & Smith, *Harry McShane: No Mean Fighter,* (London, 1978), p.107
23. *Daily Record,* 21 December 1918, p.16
24. McLean, *Legend,* p.138
25. WO32/18920, 1919 'Use of military personnel in aid of civil powers in event of civil disturbances and strikes: Great Britain'
26. Courts martial were imposed during the breakdown of the system of civil justice during the violent birth of an independent Ireland, followed by internment without trial. Martial Law was also 'proclaimed' in various counties in 1920 and 1921.
27. *Glasgow Herald,* 7 February 1919, pp.7-8
28. Kenefick, *Red Scotland: The Rise and Fall of the Radical Left, c.1872-1932,* (Edinburgh, 2007), p.10
29. Pittock, *Scottish Nationality,* (Basingstoke, 2001), p.103
30. Morgan, 1987, *Conflict and order: the police and labour disputes in England and Wales, 1900-1939,* (Oxford, 1987), p.75; Jeffery & Hennessey, *States of emergency: British governments and strikebreaking since 1919,* (London, 1983), p.75
31. Townshend, 'Military Force and Civil Authority in the United Kingdom, 1914-1921', *Journal British Studies,* vol. 28, (1989), pp.262-92
32. Ash, *The Lost Dictator: Field Marshal Sir Henry Wilson,* (London, 1968), chapter 19
33. Webb, *1919: Britain's Year of Revolution,* (Barnsley, 2018), pp.148-9. Wilson resigned from the army and his post of CIGS on 19 February 1922 and was elected as a Conservative MP for North Down on 21 February 1922. He was murdered on 22 June 1922 by the IRA.
34. Churchill, *The World Crisis,* (London, 1923), p.760
35. Milton *John Maclean,* (London, 1973), p.191; Broom, *John Maclean* (Loanhead, 1973), pp.120-1
36. Barclay, 'A "villain for all seasons": Churchill and Scottish Mythologies of Grievance', *Finest Hour,* (2020), pp.14-18. https://gordon-barclay.net/wp-content/uploads/2020/09/FH189_Article_Extract.pdf
37. CAB23/9/9, 1919, p.3

38. WO73/110, 'Office of the Commander in Chief and War Office: distribution of the army monthly returns. Jan-Jun 1919', National Archives

39. Blake, *Civil Disorder in Britain, 1910-1939: the Roles of Civil Government and Military Authority* (DPhil University of Sussex, 1979), p.85

40. TNA MUN 1/18 Ministry of Munitions: Munitions Council Daily Reports, Report 427-446 (no. 427 Monday 3 February 1919)

41. Devine, *The Scottish Nation: a modern history*, (London, 2007), ebook 811.7–813.5/1763; Lynch, *Scotland: a new history*, (London, 1991), p.425

42. Still, *Introduction to Crowd Science*, (London, 2014), p.47

43. Still, *Crowd Science*, p.50

44. British Pathe, 1919, 'Striking Workers on the Streets of Glasgow 1919' https://www.britishpathe.com/video/VLVAXTHPXEWW57XVDE 31549UKTJX-STRIKING-WORKERS-ON-THE-STREETS-OF-GLASGOW

45. Still, *Crowd Science*, p.44

46. Still, *Crowd Science*, pp.43-4

47. Pheasant, *Bodyspace*, (London, 1998) quoted in Still *Crowd Science*, pp.33-4

48. Still, *Crowd Science*, p.36

49. Barraclough, 'Historical pessimism', *Guardian*, 20 October 1961

50. Damer, 'In the Rapids of Revolution?', *Scottish Affairs*, volume 28, no. 3, (2019), pp.339-48

51. Lipstadt, *Denying the Holocaust: the growing assault on truth and memory*, (London, 1994), pp.19-20

52. McShane & Smith, *Harry McShane*, pp.106-7

53. Ten men at the two other related riot trials were found guilty, most receiving sentences of ten days or three months. Only one man, Hendren, received a sentence of six months.

Index